FOUR PLAYS OF EURIPIDES

ESSAYS ON
FOUR PLAYS OF EURIPIDES

ANDROMACHE   HELEN   HERACLES
ORESTES

by

A. W. VERRALL, Litt.D.

Fellow of Trinity College, Cambridge

CAMBRIDGE :
at the University Press
1905

CAMBRIDGE
UNIVERSITY PRESS

University Printing House, Cambridge CB2 8BS, United Kingdom

Published in the United States of America by Cambridge University Press, New York

Cambridge University Press is part of the University of Cambridge.

It furthers the University's mission by disseminating knowledge in the pursuit of education, learning and research at the highest international levels of excellence.

www.cambridge.org
Information on this title: www.cambridge.org/9781107683129

© Cambridge University Press 1905

First published 1905
First paperback edition 2014

A catalogue record for this publication is available from the British Library

ISBN 978-1-107-68312-9 Paperback

PREFACE.

THE texts of Euripides to which I refer in this volume are the following. For the *Andromache* and the *Heracles*, the only two of the four plays which are included in the published volumes of Professor Gilbert Murray, I have used his edition. For the *Helen* I use the text of W. Dindorf in the 1869 edition (with *apparatus criticus*) of the *Poetae Scenici*. For the *Orestes* I refer to the edition (and commentary) of Mr Wedd. I have used also the commentary of Mr Hyslop on the *Andromache*, those of Professor von Wilamowitz-Möllendorff and Mr Blakeney on the *Heracles*, those of Paley on all the four plays, and others. To the commentary of Mr Wedd I am largely indebted.

It has been my intention to notice doubts, whether of text or interpretation, which seem material to the purpose of my citation; if in any case I have not done so, it is by inadvertence. But doubts of either kind, when they are not for my purpose material, I do not notice.

I cite frequently the translation of Euripides in verse by Mr A. S. Way, and appreciate highly the advantage of being able to adduce a version so faithful. It will naturally be understood, that by those citations I do not pledge myself to agreement with the translator in all details. Differences or questions not material to the immediate purpose, I pass here, as in the original text, without remark.

In correcting the book for the press, I have received great help from my friend and colleague Mr J. D. Duff, for whose pains I cannot be too grateful. And I have also to acknowledge, with the special thanks due from an unskilful corrector, the excellent services of the University Press.

A. W. V.

Trinity College, Cambridge.
September 20, 1905.

CONTENTS.

INTRODUCTION.

Four plays of Euripides are discussed in this volume, which may be regarded as a sequel to that entitled *Euripides the Rationalist*, though the topics are for the most part different.

Of the four plays three, the *Andromache, Helen*, and *Heracles*, have been selected, because the present state of study and criticism suggests that a fresh discussion of them is warranted and perhaps necessary. The *Andromache* is little read for pleasure ; and it is generally agreed that the play, as now understood, is bad. The *Helen*, as a whole, is not much esteemed ; those who pronounce any positive opinion upon it, agree generally in thinking it weak. In the *Heracles*, common opinion awards high praise to a portion, which portion however is so interpreted as to require the supposition that the rest of the drama is worse than irrelevant ; and the whole has accordingly been dismissed by some, not without reason, as inconsistent and inexplicable.

Now doubtless Euripides had faults. He had difficulties, and therefore faults, peculiar to himself. The proposition that 'the genius of Euripides was at discord with the form in which he worked[1],' must be the basis of any reasonable criticism upon his work. It will be seen from some parts of these Essays, that, far from disputing that proposition, I conceive it to have some applications, which are not at present commonly recognized.

[1] Sir R. C. Jebb; Article on 'Literature' in *A Companion to Greek Studies*, p. 115.

But when we consider in what an age, and under what judgments, his plays attained celebrity, and when we consider the sifting process, by which they were reduced to the extant number, we may modestly and properly doubt whether any of the remnant can really deserve a general blame. In these cases at any rate there is room for the suggestion, that we do not yet see to the bottom of the matter. And indeed at the present time I hope and believe that such suggestions, offered with respect, will be received with pleasure.

My belief is that, with regard to each of the three plays above named, judgment is at present embarrassed by a fundamental misconception.

The *Andromache* is criticized as if it were an independent work, a complete story. So regarded, it appears to me, and has long appeared, neither bad nor good, but simply unintelligible. But what if it is part of a story, a sequel? Then to treat it as an independent whole is as if we were to expound and estimate the *Catriona* of R. L. Stevenson, without knowing or suspecting that there had ever been such a story as *Kidnapped*.

The *Helen* is estimated as a melodrama, and, so estimated, is pronounced, as well it may be, weak. But what if it were a playful imitation of melodrama, in which the vagaries of Greek tragedy are deliberately exaggerated? What if the circumstances of the production were such, that only a humorous theme and playful treatment were suitable, or even admissible?

In the *Heracles* the poet was in earnest, profoundly in earnest, with his purpose, whatever that was. This is evident, but beyond this we cannot go without encountering doubt. Starting with any presumption, with any whatever, respecting the purpose of the dramatist, the reader will soon find reason. I do not say to abandon that presumption, but to question it, to suspend his judgment. And certainly it does not become an interpreter to be trenchant, when his author is ambiguous, and appears *prima facie* to offer simply contradictions. In this case, as in the *Ion*, the main thing superficially visible is that, whatever Euripides meant, he did not mean to be plain. But in such a case, the first condition of an acceptable reading is that it should account for the ambiguity and the obscurity,

A man, or at all events a dramatist, who conceals his meaning, must have a reason for concealment. Now the current reading of the *Heracles*, which presumes the religious legend of the hero to be the basis of the story, is open, I think, to this universal and sufficient objection, that it does not account for the ambiguity and the obscurity. A drama about the passage of the Red Sea, which was meant simply to illustrate the account in *Exodus*, might have many different qualities ; but one it would certainly not have : in its general purpose it would not be obscure. But suppose that a man of some sagacity and originality, after much reading in the learned and ingenious speculations of sceptical commentators on the Pentateuch, after sadly digesting many conjectures about the possible effect of winds and tides in producing an uncommon state of the waters, were to arrive (as he might) at the conclusion, that, when all in this way had been said, the description in *Exodus* cannot really be ·accounted for as merely a loose version of a natural incident : that we must necessarily suppose either miracle or else imagination, and indeed a singularly powerful imagination, a wild and lawless imagination. Suppose this man to speculate gravely or humorously in his own mind upon the possibility that the wild imagination concerned in the product was that of him who 'slew the Egyptian,' and that the leader and historian of the Israelites, having the strongest mind and strongest character of his age, had also a touch of insanity. Suppose the man so speculating to be a poet, and to conceive (as he might) that such a hero, such a Moses, would be no mean subject for a tragedy. Suppose the poet so placed, that his tragedy, if presented to the public at all, must be exhibited on Easter Monday, in the Albert Hall, under the patronage of the State, and before an audience comprising not merely ministers of all kinds and degrees, but students from the Universities and pupils from the Schools. Would you expect the play to be transparent ?

The *Orestes*, the fourth play on our list, stands in a very different position from the other three. The general opinion of readers has placed it, as a whole and under some important reservations, very high. Under all criticisms and reservations, it is constantly read ; and this is the real test of appreciation.

And therefore an expositor, who professed to modify fundamentally the current conception of the *Orestes*, would and should be received with distrust. I have no such pretension. As to the general line and character of the play, I differ not at all from what is laid down, for example, in the edition of Mr Wedd ; or so little, that I have doubted whether I had material and grounds enough for publication. But on certain points, especially in the latter part of the play, there is, I think, something of general importance to be said. And I have thought it most convenient to place these points in a connected view of the whole.

The appendix of notes on the four plays has, much of it, no special connexion with the Essays ; and I would ask for it a different consideration. In studying the plays, I have naturally had occasion to consider points of detail, which are notoriously difficult or obscure ; and on some of these suggestions have occurred to me which seemed worth noting for consideration. But the questions raised in the appendix, those of them which do not relate to the Essays, are mostly such as do not, in my judgment, admit a positive answer ; and in the appendix, so far as it does not affect the Essays, a general *perhaps*, whether expressed or not, is to be understood.

A GREEK BORGIA.

(*ANDROMACHE.*)

Phoebus delights to view his laurel-tree.   *The Oracle.*

I myself have seen the ungodly in great power, and flourishing like a green bay-tree.   *The Psalmist.*

THE purpose of this essay, as foreshewn in the Introduction, is to prove that the *Andromache*, a play notorious in the current criticism of Euripides for its formless and unintelligible construction, owes this undeserved reproach to the fact that it is not and does not pretend to be a story complete in itself. It is a sequel, a second part. The first part was probably also dramatized by Euripides. But whether this was so or not, the first part, as a story, certainly pre-existed. The *Andromache* takes it as known, and without it is no more comprehensible than the second volume of a novel to a reader ignorant of the first.

The simplest way of presenting the matter will be first to give the preceding story, so far as it can be ascertained, and the sequel, the extant part of the story, so far as is necessary to show the connexion. The reader will then be in a position to estimate the evidence alleged, from the extant play and from criticisms upon it, that the play is not intelligible *per se*, but requires for its explanation some such a preface as we have constructed.

Menelaus, king of Sparta, at the time when with his brother Agamemnon he made the famous expedition against Troy for the recovery of Helen, left at home an only child, an infant daughter, Hermione. By a family arrangement this heiress was promised in marriage to an heir even more important, her cousin Orestes, only son of Agamemnon, king of Argos; and the children were bred in this expectation. But towards the end of the Trojan war, by the death of Achilles the success of the Greeks came to depend upon the assistance of his son Neoptolemus. To obtain this, Menelaus, a politic, selfish, and unscrupulous man, promised his daughter to that prince also. She was still far from marriageable age, and the conflict of engagements did not arise till some years later. Meanwhile Troy fell, and Agamemnon returning to Argos was murdered by his wife Clytaemnestra; Orestes was from this time brought up in Phocis, where he formed a close con-nexion with the administrators of the oracle of Delphi; a vigorous youth, but of a singularly inhuman disposition, at once cold and ferocious, he not only set himself on reaching manhood to avenge his father and recover his right, but, encouraged by the oracle, actually slew his mother with his own hand. The deed excited general horror, and Orestes became an exile once more. About this time Hermione came of age, and Menelaus, whose absence had been prolonged for some years after the fall of Troy, returned to Greece. Both Orestes and Neoptolemus claimed his promise, and there ensued a contest, in which Orestes was completely worsted. He besought his cousin to fly with him, but she refused. He tried to work upon the generosity of his rival by pleading 'the hardship of his position' (*v.* 974) but was haughtily repulsed. He urged the father to respect the prior engagement; but Menelaus, whose object now and throughout was to sell his daughter to the best advantage, preferred in the circumstances the alliance of Neoptolemus.

But though the emissary of Delphi was thus signally defeated, 'Apollo' could foresee and promise an equally perfect revenge. With Neoptolemus, a gallant man but impetuous and imprudent, Delphi had already a personal quarrel; he had had the audacity to demand of 'Apollo' satisfaction for the death of his father Achilles. By another error (which Greek sentiment would probably not have much reprehended, though Euripides thought otherwise) he had laid his domestic position open to attack. Cohabiting with his Trojan captive Andromache, formerly wife of Hector, he had become by her the father of a boy, and upon his marriage, though he quitted his connexion with the mother, he retained in his household both her and her son. The jealousy of his young wife, who loved him passionately, rose almost to madness when after some time she herself was without a child ; and the same circumstances convinced Menelaus that he had chosen the worse bargain, and that his nephew, who, apart from his temporary disgrace, was by far the more important personage of the two, would after all be the better ally. But to repair the mistake was not easy. To remove the unguarded Neoptolemus was indeed a simple matter; and Orestes, aided by the fanatics of Delphi, undertook to do this, upon the occasion of a visit paid by his rival to the oracle for the purpose of appeasing the offended god. But there remained the apparently insoluble problem, how in any tolerable and not too scandalous manner Hermione, loving Neoptolemus to distraction, could be forced to accept for her second husband the assassin of the first. The *Andromache* shows with what cold-blooded and truly Spartan ingenuity Menelaus achieves this purpose, so using the circumstances of the family and the characters of the persons composing it that his daughter is actually compelled by conjugal passion to put herself, while yet ignorant of her husband's fate and her own position, into the power of the destined successor. The action takes place at the house of Neoptolemus near Pharsalus in Phthia, and commences at the time when Orestes, having killed Neoptolemus at Delphi, has brought the news of his death to Menelaus, who has come to Phthia from Sparta for the purpose of preparing and executing at the proper moment his part of the plot.

The story, in dexterous combination and moral interest one of the best among the extant remains of Attic tragedy, is manifestly such that, like many other stories excellently fitted for dramatic purposes, it could not possibly be exhibited entirely within a single play of the Greek form. If, as seems most probable, it is essentially the invention of Euripides, then

we must necessarily suppose that the earlier part, the preliminaries to the *Andromache*, was the subject of a preceding play,
which turned upon the contest of the rivals for the hand of
Hermione, and the determination of that contest in favour of
Neoptolemus.   We shall see that for the existence of this
play there is some positive evidence.   But I would clearly
repeat that this, the embodiment of the former part
in the shape of a drama, cannot be fully proved.   It is
in my opinion probable, perhaps something more, but it is
not certain.   What is certain and demonstrable is that the
Andromache assumes for known, in some form and by some
means, a preceding story having the general outline which
we have drawn, and starts from the situation which we have
indicated, a plot between Menelaus and his nephew to transfer
the possession of Hermione, after the assassination of
Neoptolemus, to Orestes.

In colour, circumstances, and characters the story, like others
of Euripides, the *Orestes* for instance and the *Ion*, is essentially
'modern,' of his own time, and takes from heroic antiquity
really nothing but the names.   The general foundation of it,
down to the return of Menelaus to Greece, follows common
legend, and requires no special exposition.   The central
portion, from this point to the opening of the *Andromache*, is
evidenced for us by the statements and implications of the
Andromache itself.   In the extant part, the existing play, the
principal interest lies in the exhibition of the refined depravity,
probably drawn from life, which noble Greek politicians could
display in dealing with a domestic embarrassment.   The
methods of Menelaus remind one strongly of those which
are attributed, I profess not to say with what justice, to the
nobility of the Italian Renaissance, and the title of this essay
has been chosen from that point of view.

Without the facts presupposed the *Andromache* is not
merely formless, but unintelligible.   It falls into a series of
actions not only disconnected, but each of them separately
inexplicable.   In particular the proceedings of Menelaus,
which occupy most of the piece, have as a whole no conceivable purpose, no end, adequate or inadequate, to which as a

whole they possibly can be directed. The performance of
Orestes becomes so casual in the occurrence, and so obscure
in aim and result, that it does not and cannot command any
interest. And the death of Neoptolemus, appended as another
occurrence to these occurrences, without connexion prior or
posterior, and even without any definite relation in time, would
seem to fill up a congeries for which it would be difficult, and
is not necessary, to find any suitable name. It is certainly
neither story nor play, as these words are commonly understood. Nor is it any paradox to say this ; the same thing in
substance has been said repeatedly, under the form of criticisms *ex hypothesi* upon the dramatist. However, it matters
not how reasonable, or how absurd, the *Andromache* would be,
if it were an independent work ; because we are in a position
to *prove* that it is not such a work. To approach the subject
properly, I will ask leave now to state separately, though at
the expense of some repetition, those facts which are actually
narrated or performed in the extant drama itself.

A summary of the play will run as follows.

Menelaus, king of Sparta, married his daughter Hermione
to Neoptolemus of Phthia, son of Achilles, and himself one of
the principal actors in the taking of Troy. Neoptolemus, at
the time of the marriage, had already a son by a slave-woman,
Andromache, formerly wife of Hector. Though this connexion
was then broken off, the slave and her child have remained in
the household, where the little boy in particular is the object
of much affection. The wife, who is passionately attached to
her husband, detests them both, and her jealousy, rising to
fury when after some time she herself remains barren, has
made the situation intolerable. Neoptolemus, having reason
to suspect the enmity of Apollo, has gone to Delphi to obtain
reconciliation with the god. During his absence, Menelaus
has come from Sparta to his daughter's home, which is
situated near Pharsalus, the capital and residence of the aged
Peleus, grandfather of Neoptolemus and still sovereign. These
facts are narrated in a semi-dramatic prologue spoken by
Andromache, who further informs us that, believing herself
and her son to be in danger from Menelaus, she has sent the

boy to a neighbour, and has taken refuge at an altar, which
lies before the entrance of the house and composes with it the
scene of the play.   At this point the action commences.—
Andromache, learning from a Trojan woman, now her fellow-
slave, that Menelaus has discovered the boy, persuades the
informant to summon Peleus, whom previous messengers have
apparently failed to reach.   Hermione visits her rival and
commands her to quit sanctuary, but makes no impression
and returns to the house.   Menelaus however by producing
his young captive, and threatening to take his life, is more
successful; to save the boy, Andromache surrenders at
discretion, whereupon Menelaus declares that the life of the
child, though spared by him, is still liable to the sentence of
Hermione, and conducts both his victims within to receive
her judgment.   Presently he brings them out again; both are
to die; and the execution appears to be imminent, when
Peleus arrives.   On learning the situation, the aged prince
violently upbraids the invader of his family, who, he says, will
do well to depart, and take his 'barren daughter' along with
him.   Menelaus professes himself unable to comprehend this
indignation; if his friendly intentions are so received, he will
not contest the matter, which can be decided at leisure hereafter; for the present he has business at Sparta.   And
hereupon, without communicating with his daughter or even
re-entering the house, he departs as for Sparta forthwith, while
the rescued pair, Andromache and the boy, go away under the
protection of Peleus.   After a while, an uproar in the house
apprises us that Hermione has become aware of her father's
departure, and promptly she herself appears, frantic with terror
at the idea of meeting her husband, without any support,
after what has passed, and eager for instant flight.   At this
moment enters Orestes, nephew of Menelaus and cousin to
the princess.   The accident of a journey has brought him, as
he explains, to her neighbourhood, and he has taken the
opportunity to enquire after her health.   Hermione, in a
transport of relief, explains the position of affairs, and be-
seeches him to place her in safety, to conduct her to her
father.   This, after some demur, he consents to do for the

sake of old times, reminding her that, though bestowed on a more fortunate pretender, she had once been promised to himself. This reminiscence she waives as inopportune, and hurries him off, referring all questions to the decision of her father. The news of her flight recalls Peleus, who, learning that Orestes in the moment of departure has threatened machinations against Neoptolemus, is about to send warning to Delphi, when the companions of Neoptolemus arrive. They bring from Delphi the body of their master, murdered there by Orestes and others. With the narrative of the murder and the lamentations of Peleus the action ends. The prophecies of Thetis, mother of Achilles, who concludes the piece, after the Euripidean manner, with an apparition *ex machina*, portend to Peleus consolation in another world, and to the son of Andromache (Molossus) a kingdom (Molossia) in this.

Such is the action presented. Is it then—this is our first question—is it, as a fact, self-explanatory? Do we comprehend it as a whole? Do the incidents proceed one from the other, account for one another, exhibit, in the motives of the actors, a mutual relation of cause and effect? The answer appears to be unanimous. The whole, as a whole, is nothing. The play, as a whole, is worthless. A recent editor, reflecting the common opinion, expressly directs notice to considerations which 'redeem the *Andromache* from worthlessness,' considerations which deal with parts only, with single elements or separate scenes. Considerations of this kind we may find in abundance; there is scarcely any portion of the play, perhaps not one important speech, which does *not* exhibit proofs of great literary and artistic skill. But nothing of this kind affects the unanimous judgment pronounced (*ex hypothesi*) upon the futility of the whole as a whole, the lack of a story. It is agreed that the play so conceived is (to use the very inadequate term usually applied to the case) 'wanting in unity.'

The use of so mild a term is unfortunate, and though prompted doubtless by respect for Euripides, tends really to do him a monstrous injustice, by concealing the enormity, and therefore the improbability, of the charge thereby alleged against him. A play is properly said to 'want unity' when there is not any one common interest, in which all the parts converge, and which combines them into a whole. Such a defect may be exhibited in plays in which the mechanical connexion and sequence of the incidents is perfectly clear, in plays which have *a story*, a story plain and simple. It is sometimes found in the work of the most skilful and experienced playwrights, and may be alleged without improbability against any one. It is alleged for example against the *Ajax* of Sophocles, where the interest turns first upon the suicide of the hero, and then upon the question whether he shall be duly buried. These, it is said, are separate interests, and do not properly compose a single theme. Such a charge, whether justified or not—I agree with those who think it in this case not substantial—is properly signified by the term 'want of unity.'

It is not meant, and of course could not be alleged without absurdity, that the death and burial of Ajax do not make *a story*, that there is not between the incidents any natural sequence or necessary connexion whatever. So again a certain 'want of unity' may be attributed to *The Merchant of Venice*, because the marriage of Portia and the persecution of Antonio, though the mechanical link between them is plain and solid enough, are topics not very harmonious in interest, and because each topic is pursued into some developments which have little, if any, bearing upon the other. But they compose a story. The play does not leave us ignorant of any relation between the scene of the caskets and the scene of the trial, at what interval and after what incidents the one scene followed upon the other, and why Portia should be present at both. The 'want of unity' does not mean this. But this, and nothing less, must be the want of unity which shall cover the case of the *Andromache*, if we are to presume nothing which is not stated in the drama. It presents three incidents, (1) the visit of Menelaus to Phthia, (2) the visit of Orestes, (3) the murder of Neoptolemus at Delphi, not one of which is connected as cause or effect with another. The coincidence of the first two is (we are to suppose) fortuitous, while the third is so totally independent, that we need not and cannot determine (so we are told[1]) when and by what intermediary process it comes to pass. This is to 'want unity' with a vengeance! But what hypothesis could be less probable than that so insane a method of composition was practised and accepted by the rival and the audience of Sophocles?

Nor are these independent portions even intelligible separately. During the first half of the play the principal agent is Menelaus, whose action, so far as appears upon the statements of the play, is from first to last unintelligible and absurd. A man of mature years and experience takes a long journey and undergoes much trouble, that he may instigate and encourage a young wife to secure her hold upon the home and heart of a husband, whom she passionately loves, by openly murdering that husband's only and beloved child! A prince, coming privately into the territory and almost into the residence of an ally, proceeds to seize and execute there the sovereign's sole descendant, and when caught in the act, is surprised that his friendly proceeding should move the ancestor to resentment! A politician and soldier lays a design which can hardly be concealed from those who will certainly arrest it, yet allows the discovery to be made in the most obvious and preventable way, and at the first opposition postpones the affair *sine die*! A father, having deliberately involved his married daughter, acting under his authority, in a domestic situation of extreme delicacy and peril, withdraws, escapes, and disappears without bestowing upon her so much as a farewell! There is no end to the extravagances and contradictions of a portraiture in which no one, so far as I am aware, professes to find any interest. *Incredulus odi*: it is incredible and disgusting. Part of this incredibility the dramatist is actually at the pains to prove. That the murder of Andromache must disgrace both the princess and the king, and that the murder of the young Molossus[2] means ruin to

---

[1] See hereafter, and refer to commentaries upon *Andromache* 1115.

[2] It is convenient to use this name, though it is not given, and scarcely so much as implied, in the play. See *v.* 1248, and the *dramatis personae* in Prof. Murray's text.

the wife and endless embarrassments to her father, is not only obvious but is explained to the conqueror of Troy by the Trojan captive, Andromache:

> And the child's death—
> Think ye his sire shall hold it a little thing?
> So void of manhood Troy proclaims him not.
> Nay, he shall follow duty's call, be proved,
> By deeds, of Peleus worthy and Achilles.
> He shall thrust forth thy child. What plea wilt find
> For a new spouse?—This lie—'the saintly soul
> Of this pure thing shrank from her wicked Lord'?
> Who shall wed such? Wilt keep her in thine halls
> Spouseless, a grey-haired widow? O thou wretch,
> Seest not the floods of evil bursting o'er thee[1]?

She expresses amazement and almost commiseration that these and other such considerations should escape the intelligence of such a personage. How is it possible for us to suppose that they do escape him, or that he is pursuing what he really believes to be the interest of his daughter as wife to Neoptolemus? Or how can we imagine that, if really possessed by such a delusion, he, the mighty king of Sparta, will quit the pursuit of his purpose, and this with apparent indifference, for a few high words from such an opposer as Peleus? But the acme of the incomprehensible is reached in his departure, when, pleading a vague business at home, he quits the scene—and is heard of no more. For this proceeding we are shown no motive whatever. He is in no danger, and what is more, he shows no alarm. His bearing towards Peleus is cool, contemptuous, and provocative. Nor is it even suggested to him—how could such a suggestion be made without absurdity?—that he should leave Hermione, and leave her without notice of his intention. The old king, in the violence of his indignation, bids him 'take his daughter away[2]'; but that even this is not seriously meant, and that

---

[1] *Andr.* 339 foll. (Way). The play everywhere assumes that Neoptolemus is not an unfaithful husband (even if this accusation were to the purpose) and that his fidelity could be established. In 346 πεύσεται, *he will inform himself of the facts* (Kiehl, Murray) seems a better reading than ἐψεύσεται, and puts the point more clearly.

[2] *v.* 639, *v.* 708.

Peleus expects no effect from it, appears from his own behaviour both immediately afterwards[1], and again a little later, upon hearing of Hermione's flight[2]. More than this, it is something like a physical impossibility, that such a personage as the King of Sparta should vanish at a moment's notice and without any preparation, commencing a journey of many days in such a manner that his departure is not discovered till he is beyond reach of recall. In every aspect the thing is purposeless, incredible, and silly.

And to increase our perplexity, it appears that the portraiture of Menelaus is supposed by the author to have, at least indirectly, a political application, gratifying to Athenian prejudices against the Spartan character. The speech of Andromache, beginning

> O ye in all folk's eyes most loathed of men,
> Dwellers in Sparta, senates of treachery,`
> Princes of lies, weavers of webs of guile,
> Thoughts crooked, wholesome never, devious all—
> A crime is your supremacy in Greece[3]!

is always and necessarily so understood. But if the Menelaus of the play is such as he is now made out to be, stupid and cowardly, without foresight, sense, or firmness, a sort of imbecile or idiot, where is the point of the satire? If the kings of Sparta or the Spartans generally had resembled this, their power and policy would not have excited in their adversaries those feelings of detestation and fear to which Euripides appeals.

The visit of Menelaus occupies more than half the play. The visit of Orestes, filling one scene, though more intelligible, is scarcely more satisfactory. The gist of it is that Hermione, by the arrival of her cousin, is enabled to obey the prompting of her terror and to follow her fugitive father. The obvious objection here is the extravagant employment of the fortuitous. In the conduct of a story, coincidences, within reasonable limits, may no doubt and must be supposed, and will readily be

---

[1] *vv.* 747 foll.   [2] *vv.* 1047–1069; see especially *v.* 1060.
[3] *vv.* 445 foll. (Way).

accepted if a sufficient interest depends upon them. In the *Oedipus Tyrannus*, it is a coincidence that the death of the king's supposed father is announced to him while he is investigating that of his real father; and since this is necessary to the development of a most admirable and exciting intrigue, it is very well. It is a coincidence, but an admissible coincidence, that Medea, having one day in which to find a friend who will give her refuge, is visited by such a friend upon that day. But the visit of Orestes goes plainly beyond belief. He is the one man in the world who could be supposed likely to assist Hermione in leaving her husband's house. He is journeying (so he tells us[1]) to Dodona, at the end of Greece, and finding himself by this accident in Phthia, pays a call, as we should say, of enquiry. And he meets Hermione, eager for flight, at the very door! Whether the scene redeems, by its interest and truth to nature, this draft upon our credulity, I shall not discuss. The movement of it is precipitate, and the motives, on the side of Orestes, obscure. We should doubt to what it will lead, which would be a very proper effect, if we had the means of divining, or were afterwards told. But as we never are told, and Hermione after this episode is not heard of again, the scene remains hung up as it were, without development as without preparation, a fragment.

The third portion of the play, a powerful narrative of the murder of Neoptolemus, with a slight dramatic framework, is without fault, if considered apart, but to the story, as a whole, it contributes nothing. At what interval of time, and after what intermediate events, the murder follows (if it does follow) upon the proceedings at Phthia, is actually supposed by critics, as we remarked before, to be an open question ; and of interdependency, upon this hypothesis, it is needless to speak.

Such is the construction, if the word is applicable, now attributed to the *Andromache* of Euripides. Upon the external evidence against such an assumption I shall not insist, though I consider it prohibitory. 'Of all plots and actions the epeisodic,' says Aristotle, 'are the worst. I call a plot

[1] *v.* 885.

"epeisodic" in which the episodes or acts succeed one another without probable or necessary sequence. Bad poets compose such pieces by their own fault, good poets, to please the players ; for, as they write show pieces for competition, they stretch the plot beyond its capacity, and are often forced to break the natural continuity[1].' For an extant example of this just and exact remark we may cite the *Suppliants* of Euripides. The subject of that play is the generosity of Athens in rescuing the corpses of certain Argives, to which the victorious Thebans have refused burial, and which receive a solemn funeral at Eleusis. During this rite Evadne, wife to one of the dead, having escaped in distraction of mind from the care of her relatives at Argos, comes wandering to the place and throws herself upon the pyre of her husband. Now in this occurrence there is nothing obscure or unnatural : the *when* and *why* of it are perfectly clear. But since it is 'neither necessary nor probable' that such a fact should arise out of the circumstances of this particular funeral, since the fact is merely possible and has no relation to the general subject of the play, the enterprise of Athens, the occurrence is an 'episode' in the bad sense, which breaks the plot and 'stretches it beyond its capacity.' This example illustrates also the temptation, alleged by Aristotle, to please the actors and to enrich the show by introducing an effective part, the part of the *suttee*. A narrative episode, where the connexion required is of course that of the events narrated as well as of the narration itself regarded as an event, may exhibit the same fault. 'Epeisodic' in this sense has been supposed to be the description of the beacons in the *Agamemnon* of Aeschylus, and indeed all the first half of that tragedy, consisting of facts which, as preliminaries to the murder of the king, are possible merely but 'neither necessary nor probable.' This supposition is, I think, mistaken, and proceeds from misconception of the story, but it is none the less available as an illustration of Aristotle. Now the fault so defined is noted by Aristotle, not without reason, as 'the worst' which a plot can have. But it is not the worst, it is far from the worst, if we are to

[1] *Poetics* ix. § 10 (Butcher).

include such a 'plot' as is attributed to the *Andromache*, comprising events between which no connexion and no sequence is even alleged, an event A and another event A[1] (we must not call it B, for this at least suggests sequence), which are set down separately, side by side, without so much as a given order in time, and which the reader may arrange or not arrange as he pleases. To say of such a plot, that the sequence of its episodes is 'neither necessary nor probable,' or that it is 'stretched beyond its capacity,' would be criticism futile and short of the mark. But Aristotle ignores and by implication excludes such a case, not imagining, as we may naturally suppose, that it could ever occur. Nor does it nor could it occur ; it is an offence to which there is no temptation. A similar inference, perhaps even stronger in its bearing upon Euripides, might be drawn from the silence of Aristophanes.

But such *a priori* considerations, however cogent, are of little importance in view of the fact, which I now propose to prove, that the plot or story of the *Andromache* is not that which has been supposed. And in particular, as a first step in the argument, I shall prove that the play does not profess to contain the story entire, but presumes the story, whatever it was, as known beforehand to the spectator or reader. As this point is of the utmost importance, both for this play and for the general history of Athenian drama, I ask leave to explain formally the nature of the proof.

The proof does *not* depend upon any subjective judgment respecting the sufficiency or insufficiency for artistic purposes of the facts given in the play, respecting the goodness or badness, in short, of a story supposed to contain those facts and those only. If the facts given in the *Andromache* composed in themselves an excellent story, it would still be certain and demonstrable, that not the play, but something external and prior to the play, is supposed to put us partly in possession of those facts. And for this reason. The facts actually given are not disclosed either (1) in such an order, or (2) in such a manner, that their relations can be understood. The last scene, and the last scene only, reveals certain facts *as having pre-existed from a time before the beginning of the*

play. They are even then revealed in such a manner that
their pre-existence, before the beginning of the play, cannot
be ascertained without reviewing the whole, without a retrospect which a reader (as experience has amply proved) is not
likely to pursue, and a spectator could not pursue. Yet one
at least of the preceding scenes is of such a character, that a
reader or spectator of it, if not then acquainted with the pre-
existing facts, must (and actually does) totally and irretrievably
misconceive and misunderstand it. These phenomena compel
us to the inference that *something*, these pre-existing facts at
least, is assumed by the dramatist as already given to the
spectator from some source external to the drama.

The facts revealed in the final scene, or rather upon a
comparison of the final scene with the whole drama, are
these :

(1) that some time, some days, before the beginning of the
play Neoptolemus has been murdered at Delphi ;

(2) that Orestes was then at Delphi, assisting in the
murder.

We will take them in order.

(1) The corpse of Neoptolemus, carried by his attendants
from Delphi, arrives at his home, the place of action, simultaneously with the second entrance of Peleus[1]. The whole
time from the beginning of the play to this point is covered
by two summonings and two comings of Peleus, *plus* the time
(say, twenty minutes) which may elapse after the disappearance of Menelaus before Hermione learns that he is gone.
Neglecting this addition, and confining our attention to
Peleus, in the first scene we see a messenger despatched to
summon him from his house in the town of Pharsalus[2]. In
the fourth scene he arrives, and departs again to return home[3].
He is recalled by some person, or persons, who tell him that
Hermione has fled, but tell him nothing, and therefore know
nothing, about Orestes, and nothing distinct about Menelaus[4];
slaves (we may suppose) belonging to the household of
Neoptolemus, who go instantly for the old king, as they

[1] *vv.* 1047–1069. [2] *v.* 16, *v.* 22, *v.* 83.
[3] *vv.* 547–765. [4] *v.* 1060.

naturally would, when first she attempts to run away[1]. The place where they find him, and from which he returns, cannot be more distant, and is probably nearer, than Pharsalus. Now Pharsalus is close by. The town and the residence of Neoptolemus have 'common pastures'; a slave-woman may and does get to the town and back before her absence is discovered by a watchful mistress; Peleus, a great-grandfather and shaken with age, passes and repasses without difficulty, and is apparently supposed to walk[2]. No exact distance is prescribed, but Pharsalus is close by. If we put it an hour off (which is too much), three or four hours will cover the action up to the second entrance of Peleus; and almost at the same moment comes the party from Delphi. Now the play assumes as an essential condition, what Euripides and every one else knew for a fact, that Delphi is far away, a long journey. Neoptolemus there is utterly out of reach. The visitors from Pharsalus, on arriving there, spend three days[3], before approaching their business, in indulging their curiosity with a view of the strange place. The journey was in truth about sixty miles, most of it through mountain ranges; and such a conception, not precise but approximate, would be conveyed by the mere names of the places to a public who, as we may see from the history of Herodotus and other evidence, knew well enough the general features of their little country. The companions of Neoptolemus, mere personal attendants, are few, perhaps not more than the necessary five[4], so few at any rate that they do not even detach a messenger, but all return together, bringing the corpse. That such a journey must have occupied not three hours, but something nearer three days, is no matter of calculation, but obvious, a conception arising necessarily with the picture of the facts. It is therefore a datum of the play, that the murder precedes the beginning of the action by a period indefinite but certainly counted in days.

It may be worth while to point out, in view of the way in

---

[1] *v.* 823.
[2] See preceding references.   [3] *v.* 1086.
[4] The narrator of the murder and the bearers of the corpse.

which the drama and its story have been treated, that the question of the foregoing paragraph, the question when the murder happened, *has nothing to do with the movements of Orestes.* The prevalent assumption to the contrary, and the notes which it is the custom to write upon *vv.* 1115—1116, betray upon this point a confusion surprising, though, as we shall see, not inexplicable.

But *secondly,* we learn in the final scene that at the time of the murder Orestes was at Delphi and took part in it. The first half of the narrative is chiefly occupied with exhibiting his presence and activity as leader.

> Thy son's son, ancient Peleus, is no more,
> Such dagger-thrusts hath he received of men
> Of Delphi and that stranger[1] of Mycenae.

> ...While Agamemnon's son passed through the town
> And whispered deadly hints in each man's ear.
> ...Then was Orestes' slander proved of might
> In the hoarse murmur from the throng, 'He lies!
> He hath come for felony.' On he passed, within
> The temple-fence, before the oracle
> To pray, and was in act to sacrifice :—
> Then rose with swords from ambush screened by bays
> A troop against him : Klytemnestra's son
> Was of them, weaver of this treason-web[2].

By this troop, with the favour and assistance of the Delphian mob, Neoptolemus is slain.

It is therefore a fact of the story, and we by the last scene are informed, that Orestes, when he appears in the play, at the time when he consents to conduct Hermione to Menelaus, has actually come from the place of the murder, and knows that her husband is dead. But—and here is the vital point—

---

[1] 'Their ally' would be nearer the sense.

[2] *vv.* 1073-1116 (Way). Here again it matters not whether we render the idly debated *vv.* 1115-1116, ὧν Κλυταιμνήστρας τόκος | εἶς ἦν ἁπάντων τῶνδε μηχανορράφος, as above, or make them (with some) mean merely that Orestes was 'the contriver of all this.' His presence is shown by the whole narrative, and his actual part in the act by *vv.* 1074-1075, and *v.* 1242 (χερός). See Mr Hyslop's note (edition of Macmillan, 1900). Nor are the debated verses really ambiguous; the natural meaning of ὧν εἶς ἦν (cf. *v.* 614) cannot be affected by what follows.

the dialogue and relations between Orestes and Hermione are
such, that the dramatist, since he intends Orestes to have this
knowledge, must also intend that the real situation of Orestes,
his part in the murder and knowledge of the murder as an
accomplished fact, shall be known to the audience when they
witness the scene of the abduction. The contrary is inconceivable, never has been suggested, and never will be by any
one. What is now supposed by critics is that, at the time of
the abduction, the murder is really future. This, as we have
seen, is impossible ; and if the murder is then past, the
audience must be supposed then to know it. Otherwise not
only must they mistake the whole spirit of the scene, but they
must be irretrievably deceived as to the facts.

> Agamemnon's son and Klytemnestra's I,
> My name Orestes : to Zeus' oracle
> Bound, at Dodona. Seeing I am come
> To Phthia, good it seems that I enquire
> Of my kinswoman, if she lives and thrives,
> Hermione of Sparta. Though she dwell
> In a far land from us, she is all as dear[1].

These are lies, the journey to Dodona and all the rest.
But the audience, if not previously informed of the murder,
must take them, as readers now do, for truth, and similarly
throughout the scene must altogether misconceive the bearing
of everything which Orestes says or does. For such a
deception of the audience there is no conceivable motive ; it
is not a case in which Euripides can have meant his purpose
to be and remain, so far as concerns the theatre, ambiguous.
Even if the audience were afterwards, in the last scene,
effectually enlightened and undeceived, they could only say
' Then please let us have the abduction over again, now that
we are in a position to understand it.'

But in truth the result would be different and far worse ;
for as the play stands, spectators of it never would apprehend
the true facts at all, and even readers have but a poor chance.
The final scene does, it is true, disclose the facts, and makes
them certain, but only upon a retrospect of the whole play,

---

[1] *vv.* 884 foll. (Way).

a comparison of what we are finally told with what we have seen all along. But there is a particular circumstance, which does now actually prevent readers, and even students, from grasping the significance of the final disclosure and its relation to what precedes, does actually prevent them, even with the book in hand, from making the necessary retrospect and thus arriving at the truth. At the end of the abduction-scene, and when Hermione has left the stage (we will consider this point hereafter), Orestes actually describes the plot against Neoptolemus, but speaks of the murder as future:

> Such toils of doom by this hand woven for him
> With murder-meshes round him steadfast-staked
> Are drawn : thereof I speak not ere the time ;
> But, when I strike, the Delphian rock shall know[1],

with more to the same effect. Now when we have once perceived and learned that the murder, when these words are spoken, is in fact done, we also instantly perceive, that these words give us no reason for thinking otherwise. Being where he is, at the house of Neoptolemus, Orestes could not possibly describe the murder as done, and done by him. He must refer to it, if at all, as future. Nay more, it is only the past fact which (as we shall see) makes credible, in the circumstances, such a revelation of what is said to be future. If the murder were still to be accomplished, would Orestes give this warning of it in Phthia? As to the futurity he lies of course, as throughout the scene he lies. But if, not being otherwise informed, we take this speech, when we hear it, for truth, the subsequent disclosure, made as it is, produces no enlightenment, but only a sense of confusion. We feel indeed, every one feels, a difficulty. But even students have not been able to set themselves right ; and instead of correcting by the disclosure their interpretation of the abduction-scene, have either abandoned the story as unintelligible, or wandered off into unavailing attempts to make the final scene square with the abduction-scene as misread, to make the final scene also mean that the murder, at the time of the

---

[1] *vv.* 995 foll. (Way).

abduction, was future. When students do this, what would an ordinary reader do, and what could a spectator?

Once more therefore, it is certain that from some external source the spectator or reader of the play is supposed to learn beforehand this much at least, that, before the action opens, Neoptolemus has been murdered by Orestes at Delphi.

But we cannot reasonably stop at this point, or suppose that the external source gave just this fact and no more. It is but rational, it is necessary, to suppose that the information given by the external source (since there was one) was sufficient to make the whole play intelligible. We know now why Orestes comes to Pharsalus, and why he is ready to take away Hermione. But how happens it that, at the very instant when he presents himself, Hermione, the passionate lover of Neoptolemus, is ready to be taken away? How can Orestes anticipate this? Why does Menelaus pursue a course of conduct which has and must have this result, which can have no other, and which, apart from the result, is without sense or purpose? These things also the external source must have explained, by informing us from the first that Menelaus is co-operating with Orestes.

What is the motive of this alliance the play itself explains[1]. Hermione, only child of the king of Sparta, was originally promised, we are told, to Orestes, only son of her uncle Agamemnon, king of Argos—a family arrangement almost dictated by the circumstances. To buy the necessary help of Neoptolemus, as representative of Achilles, at Troy, Menelaus contracted his daughter also to him, and notwithstanding the inferiority of the match[2] preferred the later engagement to the earlier, because Orestes, before the return from Troy, made himself for the time impossible by murdering his mother Clytaemnestra. The marriage, though the husband loved the wife and she adored her husband, was from a worldly point of view a failure, partly from domestic embarrassments, but chiefly because it was barren. With time, and the persistent support of the oracle at Delphi, the heir of Agamemnon had

---

[1] See the prologue, the abduction-scene, and the murder.
[2] See *vv.* 147–154, 209–210, and the behaviour of Menelaus *passim.*

become again a person of consequence, and was perfectly ready to repair by a second murder the disastrous effects of his first. Uncle and nephew came to terms. The visit of Neoptolemus to Delphi made part of the plan easy, and it remained only to overcome an obstacle which in ordinary circumstances would have been invincible. That Hermione, such as she is, should be induced to wed willingly with the murderer of Neoptolemus, was a plain impossibility[1]. She must be made to put herself, while yet unconscious of her loss, in the power of the assassin, and to do it, if that might be managed, so as to incur the suspicion of complicity. The play shows how, by the abominable cunning of Menelaus, abusing for his purpose the confidence of his daughter, her love for her husband and fear of his displeasure, and playing upon the weak points of the family, the ambiguous position of Andromache and her child, and the inconsiderate impetuosity of the old Peleus, the obstacle is triumphantly turned.

But now, as to the 'external source,' how, it will naturally be asked, are we to conceive that? So imperfect, so very small, is our knowledge of literary and theatrical conditions at the time and place, that any answer to such a question must be given with reserve. Subject to this I will say, in this particular case I can imagine nothing which would completely meet the requirements except a preceding play, a 'First Part,' to which our *Andromache* was the sequel. A sequence of plays was a thing familiar to the Athenians, and composition in this form was not abandoned, as we know, when, for the purpose of competition at the festivals, the practice was introduced of 'contending with play against play' and not 'by trilogies.' For many excellent stories, and this is one of them, a single play of the Athenian type is an impossible form. There are in the *Andromache* indications of the preceding play, and traces perhaps, but dubious, in the fragments of ancient commentary. Of the two Greek 'arguments' prefixed

---

[1] See *vv.* 170–176 and Hermione *passim*. Also *vv.* 37, 403, etc.

to our play the first is worthless, an abstract, not even correct[1], of the existing drama.   But the second, supposed (but this is uncertain) to represent in some way that of the Alexandrian scholar Aristophanes, contains one sentence which looks ancient and possibly interesting, because in itself it has no clear meaning : τὸ δὲ δρᾶμα τῶν δευτέρων, 'the play (*Andromache*) is one of the second plays.' This has been taken to signify that it is *second-rate*, one of a class inferior in artistic merit.   Since the writer of the argument, as it now stands, proceeds to praise certain details (ὁ πρόλογος σαφῶς καὶ εὐλόγως εἰρημένος κ.τ.λ.), it is probable, perhaps certain, that he understood the preceding words as depreciatory[2].   But then they cannot be his words, for he takes them unnaturally.   A 'second play' is not the same thing as a 'second-rate,' and no one surely would of his own motion put so simple a meaning in such inappropriate and unintelligible terms.   Nor can we accept another suggested interpretation, that the play was second in the competition. That, if it was so, would be expressed in the regular and natural form, by saying that 'Euripides was second with the play.' Now these ancient prefaces, as they come to us, not unfrequently contain notes (which are indeed the best part of them) older than our copies, older even than the bulk of the prefaces, notes not intelligible except by reference to notes which have perished ; such for instance is the παρ' οὐδετέρῳ κεῖται ἡ μυθοποιία in the preface to the *Eumenides* of Aeschylus, signifying 'the story of this drama is not found in either (Sophocles or Euripides).' 'This play is a second play' or 'one of the second plays' has the appearance of such a note.   What are 'second plays'?   What can they be, except plays which are sequels, plays preceded by a 'first'?   The note may refer to a list, distinguishing those of the plays contained in some collection which were known or conjectured to be sequels; and it may possibly signify that the *Andromache* is one of them.

[1] ἡ βασιλὶς ἐβουλεύετο κατὰ (τῆς Ἀνδρομάχης) θάνατον, μεταπεμψαμένη τὸν Μενέλαον.   For the last statement there is no evidence, and it is inconsistent with the story.   Andromache in the play attributes to Hermione (*vv.* 39–42) apart from Menelaus only the 'desire' to kill her.   Even ἐβούλετο κτανεῖν, as we shall see, would not be completely true.   The plan and the original action belong wholly to Menelaus.

[2] Cf. *Hippolyti hypothesis* s.f.

From the same hand comes, we may guess, also the next clause of the argument. 'The prologue is clear and appropriate in statement,' ὁ πρόλογος σαφῶς καὶ εὐλόγως εἰρημένος[1]. The person, who actually wrote or framed the argument as we have it, took this to refer to the 'prologue' spoken by Andromache in our play; for he adds, 'Also the elegiacs[2] in the lament of Andromache (are good),' and then notes other points as good or 'not bad.' But that any man, not copying another but expressing naturally his own opinion, selected the Euripidean prologue (so called) for exceptional praise, is a thing hard to believe or understand. The speech of Andromache is certainly neither obscure nor, so far as it goes, inappropriate ; it gives the necessary facts, so far as they are known to Andromache. But it scarcely pretends to dramatic merit, or any merit other than mechanical, and to note it for one of the better parts, a thing exceptionally commendable in Euripides, is irrational. The 'prologue' commended, in the first instance, as 'clear and appropriate in statement' must surely have been the work of some one in whom such an achievement was commendable. Now if the play was really a sequel, we can understand this. Divorced by accident, or the needs of representation, from its predecessor, it wants a 'prologue' properly so called, a literary introduction in verse, like those of Roman and modern times. Somebody wrote one, and it is to this that the note really referred, recommending it as useful and giving it the only praise that it could deserve. Unluckily, not being by Euripides, it was not always copied with the play, and we have now to make it, in verse or in prose, for ourselves. Similarly, prologues were written to the *Rhesus*[3].

Further there is reason to think that we know the name of the prologue-writer—Democrates. At least this would explain what has not been explained, the extraordinary statement, rightly or wrongly attributed to Callimachus, that our

---

[1] Note the absence of a conjunction, indicating that this clause was not originally meant to qualify the preceding clause τὸ δρᾶμα τῶν δευτέρων. If it were, we should expect a 'but,' δέ, ἀλλά, or μέντοι. In fact, there is or was no connexion between the two remarks, as the *asyndeton* properly indicates.

[2] ἔτι δὲ καὶ τὰ ἐλεγεῖα κ.τ.λ.—ἔτι Hermann, ἔστι codd.   [3] *Hyp. Rhesi.*

play 'was superscribed *Democrates*[1]'! Assuredly there is misunderstanding here, if it is implied that the 'superscription' signified either the title of the play or the name of the dramatist. But if 'Democrates' was author of a prologue sometimes prefixed, the superscription of his name was in such copies proper and necessary, and may easily have crept without right into others.

But stronger and steadier than these broken lights from without is the evidence in the play itself, the allusive retrospect in which Orestes describes to Hermione the circumstances of her marriage to Neoptolemus[2]. Not only is the narrative so summary that a theatrical audience, unacquainted with the facts, could scarcely follow it with interest, but upon examination more than one point will be found unintelligible. 'I came to Phthia,' says Orestes, '*though disobedient in this to thy injunction*, with the purpose of assisting thee to escape[3].' When did Hermione forbid Orestes to come? Against any communication between them since her marriage we have presumptive and even conclusive evidence in the whole play and particularly in this scene. Does Orestes only pretend the prohibition? If so, what is his motive, how

---

[1] Scholium to *Andr.* 445 ὁ δὲ Καλλίμαχος ἐπιγραφῆναί φησι τῇ τραγῳδίᾳ Δημοκράτην. It will further explain why this remark now appears in connexion with a subject to which it is not apparently relevant, the date at which the play was written. The observation that 'the *times* of the play cannot be simply grasped' (εἰλικρινῶς δὲ τοὺς τοῦ δράματος χρόνους οὐκ ἔστι λαβεῖν schol. *ib.*) referred, when it was originally made, to the *times* of the action, the interior *times* (not the date of composition), which in the play itself are not easy to be grasped, as modern scholars have too much reason to know. It was in connexion with this that 'Democrates' was originally mentioned, because his prologue of course made the *times*, the succession of events, clear. The scholium implies a misunderstanding.—The conjectural substitution of Τιμοκράτην for Δημοκράτην in this scholium, and the dependent conjectures cited, but not affirmed, by Prof. Murray (in his note on the *dramatis personae*) seem more than hazardous.

[2] *vv.* 964–984.

[3]
ἦλθον δὲ σὰς μὲν οὐ σέβων ἐπιστολάς,
εἰ δ᾽ ἐνδιδοίης, ὥσπερ ἐνδίδως, λόγον,
πέμψων σ᾽ ἀπ᾽ οἴκων τῶνδε.

By the order of the words the negative οὐ falls upon σέβων, *disregarding*, and the ἐπιστολάς (which may or may not mean a 'message') must be a command *not* to come; and εἰ δ᾽ ἐνδιδοίης λόγον implies the same.

could an audience comprehend it, and how is it that a plain falsehood, relating to herself, does not surprise Hermione nor awake in her any suspicion ?

Presently we are told that, when Orestes humbly besought Neoptolemus to resign his claim upon Hermione, 'he not only was insolent about the slaying of my mother, but made the gory-visaged fiends a reproach against *me*[1]!' Why 'against *me*'? To whom else but the murderer should the Furies of Clytaemnestra be a reproach? The expression implies a conception of Orestes and of the Furies different from any of the various views which Euripides presents elsewhere, in the *Orestes* for example and the *Iphigenia in Taurica*[2]. In both those plays the Furies are indeed an illusion, in the one an illusion of fever and in the other of mania ; but it is the murderer who imagines and 'sees' them. Imaginary, unreal, they must always have been in Euripides ; but it was a good variation of the well-worn theme to attribute the superstitious imagination to others, who fancied or 'saw' the matricide so pursued, while he, impervious to vulgar beliefs as to common feelings, confronted the general horror with genuine contempt. Such an Orestes, and only such an one, could repudiate 'the reproach of the Furies' in the language of our play ; and the trait is in keeping with his character in this story. As we shall see, the Orestes of the *Andromache* can scarcely be supposed to have known either fancy or fear. But then, if the audience are to understand the tone of his allusion, they must know his mind, and must have seen how he bore himself in the scenes to which he refers.

These and other like touches confirm us in the conclusion that the audience, as well as Hermione, must be acquainted with the subject of these reminiscences, and that what we have here is a summary, from one aspect, of a foregoing play[3]. It represented the contest for the hand of Hermione, and the

---

[1]   ὁ δ' ἦν ὑβριστὴς εἴς τ' ἐμῆς μητρὸς φόνου
        τάς θ' αἱματωποὺς θεὰς ὀνειδίζων ἐμοί.
The form ἐμοί (not μοι) is necessarily emphatic.

[2]   Of the *Electra* we can hardly speak in this connexion, since in that play the action of the Furies is only predicted in the finale, and any conception of it is admissible.   [3]   See also Appendix, notes on *v.* 1032, *v.* 1151.

triumph of Neoptolemus over his opponent, of which triumph, as Orestes here repeatedly reminds us, the *Andromache* exhibits 'the reverse[1].'

> Soon as to Greece returned Achilles' son,
> Thy father I forgave ; thy lord I prayed
> To set thee free. I pleaded mine hard lot,
> ...that I might wed
> From friends indeed, but scarce of stranger folk,
> Banished as I am banished from mine home[2].

In the hesitation or decision of Menelaus[3], in the relations of the rivals to each other and to the bride, we see, partially but sufficiently, very apt material for a Euripidean drama. The interview, in which Hermione forbade Orestes ever to visit her future home, must have been a scene in that drama ; and since, in now consenting to be her conductor, he tells her that 'her situation is *reversed*[4],' it would seem that on the former occasion it was he who besought her, but vainly, to cut the knot of his distresses by an elopement. The Hermione of the second part would certainly have refused such a petition, and that with no little asperity. At the close of such a play, the discomfited matricide, in cursing the oracle which had encouraged and betrayed him (as he does always on the Euripidean stage but not always exactly in the same vein[5]) would be consoled as in the *Electra* and the *Orestes*, by a *deus ex machina*, probably Apollo himself. This personage, a mere piece of theatre-machinery, would play the regular part of his kind by sketching the future. But whereas more commonly, as in the *Orestes* and the *Iphigenia*, the deity of the machine offers only a legendary sequel, indifferent or even contrary to the Euripidean story with which it is

---

[1] *vv.* 982, 1007 etc.

[2] *vv.* 971 foll. (Way). The words omitted 'The fate that *haunted* me...' are a modification of the original (τὸν παρόντα δαίμονα) and scarcely in character.

[3] That Menelaus returned to Greece before the marriage of Hermione is not stated in the *Andromache*, but that was the commonly received chronology (see Euripides' *Orestes*), and it gives a situation for the story of the choice between his two promises so much better dramatically that we may fairly presume it.

[4] περιπετεῖς ἔχεις τύχας *v.* 982.

[5] *Orestes* 285 etc., *Iph. T.* 77, 570 etc., *Electra* 1190.

formally connected, here he would promise the sequel exhibited in the second play. Orestes should yet have his revenge. Delphi would itself provide him with place, time, and opportunity for making away with one who had insulted both her obedient servant and her patron-god. And Menelaus, repenting of his treachery, should himself devise and achieve the means whereby the discarded nephew should recapture 'his lawful bride[1],' herself helping, for his better satisfaction, and praying to be taken. With this, or something like this, we are ready to follow the *Andromache*.

When we learn, in the Euripidean prologue, that Neoptolemus has gone to Delphi, and Menelaus arrived in Phthia, we know that the revenge of Orestes has come; when we hear that Menelaus is already at strange work in the house, we know that the revenge is partly executed, that Neoptolemus is dead and Orestes has come for his bride. And our curiosity is highly excited; for so clever a villain is Menelaus, that not one spectator in ten thousand could divine his plan, or perceive how the position of the slave could bear upon the abduction of the mistress. And other points are mysterious. Andromache has concealed her child and has taken sanctuary; why have these things been permitted? Menelaus is respecting the sanctuary, though even Andromache has doubts about the sufficiency of its protection[2]; is this his piety, or what is it? Peleus lives close by, yet he has not interfered. Why?

This last question indeed we are already better able to answer than the innocent Andromache, who cannot understand why, though she has sent several times for the head of the family, there is no word of his coming[3]. She supposes the messengers negligent of her interests. Since the concern is that of Peleus and Neoptolemus and the whole house, her explanation will not hold, as she herself afterwards recognises, returning to the even less tenable supposition of neglect in Peleus[4]. However she has now the chance to send another summoner, who, as we guess, is likely to be more successful.

---

[1] *Andr.* 1001. [2] *vv.* 42–46.
[3] *v.* 79 foll. [4] *v.* 560 foll.

Peleus will of course be summoned if and when the conspirators choose, and not before; but we are given reason to
suppose that they desire it now. For Menelaus, who knows
where the young boy is and has gone to seize him, has
announced the intention of putting him to death in the
hearing of a Trojan woman devoted to Andromache[1]. To
Andromache she of course reports it, and conquering a terror
not the less pathetic because we can perceive it to be mistaken, undertakes also to report it to Peleus. Our interest in
the victims of these machinations is heightened by the exquisite song with which Andromache consoles her loneliness
(the elegiacs admired by the author of the Greek argument),
and by the dread which the mighty Lacedaemonians are seen
to inspire, even in the Phthiote women (the Chorus), who now
bring her their sympathy and advise her to submit. In the
moment of expressing their fear of Hermione, they are
surprised by Hermione herself, between whom and Andromache
passes a scene full of interest.

It is pitiable that creatures so incapable of defence, and so
unhappy, should be counters in so deadly a game. The past
and present sufferings of the one, the horrible shock which
awaits the other, their torturing relation to one another, and
complete mutual misunderstanding, unite to move our compassion. Hermione, a dependent being, is dominated by two
feelings, confidence in her father and passion for her husband.
Her pride in Menelaus, her sense of importance as his heiress,
her conviction that all the world is or should be obedient to
him and her, are displayed in her first words, when she silences,
to her own destruction, any possible remonstrance from the
women of Phthia:

> With bravery of gold about mine head
> And on my form this pomp of broidered robes,
> Hither I come :—no gifts be these I wear
> Or from Achilles' or from Peleus' house ;
> But from the Land Laconian Sparta-crowned
> My father Menelaus with rich dower
> Gave these, that so my tongue should not be tied.
> To you I render answer in these words[2].

---

[1] *v.* 68, *v.* 72.   [2] *vv.* 147 foll. (Way).

Here the 'irony of the situation,' in which no play, not even the *Oedipus Tyrannus*, is stronger than the *Andromache*, is already seen. It is because the princess of Sparta is indeed no less important than she thinks herself, that her life in a few hours will be shattered for ever. Sharper still is her unconscious satire when, in the blindness of her jealousy, she reproaches Andromache for her obedience to Neoptolemus;

> With this son of him who slew thy lord
> Thou dar'st to lie, and to the slayer bear
> Sons! Suchlike is the whole barbaric race :—
>   ...Kin the nearest wade
> Through blood; no whit hereof doth law forbid.
> Bring not such things midst us[1].

One wonders, not without a shiver, whether the wife of Orestes remembered these words of nights. That her two dominant sentiments are in deadly opposition, that the hour is now past when she can be at once daughter to Menelaus and wife, or even widow, to Neoptolemus, she has not a suspicion. But she does see—and for consistency in the character and truth to nature this must not be overlooked—frantic as she is, she does see, that Menelaus is going farther than she can safely desire. Her very presence at the sanctuary is proof that her fear of her husband, the obverse and the necessary complement of her love, is uneasy. She comes, as at last we discover when the explosions of mutual hatred permit, to persuade Andromache, if possible, into leaving her refuge[2]. She knows[3], as already we know[4], that she will soon have, in the person of the boy, an irresistible means of compulsion. If then she tries to forestall this method, it is because she is unwilling, as well she may be, that the child should be attacked. Nor does she really intend or deliberately desire, however Menelaus may talk or tempt her, that even Andromache shall be put to death.

> This the Nereid's fane shall help thee nought,
> Altar nor temple ;—thou shalt die, shalt die!
> *Yea, though one stoop to save thee, man or God,*
> Yet must thou for thy haughty spirit of old

---

[1] *vv.* 170 foll. (Way). [2] *vv.* 251–253. [3] *v.* 262. [4] *v.* 70.

> Crouch low abased, and grovel at my knee
> And sweep mine house, and sprinkle water dews
> There from the golden ewers with thine hand,
> And where thou art, know[1].

Here, in her first speech, before the heat of conflict has made her quite mad, is her real mind. What she expects is, if we may use a plain term, to bully her rival, to abase her, for the time, into the mere slave, which as yet she has never been. Kill her she dare not; she cannot even threaten it without unsaying her words; and the child she would fain not molest, if she could find any other way to her will. Here, in her fear of her husband, is the assailable point for Andromache, and the one way in which the scheme of Menelaus, though unsuspected, might have been crossed. If Andromache would have calmly pressed upon the daughter but a little of the plain truth about Neoptolemus which she afterwards expounds, as vainly as complacently, to the father[2], Hermione might have been scared into opposing her father, or at least (which would have been enough) into manifesting her reluctance. But Andromache never once touches upon this visible and vibrating chord. Nor must we miss the fact that this is due, if we may not say to a fault in Andromache, yet to a dulness, or a lack of sensibility. Euripides almost never takes sides, never presents that mere opposition of good and bad which nature eschews. Andromache no more understands Hermione than Hermione her, and is, so far as she can be, not less unjust. Andromache is a woman (there doubtless are such) who does not know what love is, who has never felt it, and perhaps never could. In the lecture upon conjugal jealousy, sensible enough in part but totally inopportune, which she reads to the young queen, she makes capital of the fact that her affection for Hector had been wholly free from jealousy:

> Ah dear, dear Hector, I would take to my heart
> Even thy leman, if Love tripped thy feet.
> Yea, often to thy bastards would I hold
> My breast, that I might give thee none offence[3].

This may or may not be an adorable sentiment, and

---

[1] *vv.* 161 foll. (Way).   [2] *vv.* 319 foll.   [3] *vv.* 222 foll.

Euripides may or may not have approved it; but it is neither connected nor compatible with the passion of love. And accordingly Andromache is so far from conceiving what the feeling of Hermione for Neoptolemus really is, that she describes it, in words which one dares not translate, as ἀπληστία λέχους, and likens Hermione to her mother Helen! That Hermione receives the admonition, terminating as it does in this stupid insult, with a protest more of grief than of anger—'Why take so proud a tone?'—is an astonishing proof of her singular and fatal openness to every kind of influence. And when Andromache a second time, and with even less relevance[1], cites the paramour of Paris as a reproach against the wife of Neoptolemus, we cannot be surprised that the outraged girl furiously closes the interview, and goes, beyond salvation, to her fate[2].

Menelaus soon comes with the boy Molossus—it is convenient to use this name, though there is no clear authority for it in the play[3]—and is the principal figure of the next two scenes, in which he executes his design. The performance, as well as the conception, justifies the terror, no less than the detestation, which he and the name of Sparta are said to inspire. The urgency of the occasion, the improbability and indignity[4] of the part which he has to play, never disturb for an instant his progress to the mark. We soon understand now why Andromache has been suffered to take sanctuary. It gives Menelaus not only a presentable pretext, which otherwise might have been hard to find, for proceeding against Molossus, but also the opportunity of making Hermione, to all appearance, specially responsible for condemning the boy to death. The king promises to spare him, if the mother surrenders herself; and he keeps his promise, in the

---

[1] *v.* 249, where καὶ πρόσω means 'at the farthest distance,' *i.e.* 'however little to the purpose.'

[2] The words at the end of the scene (*v.* 272) οὐδεὶς γυναικὸς φάρμακ' ἐξηύρηκέ πω | κακῆς· τοσοῦτόν ἐσμεν ἀνθρώποις κακόν are commonly mistranslated. The last verse means 'when she is evil; so far (and so far only) are we an evil to mankind.' To make Andromache say that women as such are evil would be contrary to her feelings and character. *v.* 353 is ironical.

[3] See *vv.* 1243–1249, which suggest it.   [4] *v.* 366.

treacherous fashion to which the Greeks had been but too well accustomed, by referring the fate of Molossus to the separate decision of the princess. Since the Spartans were sticklers for the forms of religion, and had recently (but, as the Athenians held, dishonestly) urged against Athens the guilt of violating sanctuary[1], it is possible to think that Menelaus really feels the scruple which he formally satisfies. But this is not my impression ; the scruple, like everything in Menelaus, is a trick, bearing upon his true purpose and successful in its object. All through the scene the irony of the situation continues to work, notably when Andromache, in the speech already often mentioned, explains to the short-sighted father how he is ruining all chance for his daughter of happiness with Neoptolemus[2], and the other women point out to him how much better he might use his influence in appeasing his daughter's unfortunate jealousy[3]! His plausibility, considering the nature of his pretences, is admirable.

> Woman, these are but trifles, all unworthy
> Of my state royal—thou say'st it—and of Greece.
> *Yet know, when one hath set his heart on aught,*
> *More than to take a Troy is this to him.*
> I stand my daughter's champion, for I count.
> No trifle robbery of marriage-right.
> Nought else a wife may suffer matcheth this.
> Losing her husband, she doth lose her life.
> Over my thralls her lord hath claim to rule,
> And over his like rights have I and mine.
> ...Waiting the absent if I order not
> Mine own things well, weak am I, and not wise[4].

It is all sheer nonsense, as an explanation of his supposed desire to take the lives of Andromache and Molossus, and even the sneers in it (such as *waiting the absent*) are transparent to the spectator. Yet it sounds like self-deception, and could not raise any suspicion of the true facts and the real intent. The pathos of the mother's self-surrender is obvious, being indeed one of the few points in the play which the current interpretation leaves intelligible ; and

---

[1] Thucydides I. 126–127. [2] *v.* 319. [3] *v.* 421. [4] *vv.* 366 foll. (Way).

though of subordinate interest, it serves to feed the emotions of fear and hatred against the deceiver.

It should be noticed in passing, however, that Andromache, here as before, is scarcely less imprudent than unhappy, and shows, good woman that she is, the same inexpugnable conceit of her own wisdom, which appears in her treatment of Hermione. The tone of superiority, in which she enlightens the supposed blindness of Menelaus, would be dangerous indeed if he were really blind; and when she insults the man, who, as she thinks, has her fate and that of her child in his hands, with the foolish and pointless epigram that he may perhaps prove as zealous for his daughter as formerly he was for his wife—

> but one thing in thy nature
> I fear—'twas in a woman's quarrel too
> Thou didst destroy the hapless Phrygians' town[1]—

when one hears this, one can but say in excuse that she seems, poor woman, to have Helen, as it were, on the brain.

At the close of the scene Menelaus takes his prisoners into the house, ostensibly in order that the fate of Molossus may be referred to the decision of Hermione. We say ostensibly, because there is nothing, except the word of Menelaus (which is nothing), to prove either the intention or the fact. It is Menelaus who announces the project, and afterwards declares the result[2]; we notice that neither Andromache nor Hermione ever refers to a scene which, if it had really occurred, was not likely to be forgotten by either; and we may therefore assume with confidence that Menelaus, in this matter, does not give his daughter fair play. From what we know of her mind it is most improbable that, if really consulted, she would have taken upon herself any part of the crime, or even have allowed the king to proceed further without a protest. She has not the courage for it, nor, to do her justice, the cruelty. He on the other hand says and does enough to make her seem guilty in the first degree both to others[3] and, as we shall see, to herself. To give her at this

---

[1] *v.* 361.   [2] *vv.* 431–444, *v.* 518.   [3] *v.* 489.

moment the chance of interference would be an error of which he is certainly to be acquitted.

When after an interval he leads out the miserable pair as for death, their appearance is almost immediately followed by that of Peleus, a coincidence which could scarcely surprise the spectator, even at first sight. It is certain that Menelaus does not intend execution, and will not approach it until he is sure of being stopped. To cut the throats of the woman and the boy would doubtless have been indifferent to him, perhaps rather agreeable, in itself; but it could not be done without compromising the freedom of Hermione, which is essential to his purpose; and as he truly says, 'what a man wants at the moment is more important to him than the capture of Troy[1].' His part in the plot now runs smoothly to the final stroke. Peleus, an honourable and noble man, but of violent temper in his best days[2], and now long past the age of self-control[3], has no chance at all, and simply plays into his adversary's hand, unpacking his heart in extravagant insults[4], which he himself disproves[5], and futile threats, which give Menelaus exactly the lead which he expects. Menelaus is all himself, provocative and plausible, resigning the slaves with indignant acquiescence, and maintaining without embarrassment the preposterous doctrines of domestic law, upon which he pretends to have proceeded[6]. If he boggles a moment over explaining the necessity of his instant departure for Sparta[7] (here to the spectator his plan becomes finally clear), he promptly recovers himself, and actually disappears with some dignity. The figure of the old, old man, utterly unconscious of the stroke which has orphaned him, and of the sport which he is affording, but pursuing with pride his imaginary triumph, has in the highest degree that stinging pathos, not tragic, not tearful, but cruel, which Euripides wields supremely. One touch of irony may be quoted as giving the innuendo of the

---

[1] *v.* 368.   [2] *v.* 687.
[3] *vv.* 642, 678, 728, etc.   [4] *vv.* 590 foll.
[5] *vv.* 703–705. See also *v.* 678. [6] *v.* 585 and *passim.*

[7] *v.* 733 ἔστι γάρ τις οὐ πρόσω | Σπάρτης...πόλις τις κ.τ.λ. Prof. Murray rightly marks the hesitation.

whole. Peleus, like Andromache, has his word to say about
Helen:

> Helen...who forsook
> Thy love, and from thine halls went revelling forth
> With a young gallant to an alien land.
> Yet for her sake thou gatheredst that huge host
> Of Greeks, and leddest them to Ilium.
> Thou shouldst have spued her forth, have stirred no spear,
> Who hadst found her vile, but let her there abide,
> Yea, paid a price to take her never back.
> But no wise thus the wind of thine heart blew.
> Nay, many a gallant life hast thou destroyed,
> And childless made grey mothers in their halls,
> And white-haired sires hast robbed of noble sons ;—
> *My wretched self am one, who see in thee,*
> *Like some foul fiend, Achilles' murderer*[1].

So speaks the grandsire of Neoptolemus—to the accomplice
of Orestes. And the Chorus celebrate his victory : he too, as
they remember with pride, had been in his youthful days a
conqueror of Troy[2].

The scene which shows the distraction of the deserted
Hermione, though full of nature, and in the 'spoken' parts
unimpeachable, is open in the lyric part to an objection
touching not so much the dramatist as the limitations of
Attic form as fixed by Aeschylus. Shakespeare, though he
could not have bettered the conception, would have been
better served in the presentation of it. The musical, symmetrical, operatic mould, for Euripides inevitable, suits well
enough with a high passion, such as that of Andromache and
Molossus in face of death[3], but not with a passion like that
of Hermione. A naughty, conscience-stricken child (and
Hermione at the moment is very near this) is not a convenient subject for stanzas. But the substance of the scene
is admirable. It is a merit, not a defect, that the young wife
exaggerates both her offence and her danger. In vain does
her waiting-woman assure her that Neoptolemus will forgive[4],
and that mere prudence will restrain him from punishing[5].
Conscience cannot so argue, and the conscience of Hermione

---

[1] *vv.* 602 foll. (Way).   [2] *vv.* 775–801, especially 789 foll.
[3] *vv.* 501–544.   [4] *v.* 840.   [5] *vv.* 869–875.

is in the imagined frown of the man that she loves. Abandoned by her guide and encourager, she knows that her heart is guilty of all that he did, and of more ; and she is in no mood for favourable distinctions. She 'devised,' she 'plotted' those deaths which she did undoubtedly desire[1], and if her husband kills her, it will be no more than she deserves[2]. Even her father she will not accuse of anything but the desertion, and she makes the best of that[3] ; for he is still her one conceivable refuge from the anger of Neoptolemus. And in this mood Orestes takes her.

The interview between them is the acme of the drama. Orestes, who, as we have inferred, is already known to the audience from the preceding part, surpasses even Menelaus in the qualities which make villainy formidable. His nerve is astonishing. He is in extreme danger. Menelaus has of course guards[4], and can protect himself otherwise against surprise. But Orestes must come alone to the house of his victim : he is a 'pilgrim to Dodona,' and the least appearance of distrust would destroy his assumed character. How much time he has before him for the achievement of his purpose, we do not exactly know, nor probably does he ; but we can guess, as proves to be the case, that it is not more than enough. The uncle and nephew had, for their whole operation, whatever time the unburdened assassin might gain upon the bearers of Neoptolemus in the journey from Delphi ; but how little was this, and how much of it is gone ! Nor does the eagerness of Hermione make the part of the abductor easy ; because they are under hostile observation, and he, on pain of detection, must appear considerate. Though he himself prompts her confession[5], he must seem to pause upon it[6] ; and when she thereupon breaks into a long rambling plea of 'evil influence,' he must hear it out, and pretend to be convinced[7], and morally justify his consent to be her guide, not forgetting to note (since in his future account of the business she is to

---

[1] *vv.* 806, 912 and *passim.*   [2] *vv.* 920, 927.   [3] *v.* 918.

[4] A tragedy-king always has. The δμῶες of *v.* 715 are probably Helots in his service ; note also the plural οἶδε in *v.* 753.

[5] *v.* 906, ὑπηγάγου, 'you give me a lead.' See *vv.* 911, 913 etc.

[6] *vv.* 919, 961.   [7] *v.* 957.

figure as a confederate) that he once had claims upon her—claims which she, poor soul, refers to the decision of her father! Even when in agony 'lest my husband should arrive,' she actually hurries away[1], he will stay yet a minute to tell her —when she cannot hear him and others do—that he, the companion of her flight, has 'projected' a sure plot against her husband's life. When it is considered that within an hour of this time the body of Neoptolemus is laid where Orestes stands, one cannot but allow that the devil has at all events the courage of his part.

Here ends the action, properly so called. The story brought from Delphi, though necessary as a conclusion and brilliantly told, has perhaps, even when its relation to the play is understood, a somewhat detached effect, now that we read it with this play only. The acts and fate of a person, whom we do not know and have never seen, cannot well be conceived dramatically. Those who had seen Neoptolemus in the preceding play[2] could doubtless annotate the narrative of his death with recollections which would make it almost as visible as if enacted before them. From a moral point of view the story is designed to associate the fanaticism of Delphi with the militarism of Sparta, as joint contributors to the triumph of wickedness.

To this triumph there is no drawback. The 'Thetis' of the epilogue, though she is not, like some of these machine-gods, self-satiric, but paints the miraculous after-life of Peleus in verses of singular beauty[3], is still, like almost all of them, unreal and irrelevant. The drama itself is purely realistic, all the more so because one incident at Delphi is invested in the narrative with a supernatural colour plainly attributable to the imagination of the narrator[4]. However much the sea-bride of Peleus may have affected a solitary place of residence[5], and however the family may choose, by sanctuary and posthumous worship, to 'interpret[6]' her singular quality, no intelligent

---

[1] *v.* 992: see note in Appendix.   [2] *vv.* 971 foll. and *supra* p. 24.
[3] *vv.* 1253-1269.   [4] The 'voice' from the temple, *v.* 1147.   [5] *v.* 18.
[6] ἑρμήνευμα (*v.* 46); to mistranslate it 'witness' spoils the point, which (as is permissible in the 'prologue') belongs not to Andromache but to Euripides.

spectator of the play could suppose that the Peleus whom we see and hear did, in the world where the scene passes, really marry a mermaiden; and his future as a merman, however consoling to the sentiments of a vulgar audience, has nothing to do with the future of Menelaus and Orestes.

This at least is unclouded. We see well enough, and the epilogue indicates[1], that upon Delphi would fall whatever scandal personages so powerful, in an intrigue outwardly so obscure, might not be able to prevent. How Hermione took her destiny we do not know; but this is certain, that neither her father nor her husband would be troubled about her. They at least, we may assume, lived happily ever afterwards, and remembered the day of her abduction as one of the pleasantest that ever they spent. 'Αδίκως εὐτυχεῖτε, *In wickedness ye prosper*, says Andromache at the height of her passion[2], and sums the impression of the play. It is part of their plan and of their triumph (for their villainy is a delicate villainy, the product of an age not less refined than corrupt), to escape not only responsibility but even censure. Orestes himself sounds the expected note[3]; already we hear it said that Neoptolemus, who dared to demand satisfaction of Apollo for the death of Achilles, received but his due from the offended god and from the Delphian people, and that Hermione fled with good cause from her unfaithful husband, nay, that Peleus turned her out of doors[4]. If the Phthiotes, enlightened by suffering, make a stride towards a bolder theology, and complain that the Judge of human virtue has shown himself implacable as the basest of men[5], not every one even in Athens was ready for so modern a view ; and at the anger of Phthia Lacedaemon could afford to laugh.

The emotion provoked by such an issue is certainly not the tragic emotion, but it is none the less wholesome or less powerful for that. Nothing is more superfluous than to complain that this or that element in the play is not tragic. Nothing in it is tragic, nor ought to be. The current commentaries, finding in it nothing really intelligible except the pathos of

---

Andromache, exaggerate that element, and dispraise all that does not contribute to it, that is to say, nine-tenths of the piece. Even Andromache is not, properly speaking, a tragic figure. A pathetic figure she is : her past is pathetic, her mortal and maternal fears are pathetic ; but it is a necessity of the situation that she shall not now and actually suffer any injury at all; and this, with the limitations, not to say the littleness, of her character and temperament, excludes the portraiture, and properly, from the sphere of tragedy. Nor is Peleus, though in his present sufferings more pathetic than Andromache, a tragic figure. Both personages, in their relation to the essence of the story, are after all mere puppets in the successful game of the Spartans ; both, and Peleus especially, are necessarily spotted with ridicule ; and their woes, under this colouring, excite no sentiment more profound than may be soothed away by the fairy-tale of the theatrical goddess, and discharged with an easy tear.

But for all this, the play is not inferior in species to tragedy, nor shallower. It might as well be called deeper, if either comparative had meaning. It would be surely a childish view of the world and of art, which would exclude from repre-sentation τὸ ἀδίκως εὐτυχεῖν, the prosperity of the wicked, in all the unrelieved incisiveness of its formidable truth. The thing is a fact, and to consider its causes for a while is a mental and moral exercise not less profitable than fascinating. First among these causes Euripides places, and with reason, the possibility of such characters as those of Menelaus and Orestes, in which the extreme degree of unscrupulous selfishness is united not only with intellectual power but with qualities which must be called moral—self-command, self-control, the accurate subordination of means and faculties to the desired end. To see this possibility we have but to look about us, and the *Andromache* powerfully incites us to the observation. As a secondary cause we have the fault or the imprudence of the adversary, against whom villainy has to operate. It is the false position of Andromache in the house of Neoptolemus, created by Neoptolemus himself, which alone lays him open to the design of his enemies ; for which reason the slave-mistress, though in no sense the principal figure of the group, not improperly gives the title to the piece, because she is the mechanical fulcrum of the intrigue. The obvious moral, now happily out of date among ourselves but vital to a society of slave-holders, is sharply enforced by the Chorus[1].

Not out of date, and not less interesting because open to controversy, are the assaults which the poet directs against two species of social institution, which are always with us and which he evidently detested, the military and the religious, or rather, if we may be allowed an anachronism more apparent than real, the ecclesiastical. These, says Euripides in this play, are mighty assistants in the prosperity of the wicked: military institutions, because it is of their essence to put power in a single hand[2], which may (and this is a mere truth) be in some respects most unworthy of the trust; religious institutions, because their power, though founded upon a moral superiority, survives corruption, and generates the virulent poison of fanaticism[3]. Both these elements of society Euripides saw in a peculiar form and in a disadvantageous light. Sparta, the military state, and Delphi, the nearest approximation in Hellas to an ecclesiastical state, composed together the core of the mighty power banded against Athens, or rather, Euripides would have said, against humanity. Now Menelaus would be nothing without Sparta, nor Orestes without Delphi. It does not therefore follow, and the contrary might be shown, that the dramatist was blind to the virtues either of military or of religious devotion. But these are not here his theme. To discuss the charges which he makes or insinuates would take us beyond the bounds of literary or artistic criticism. I will only say for myself that I find in them a portion of truth which, however it should be qualified by other considerations, cannot be disallowed but by prejudice.

Highly significant, from a historical point of view, is the connexion which Euripides traces between the conquest of

---

[1] *vv.* 464–493.   [2] *vv.* 693 foll. and the references to Sparta *passim*.
[3] See the whole narrative *vv.* 1085 foll., a horrible picture of Delphi on its worst side, probably not untrue so far as it goes; and compare the similar picture in the *Ion, passim*.

Troy and the corruptions of Hellas. The impressive ode which follows the abduction of Hermione[1], associates closely with the Greek victory both the alliance between 'Apollo' and such a villain as Orestes, and the general triumph of mischief and violence, which the play presents to us. The Chorus speak more truly and pertinently than they yet know, when they say that from conquered Troy 'wailing for children' and 'rape of wives' have come to the conquerors also. 'Not on thee alone, O Troy, not on thine alone have lighted cruel pains: Hellas hath taken the plague; and from the fields of Phrygia the blood-raining bolt of Death has passed to fields which war wasted not'—a transparent parable of the poet's own times, when the victory over Persia, and the consequent expansion of Greek politics, had led from stage to stage of restlessness up to the devastating struggle of the Peloponnesian war. Menelaus contends for the opposite view of the contemporary evolution[2], which also had something to say for itself, as Euripides is careful to show. For a mighty agitator of mankind, which he was, he was strangely little of a partizan.

As in these opposed reflexions, so in the whole story, it is the fifth century that we have before us. The kingship of Menelaus is indeed rather that of heroic than of historical Sparta ; but this is an inoffensive anachronism. Neither plot nor characters have any tincture of antiquity, and when Hermione in her passion of flight cries out for the wings of Argo, 'first passenger between the Cyanean shores[3],' the theatrical convention might well provoke an involuntary smile. The main intrigue produces so vivid an impression of reality, that one cannot but wonder whether it had not some basis of contemporary fact. Though the death of Neoptolemus at Delphi seems to have rested in some way upon ancient tradition[4], the colouring and connexion here given to it are specifically Euripidean. The frame of the play, whatever materials may be used, must be substantially the poet's own work.

[1] *vv.* 1009 foll.; especially the conclusion of the ode. [2] *vv.* 681–684.
[3] *v.* 865.
[4] This point is obscure, and for the purpose of the *Andromache* not worth investigation.

Of the characters Menelaus is the most elaborate and interesting, though that of Orestes offers tantalizing glimpses, which in the foregoing part had probably been more fully developed. Menelaus is a sinister personage and not easily to be forgotten. The declamations of Peleus about his cowardice are extravagance, self-refuted, refuted by his history and by what we ourselves see of the man. That in the Trojan field he did not often sully his magnificent arms[1] is likely enough ; fighting is not commonly the business of a commander in chief, and certainly Menelaus was not the man to risk himself without necessity. But like Scott's Louis XI, he is 'brave enough for every useful and political purpose.' The essence of him is an intense, cold, reasonable egoism. 'What a man wants'—to quote once more his illuminating words—'is more to him than the capture of any Troy.' He is one to whom supreme gifts of birth, place, mind, and fortune are simply means for calmly gratifying his desires. He plunged the world into ten years of war simply because, having married the most beautiful of women, he did not choose to be robbed of her. In the same spirit he treads into dust the life of his son-in-law and the heart of his daughter, simply because he does not choose to sit down with the loss of a matrimonial speculation which has gone wrong. He sees the way to his will with unerring judgment, and pursues it without a qualm. Such is ὁ ἀδίκως εὐτυχῶν, and he is worth consideration.

Upon the merits of the piece, as a work of literary and dramatic art, it would be impertinent to enlarge. There are things which must not be praised. Acted with any reasonable skill, it would rivet attention throughout ; nor is there a page which does not deserve and repay minute study. Whether the sensations to be derived from it are conveniently described as 'pleasure,' is a possible but not a profitable question. They are sensations of which almost all mankind are capable, and which all that are so will desire to repeat and to encourage.

---

[1] *vv.* 616 foll.

EURIPIDES' APOLOGY.

(*HELEN.*)

If we shadows have offended,
Think but this, and all is mended.

SHAKESPEARE.

RICH but weak, brilliant and yet baffling—these and such like are the epithets which have recently` been applied by sympathetic readers to the strange piece in which Euripides celebrates, or professes to celebrate, the virtue of Helen. Here we have a problem (let it be said at once) differing altogether in the nature of the difficulty from that which arises in the *Andromache*, or again from that which meets us in the *Ion* or *Heracles*. The *Ion* is on the face of it ambiguous, and any acceptable explanation must account, among other things, for the ambiguity. The current exposition of the *Andromache* is not defective but null. What it leaves unexplained is just everything, the story, the meaning, the main lines of the piece. In the story of *Helen* all is at least superficially clear; and though we must not therefore assert that no doubt should be raised, yet neither do I intend to raise any. What baffles us here is the singular quality of the play, the fact that in spirit and tone it is unique in the drama of Euripides (and indeed of Athens, so far as known to us) and the question why this difference should be. If this question may be answered, we shall be so far the better off, even though we should conclude that a complete understanding of details is in this case not to be expected. We shall at least see more when we know what to look for.

Let us first ascertain where the singularity lies. Even Paley, who evidently enjoyed the play, and comments in the right spirit upon many parts of it, does not perhaps sufficiently mark its peculiarity as a whole. Euripides here takes, in the choice and treatment of material, precisely the course which everywhere else he carefully and even painfully avoids. Instead of the familiar realities of common experience, 'the things we handle and with which we live,' he suddenly gives us, for the foundation and essence of his story, the utmost extravagance of imagination, and introduces into the very heart of the action a stupendous miracle, which takes place almost before our eyes. Habitually he eliminates whatever in tradition was marvellous, or at all events reduces it to a mere formal supposition, which we are at liberty to vary without affecting the substance of his theme. Thus he permits his Medea to say, in accordance with the Argonautic legend, that she delivered Jason from fire-breathing bulls and other supernatural monsters ; but he uses this supposition, for the purpose of his drama, only so far as it signifies that she saved her lover from terrible dangers. Ordinary and not miraculous dangers would serve equally well to produce the Euripidean situation ; and the bulls are preferred or admitted only in order to spare both dramatist and reader the trouble of an unfamiliar invention. Iphigenia came to Taurica (so she supposes) by divine conveyance; but so far as the play of Euripides is concerned, any conveyance would do, and a non-miraculous conveyance would be manifestly preferable. Similarly the gods of the popular religion, as a general rule, either do not act upon the story at all, or act only as conventional suppositions, accounting for effects which are in themselves open to other explanation. The debate between a Poseidon and an Athena at the opening of the *Troades* is a possible, but not an indispensable, foundation or preliminary for the mundane facts which that play presents or anticipates, facts equally real and equally acceptable to the imagination whether the existence of Poseidon and Athena be supposed or not supposed. But in *Helen* the astonished reader is introduced by Euripides to a world of which

Olympus (and such an Olympus) is an indispensable part, to a train of events and actions no more conceivable apart from the jealousies and mutual malice of Zeus and Hera and Aphrodite than the story of the *Oedipus Tyrannus* is conceivable without the deity of Delphi, or that of the *Trachiniae* without the deity of Dodona, or the *Eumenides* itself without any Furies at all.

The allegations propounded are these. When Aphrodite had purchased the judgment of Paris by promising him the possession of Helen, Hera defeated the performance of the bargain, by bestowing upon the seducer a 'living image' of the lady, composed of air. Zeus, not negligent of his daughter, the true Helen, conveyed her by the agency of Hermes to Egypt, and placed her in the care of the virtuous king Proteus, with promise to be restored hereafter to her home, her husband, and the enjoyment of an unblemished character. Menelaus, her husband, has spent ten years in recovering the supposed Helen, the phantom, by the conquest of Troy, and seven years more in vain attempts to convey the phantom to Greece. Storm and shipwreck then bring him and his companion to Egypt. Here, since the death (apparently recent) of King Proteus, the true Helen has been exposed to the unwelcome courtship of his son Theoclymenus, and to escape this solicitation has taken up her abode in the late king's mausoleum. There Menelaus finds her; and his doubts of her identity and story are removed by the opportune declaration and retirement of the phantom, which vanishes into the sky with a suitable speech. Theonoe, the pious and 'all-wise' daughter of the deceased king, is aware of these events by her supernatural power, but favours the performance of her father's pledge. With her permission and connivence, the re-united spouses deceive Theoclymenus into furnishing them with a ship, in which they and the shipwrecked crew of Menelaus depart triumphantly for Greece.

Now the first impression suggested by this story, an impression which further reflexion only confirms, is that it could not possibly be made the basis of a drama seriously appealing either to the imagination or to the feelings. The works which the Greeks classed as tragedies have in general the common character, that they do make such an appeal. Here Aeschylus, Sophocles, and Euripides are at one. Differing as to the kind of suppositions which they ask us to make, and the kind of feelings which they endeavour to excite, they agree in this, that *something* is to be supposed, and to be grasped by the imagination as firmly as possible, *something* is to be felt, as fully and profoundly as the dramatist can make us feel it. But this story is in the first place too fantastic to be seriously supposable, and if it be supposed, is intrinsically incapable of exciting any serious emotion. It is in these respects on a par with the story of *A Midsummer Night's Dream* (a comparison which for more reasons than one we may conveniently bear in mind), a story acceptable only upon the understanding, declared beforehand in the case of *A Midsummer Night's Dream* by the very title, that nothing solid or substantial is to be expected.

Whether the cardinal miracle of the phantom Helen and its astounding disappearance could by any treatment be made credible to the imagination, we need not speculatively enquire. What is certain is, that Euripides does not so treat it. Never for an instant do the personages of the drama exhibit the sort of emotion which such an event must be expected to excite. They neither speak nor behave as if it were real. A single quotation will settle the point. *Where then is the evil thing which was sent to Troy instead of you?* asks Theoclymenus of Helen when he has been informed that Menelaus has died at sea. *The cloud-image, you mean,* she answers; *it vanished into air. Ah Priam!,* sighs the amiable prince, *and ah Troy town, destroyed for nought!*— and then without another word on the subject they settle the details of a funeral ceremony for Menelaus[1]. We do no disrespect to the author of such a dialogue, but conceive on the contrary that we are following his clear direction, when we say that it recalls not even the midsummer night's dream, but another famous dream, which I need not specify, in

[1] *v.* 1218.

which the cat asks what became of the baby. 'It turned
into a pig.' 'I thought it would,' says the cat, and closes
the incident by vanishing. Or again we may find a standard
for comparison in Euripides himself. Very much in the same
tone and with the same persuasive terseness does Heracles,
in a play which we are to discuss hereafter, narrate to
Amphitryon his experiences in Hades[1]. In that case and
in this, the manner of narration, coupled with the quality
of the thing narrated, impose upon the reader, if he has
any respect for the author, a plain dilemma. Either the
dramatic speaker is to be supposed insane, or else the whole
presentation is to be taken as insane, in the sense that it is
purely fantastic. In the case of Heracles we shall conclude
for the first alternative ; in that of Helen and Theoclymenus,
who are certainly no more insane than any body else, we are
driven to the second. Not a bit more conceivably real, in
relation to the miracle, is the behaviour of the old man-
servant by whom the disappearance of the phantom is
reported to Menelaus. No sooner does he grasp the fact
that his master has simultaneously discovered the genuine
wife, than the whole tremendous and world-shattering event,
all the seventeen years of futile bloodshed and misery, pass
away into the background of his contemplation, and he falls
to pleasing meditations on the domestic prospect ; it will be
like having the mistress's wedding-day over again ; he
remembers running beside the carriage[2] ; and this although
master and mistress and servant and all, if the situation as
given is to be taken seriously, are at this moment in instant
danger of death. Upon one condition only could such a
picture give pleasure, and that is that it shall be first agreed
between us and the painter, as it is agreed when we are
promised a 'Midsummer Night's Dream,' that the whole thing
shall be capricious and nonsensical. But the question to
which we are then brought, and to which every path in
Euripides' play will lead us back, is this. How in his case
was it fore-known to his audience that this particular tragedy

---

[1] *Heracles* 607–621.   [2] *Hel.* 711–733, 744–757.

was to be a jest? Where does the jest lie, and what is the
nature of it?

The allegations of the story, even if accepted as fact,
could not be the instrument of evoking emotion or sympathy,
otherwise than in a sort of humorous and satirical pretence.
Inner contradictions and moral incompatibilities meet us
everywhere, the moment we take the author at his word.
The manœuvres of Zeus, Hera, and Aphrodite are here as
petty as those of Oberon and Titania; and the tremendous
consequences, exceeding the worst which mankind is said to
have suffered from the quarrels of the Shakespearean fairies,
would be hideous, if we faced them as an imaginary fact.
Doubtless it is possible, only too possible, to conceive with
force, or even actually to believe, that

> As flies to boys, so we are to the gods ;
> They kill us for their sport.

But upon such a basis the only type of drama which can
be tolerably built is a drama like *King Lear*, gloomy, terrible,
and bitter. It would be a blunder monstrous, disgraceful,
and suicidal, to found upon it a drama like this *Helen*, where
the action proceeds to a happy and foreseen conclusion with
scarcely a hitch, and certainly without ever arousing a grave
apprehension, where we are constantly invited to smile and
not once compelled to weep. Against Oberon and Titania
we do not revolt, not even when they tell us that blight and
famine are the fruit of their little intrigues, because Oberon
and Titania by their very names proclaim themselves nought:
they are symbols to which no one does or ever did attach any
serious meaning. But Aphrodite and Hera were in the days
of Euripides symbols of awful significance, to which Euripides
himself elsewhere pays the homage of a sincere and persistent
hostility. If the Aphrodite of *Helen* is to be identified with
that Aphrodite whom he paints and condemns in *Hippolytus*,
or the Hera of *Helen* with that Hera whom he derides and
decomposes in *Heracles*, then his *Helen* offends grossly against
art, sense, and manners. How did his audience know, what
from the very beginning he seems to assume them to know,

though he does not say it and in the theatre had no means of saying it, that for the nonce the symbols are void and the story phantasmal, that he, the tragedian, is for this time just playing at tragedy, and is entitled to all the privileges of parody and the comic Muse?

And if the theology, so to call it, of the play is baffling, still more disconcerting and paradoxical is the morality. Our sympathy is asked for a faithful and virtuous wife, re-united to her husband after long separation and unmerited disgrace ; yet a story is chosen, in which the alleged facts destroy the whole moral foundation upon which such a sentiment must repose. Fidelity in a spouse is admired and valued because it is precious to the other spouse. If faithful wives and unfaithful were equal, *caeteris paribus*, in the estimation of husbands, they would be equal for all purposes ; the conjugal bond would not be a respectable thing, and would not in fact exist. And the same is true for a particular case. Why should we rejoice, and how can we, because a virtuous woman is given back to a man, who liked her as well without the virtue ? Yet such in this story is the absurd position of Menelaus and Helen. Ten years Menelaus fought to possess, and seven years he has possessed, a Helen differing from his true wife in this, and in this only, that she was the paramour of Paris. For seventeen years he has ignored this circumstance, and behaved as if his natural, proper, and only desire was to get the false Helen back to Sparta. He never even says, what his acts emphatically deny, that the moral defect of the imitation has given him any concern. When the discovery of the real woman opens the prospect of exchange, does he grasp at it? Of course not. He treats the real story, the story of the substitution, as simply disproved by the existence of the false woman, refuses any further investigation, and is actually returning to the beloved phantom, when he is arrested by the news that it has gone[1]. The obvious fact, that to such a husband, to such a Menelaus, nothing but a corporal distinction between the two Helens would be significant, and that no such distinction

---

[1] *vv.* 546 foll.

exists, is actually brought out with ludicrous completeness and emphasis. In an earlier scene the true Helen has observed that, if she could but meet her husband, she could prove her identity by 'signs which they only knew[1].' Considering that her double is a creation of Hera, this confidence seems questionable, and it proves fallacious. In vain does she exhibit to Menelaus a private mark (something, it would seem, like the mole of Imogen), and remind him that in the requisite knowledge of her person 'no one, no one is his superior[2].' The divine imitation, as might be expected, is not without the mole; and Menelaus, who cannot be the husband of two, continues to shake his head; 'she is like, oh certainly like, but—the difficulty is, that he has another'! And so to the other he goes. After this, how is it possible to take seriously the rapture with which, when no choice is left to him, he salutes the recovery of the original bride? The sentiment of such a scene is unreal, and if taken for real, would be disgusting. It is possible only if proffered and received as a humorous mockery; and of this Euripides, whose mastery of sentiment is supreme, must have been perfectly aware. He is playing with his subject, exactly as if that were what his audience would expect from him. But how should they expect it, and, not expecting, how were they to understand?

It was said above that Euripides claims in this play the liberty of parody; and this is true not loosely but literally. For the play is a cento of parodies, and the chief object of parody is Euripides himself. The *Helen* consists of a situation and a movement, both depending upon the supposed persecution of the heroine by the tyrant Theoclymenus. During the first part she is, or rather is supposed to be, in sanctuary,

---

[1] *v.* 290.

[2] *v.* 578 σκέψαι· τίς, οὗ δεῖ, τίς ἔτι σοῦ σοφώτερος; *i.e.* τίς ἐκείνου, οὗ δεῖ, σοφώτερός ἐστιν ἢ σὺ εἶ; where σοφός τινος (neuter) signifies *acquainted with* (*a matter*). So read, for τί σου δεῖ τίς ἐστί σου σοφώτερος; The action explains. That σκέψαι, *look* (cf. Aesch. *Cho.* 230), refers to something particular, is shown by the context; the general resemblance Menelaus has already admitted (*v.* 577); and note also the appeal to his special knowledge.—Wyttenbach's correction τὸ δ' οὐδείς ἐστι σοῦ σοφώτερος gives the same sense, but not so well.

having put herself under the protection of the deceased Proteus, by taking up her abode in his tomb or chapel before the palace gate. In the second part, she, with Menelaus, deceives Theoclymenus into abetting her escape. The sanctuary recalls the *Andromache*, the escape has a close parallel in the *Iphigenia in Taurica*, with this difference in each case, that whereas the rival scenes are pathetic, and exhibit real distresses and terrors, these exhibit nothing but the pretence. That a voluminous writer should repeat himself is not surprising, but surely it is odd that he should repeat himself in this way. Of the escape particularly we may say that, if this part of *Helen* had survived as an anonymous fragment, and no external information about it had existed, the Euripidean authorship would certainly have been disputed, and with reason, on the ground that Euripides could have no motive for producing so weak a copy of his *Iphigenia*. In both, a Greek woman escapes by sea from a `barbarian master, carrying off with her in one play her husband, and in one her brother. Both, in order to reach the sea, pretend that this is necessary for the performance of a religious rite. Both also pretend affection for the tyrant. Both are supported by a Chorus of fellow-captives. In both cases there is eventually a fight, in which the barbarians are beaten, Orestes in the one case, Menelaus in the other, having first proclaimed his identity. In *Iphigenia*, Orestes surprises the barbarians by his athletic vigour in carrying his sister on board ; in *Helen*, the Greeks in a body produce a similar effect by carrying— a bull ; and so on. There are even verbal parallels[1], and a resemblance throughout of language and thought more obvious to perception than to analysis. In short, the episodes are in external features as like as they well could be.

But in spirit and emotional effect one is real, the other a semblance. The peril of Iphigenia and her companions is certain, hideous, and desperate. The king of Taurica practises human sacrifice and punishes with impalement. Orestes and his friend are actually under sentence of death.

---

[1] *e.g. Iph. Taur.* 1386 ὦ γῆς Ἑλλάδος (ναῦται), *Hel.* 1593 ὦ γῆς Ἑλλάδος (λωτίσματα), to the respective crews.

Even if the Greeks should get to sea, the circumstances are such that they must almost certainly be caught; and above all, they do not get to sea. They fail; they are driven on shore; and the appalling catastrophe is evaded only by a theatrical miracle in no way affecting the tragic excitement of the story. Theoclymenus, the king of Egypt, is such a 'tyrant' as we might expect on the stage of Mr Gilbert. He has a profound respect for the memory of his virtuous father, and an aversion (for which he blames himself) to capital punishment[1]. His whole crime, so far as appears, is that he is paying unwelcome addresses to a married woman, formerly entrusted to the protection of his father, *who has heard nothing of her husband for seventeen years*; that he has supported his suit (so she says) with 'insolence[2]'; and that he has prohibited visitors from her country (from which practically it seems no visitor ever comes) under the threat of death. Unchivalrous conduct this is, not in good taste, and in a pious man highly blameable; but where is the tragedy? His behaviour to Helen, what we see of it, is decorous and even gentle; he is even polite and sensible enough to express regret for the alleged death of Menelaus though in a way fortunate, he says, for his own wishes[3]. He supposes, and surely well might suppose in the circumstances, that she may prove not inconsolable; but his only present suggestion is that she should now cease to make an apartment of the mausoleum[4], a reference to her seclusion which, be it observed, she herself complains of as 'a jest.' It is she, and not he, who, treacherously of course, proposes that he should wed her in her tears[5]; and the fact that he accepts this proposal, as a knight of Provence would doubtless not have done, is really the sole visible fault in act of which the tyrant is guilty. No violence is even imputed to him, and indeed he makes it clear that he seeks the heart as well as the hand, and

---

[1] *vv.* 1165, 1171.   [2] *v.* 785.

[3] *v.* 1197, οὐδέν τι χαίρω σοῖς λόγοις, τὰ δ' εὐτυχῶ, omitted by some because it 'breaks the stichomythia.' But this is right. After this verse there is a decent pause; then Theoclymenus resumes.

[4] *v.* 1228, πῶς οὖν; τόνδ' ἔτ' οἰκήσεις τάφον;   [5] *v.* 1231.

that it is the conjugal piety of Helen, as displayed in her
fidelity to Menelaus, which is so irresistibly attractive to his
pious disposition[1]. Of her beauty (I think) he never speaks,
and indeed this may be supposed to be a little overblown.

The effect of this scene, and of the whole play, if it were
possible to take the situation seriously, would be to make us
wonder, why Theoclymenus must be deceived at all, why he
should not be called upon to fulfil the pledge given by his
revered father to the gods, now that the legitimate claimant
has so strangely appeared. Nothing is less probable, upon
the facts exhibited, than that in that case the pious son and
suitor would have chosen the part of a traitor, a ravisher, and a
murderer. If the Greeks, and his own still more pious sister
(of whom more anon), deceive him, that is not because they
manifestly must. He might have willed right; and what is
more, he could not have done wrong if he would. For if
anything is plain in the whole proceedings, it is that under
this remarkable 'despotism' the despot is powerless. In
spite of his present order that Greeks (on pain of death)
shall have no access to his palace or his domain, Greeks on
this day (though not before apparently for seventeen years)
keep arriving all the time—first Teucer, then Menelaus, then
another, and are not once molested by his 'watchers[2],' or by
any one else; walk up 'openly,' as he complains, to his door,
and parley with his servants; and when told that 'they come
at an inconvenient time,' that 'the family is in disorder,' and
that 'if they are in distress they had better go elsewhere[3],'
they continue for hours to carry on their concerns, including
conspiracies against his peace and person, in his own front-
yard and beneath his battlements, without the least caution,
interruption, or even embarrassment of any kind! The king
himself has gone hunting[4], and it seems to be correctly
assumed that, beyond the actual range of his eye, he does
not count. The Portress at his gate is so afraid of him (she

[1] v. 1278 πρὸς ἡμῶν ἄλοχον εὐσεβῆ τρέφειν.
[2] vv. 1171 foll.
[3] See the whole scene between Teucer and Helen (v. 68 foll.) and between
Menelaus and the Portress (v. 437 foll.) especially vv. 450, 477–482.
[4] vv. 153, 1169.

says) that, though she likes Greeks herself, she actually shakes her fist in the face of a Greek beggar (Menelaus) and warns him that he will be in danger of his life if he hangs about. Truly does the tyrant observe that his people presume upon his lenity. Not a prince in all the realm of opera could have better reason to say so. We hear from Helen herself that Theoclymenus, in his offensive proposals, has not a single supporter; all the palace, except the king, are 'friends to her[1].' And verily so it proves. With the permission of the king's sister, and with the practical connivence of his subjects generally, the escape is so arranged as to sacrifice the lives of some fifty innocent and helpless Egyptians[2],—another feature of the story, be it noticed in passing, which would be repulsive if it were not too silly. However so it is, and the massacre is duly reported by a survivor. The tyrant is really furious, draws his sword, and threatens to kill his treacherous sister with his own hand. But not even now will the guardians of his virtue permit him to do any such 'injustice.' The bystanders[3] throw themselves in his path, ready to die in the cause of right, an act of heroism which, as the despot neither receives nor even calls for any assistance, and as we happen to know that he would call in vain, does not somehow seem so perilous as to require the divine intervention by which it is promptly rewarded. From first to last 'justice' has all the cards in her hand ; and one can only wonder, as we said before, why she condescends to cheat.

As for the deception itself, the merit of which, as a stroke of wit and courage, is supposed to supply the main interest of about 600 verses, a hollower business can hardly be imagined. Regarding it as serious melodrama, all find it, with Hermann, languid ; and Euripides is good enough to let us see why this is. 'Nothing,' says the conclusion[4], 'is more useful to man-

---

[1] *vv.* 313–314.   [2] *vv.* 1022, 1069 foll., 1267, 1380, 1412, 1526 foll.

[3] *vv.* 1627 foll. Who the speaker is, whether the leader of the Chorus, or (as Clark suggested, and Paley agrees) a man-servant of the king, makes no difference, though I think Clark right. Note the masculine singular δοῦλος ὤν, *v.* 1630, and ἀρχόμεσθ' ἄρ', οὐ κρατοῦμεν, *v.* 1638, a protest scarcely applicable to actual slaves. The δοῦλοι of *v.* 1641 may well mean only 'subjects of a queen.'

[4] *v.* 1617.

kind than a reasonable distrust.' And nothing therefore, we might add, less exciting to mankind than the deception of a dolt. In the deception of the king of Taurica by Iphigenia, though the trick as a trick is nothing very clever and the interest is amply secured otherwise, still the Greek woman is inventive, and the savage is no fool. Thoas has no reason to suppose that his new captives are interested in Iphigenia, or she in them ; he does not know that they have a ship; he assumes (and the event justifies him) that escape is in any case impossible; and he allows them, upon a pretext not unplausible, to go down to the beach. But Theoclymenus starts with the suspicion that the visitor comes to carry off Helen[1]. He is actually told that the visitor is 'a companion' of Menelaus, a survivor of the shipwreck in which he perished, whom some sailors' accidentally picked up[2], and this he accepts without enquiry. He is asked to furnish the pair with a ship, because Greek religion (so they say) requires a funeral ceremony to be performed, for the benefit of Menelaus, *at a considerable distance from the land*[3]. He consents, and (that Helen may return the sooner) he promises, unasked, that *the ship shall be swift*[4]. He is told that ship and crew must be under the command of the stranger who is to 'celebrate the funeral,' and that *he must make this perfectly clear.* He gives the order cheerfully 'once, twice, and again[5].' And with all this we are to admire (it is supposed) the cleverness of the Greeks in outwitting him and effecting an escape.

The sense of futility in these scenes is strengthened by the misapplication of a conventional form, the dialogue in alternate verses (*stichomythia*), and by the abuse of 'dramatic irony.' The dialogue in alternate verses, an artificial but useful type, is manifestly more or less serviceable according as the situation requires development, a progression from stage to stage and from point to point. For scenes of discovery, as in the *Oedipus Tyrannus*[6], where the truth emerges bit by bit, it is admirable. The scene in which Ion examines Creusa

---

[1] *v.* 1175. [2] *vv.* 1207–1217. [3] *vv.* 1266 foll.
[4] *v.* 1272. [5] *vv.* 1414 foll. [6] *O.T.* 1007 foll., 1149 foll.

upon her knowledge of the supposed tokens of his birth, could not be better shaped than in the terse symmetrical question and answer, each marking a new turn in the investigation[1]. Even in circumstances not so specially favourable, it has advantages, in fixing and guiding the attention, so long as there is something to look for, something to come out. The long and desultory conversation, in which Ion and Creusa, the orphan boy and the sonless mother, become gradually interested in each other[2], or that in which Menelaus ascertains the whole desperate situation of his nephew Orestes[3],—these strain the instrument, but a sympathetic spectator would hardly have them recast. But in the 'deception' of Theoclymenus this treatment approaches the grotesque. We know exactly what is going to happen. The artless scheme of the mock funeral has been evolved before (in alternate couplets) between Helen and Menelaus[4]. Before it can even be propounded to Theoclymenus, he, oddly enough, plays up to the adversary's game, by raising the question, which interests his piety, whether Menelaus has had any funeral[5]; and his desire that the rites shall be of the proper 'Greek' sort proves scarcely less keen than that of Helen herself. The thing is thus given away ; yet we have 50 more lines in altercation, the whole of which come to this, that Theoclymenus will do whatever he is asked. And to make things more natural, the part of Helen is filled with ponderous ambiguities, in which the audience, but not Theoclymenus, are to perceive the meaning, that Menelaus is not really dead. We all know that the Athenians loved this sort of irony, and telling it often is ; but it was a hazardous business, easily overdone. And here it is turned, so to speak, clean inside out.

> ΘΕ.   λιπὼν δὲ ναὸς ποῦ πάρεστιν ἔκβολα;
> ΕΛ.   ὅπου κακῶς ὄλοιτο, Μενέλεως δὲ μή[6].

Theoclymenus. 'And where did the man leave the wreck of his ship?' *Helen.* 'There where I hope it may perish, and

---

[1] *Ion* 1406 foll.   [2] *Ion* 264 foll.
[3] *Orestes* 385 foll.   [4] *vv.* 1032 foll.
[5] *v.* 1222.   [6] *v.* 1214.

Menelaus not!' What can Theoclymenus say to this cryptic exclamation but 'Menelaus...*has* perished' (ὄλωλ᾽ ἐκεῖνος)? And what is the use of thus rubbing in, what we perceive only too well, that Helen's tale and behaviour are not natural, and that the blindness of Theoclymenus must be wilful?

From the king's order, obtained in this highly probable manner, that the disguised Menelaus shall be put in command of a ship, flow consequences momentous to the topsy-turvy kingdom. The tyrant, never obeyed before or afterwards, is, in this business obeyed to perfection. He has ordered 'a swift' ship, and his agents launch 'the best sailer' of his fleet[1]. He has directed them to take orders from Menelaus; and accordingly, when other shipwrecked Greeks appear, sufficient in number to man the vessel, and when Menelaus invites all these strangers to 'take part in the funeral,' the Egyptians, though 'suspicious,' decide after deliberation that they cannot object, since the royal command was absolute, and clearly covers the case. 'It was that command of yours,' says the reporter to the monarch, 'which caused the whole mischief[2].' One can only say that, if the Egyptian language had a word for *Pinafore*, this surely must have been the name of the ship.

We said of the deception that a hollower business can hardly be imagined. If any can, it is that of the sanctuary, the hardship of Helen in being forced to inhabit the tomb or chapel of king Proteus. This is the main factor in the first part of the action, as the 'deception' is in the latter part. Here again we have in appearance a variation upon a common theme of Greek drama. For obvious reasons an altar was a favourite property of tragedy, and the situation of suppliants and fugitives a favourite opening, from the Danaids of Aeschylus all down to the Thebans of Sophocles, and the Argives, Heracleids, Andromache, Amphitryon etc., of Euripides himself[3]. Nearest to *Helen* is *Andromache*, where the solitary woman, an oppressed foreigner, the nature and position of the sanctuary, a mausoleum before a mansion,

---

[1] *vv.* 1272, 1413, 1531.   [2] *vv.* 1537–1553.

[3] Aesch. *Suppl.*, Soph. *Oed. T.*, Eur. *Suppl.*, *Heracleidae*, *Andr.*, *Heracles.*

the Chorus of friendly women-visitors, and other traits, offer
a parallel which no one could miss.   But here again, if we
attend to the action presented, we see that the interest is
given away, is treated in such a fashion that it dissolves into
a mockery.   The suppliant in sanctuary must be *ipso nomine*
a prisoner : the distresses of the position, the exposure,
loneliness, risk of starvation, and the rest, all depend upon
the essential point, that the   fugitive   is   confined to the
protecting place.   The *Andromache* or the *Heracles* will supply
illustrations *passim*, if wanted.   Now consider the confinement
of Helen.   For a few scenes, the hunted hare abides in her
form, while visitors, one of them a Greek voyager, supposed
upon the allegations to be strictly excluded from the country,
repair to her, converse with her freely, and depart un-
challenged.   The conversation raises doubts and anxieties
about the fate of her husband ; and it is suggested to her
that there is a person in the house (Theonoe, the king's sister)
who may or must be able to relieve them.   And thereupon
not only her friends in a body, but she herself, the fugitive in
sanctuary, *go peacefully indoors to enquire*[1]—a movement
especially conspicuous in a Greek tragedy, because the
withdrawal of the Chorus, and an empty scene, is a thing not
common.   In their absence comes Menelaus, who, recognizing
Helen when she re-enters, tries to prevent her return to the
chapel.   She, for the moment, actually supposes that the
'impious' Theoclymenus has set a spy upon her!   'What!
An ambush !,' she exclaims in indignant horror.   However,
she struggles back to her seat of safety, and having 'reached
that ground,' surveys her adversary and discovers her mistake;
and the business of the recognition proceeds accordingly[2].
When, after long and leisurely episodes, it becomes necessary
to the Greeks' plot that Helen should go indoors again, in
order to make up as a mourner, she goes unharmed; while
Menelaus, who asks whether he shall go with her or 'sit quiet
here at the tomb[3],' is told to remain, for 'the tomb and his
sword will protect him.'   As a situation for tragedy, this
could hardly be surpassed by Mr Puff.   Whatever the

---

[1] *vv.* 306–385.   [2] *vv.* 541, 550, 556.   [3] *v.* 1083.

suppliant may say, the fact, the staring fact is, that her
'inhabitation' of the mausoleum is voluntary and fictitious ;
the 'mattress,' which (alas !) she keeps there[1], is an empty
symbol ; and the so-called sanctuary, which she quits and
enters whenever she chooses, is a retreat about as painful as
a summer-house.

And so it is with all parts of the machinery. Wherever
we look, we seem to find dummy levers, springs of plaster,
and wheels that cannot revolve. Take yet one more leading
theme, the omniscience of Theonoe. This personage, the
king's maiden sister, is the good fairy, we may almost say the
goddess, of the story. Her superhuman intelligence, her
universal knowledge of 'all things that are and are to be' is
asserted in terms that might have contented Apollo or
Ammon. She is a living oracle. The world consults her,
like Apollo, about the foundation of colonies. Nothing can
possibly be hidden from her[2]. She foretells the approach of
Menelaus and knows when he comes. Her solemn consent
has to be obtained before anything can be attempted against
Theoclymenus ; and he, in his one instant of puzzle, rather
than suspicion, about the manœuvres of Helen, is promptly
reassured by the suggestion that Theonoe must know[3]. In
short, her omniscience is the key-stone of the arch. And yet
it is ignored, as well as assumed, with the most impudent
caprice. With Theonoe for a companion and friend, Helen is
nevertheless ignorant, speaking broadly, of everything that
has befallen the Greeks since she was removed from them,
and now, seven years after the taking of Troy, learns this and
the intermediate history, in the play, from a Greek voyager[4].
Nor is the strangeness, or rather the absurdity, of this
situation allowed to escape our notice. Teucer, the informant,
cannot say what has become of Menelaus ; he has not
reached home and is supposed to be lost[5]. Presently Helen
bewails this uncertainty to her female friends. ' But why be
uncertain ? ' is their very natural observation. ' Why not

---

[1] *vv.* 797–799.

[2] *vv.* 13, 144 foll., 317 foll., 530, 818 foll., 922, 1198, 1227 and *passim*.

[3] *v.* 1227 (λαθεῖν Jacobs, for θανεῖν).   [4] *vv.* 107 foll.   [5] *vv.* 123 foll.

consult Theonoe? *From her you will know everything. With
such an informant at home, why look elsewhere*[1]*?*' And to
Theonoe, as we have already seen, they accordingly go. We
might follow this matter further, but for the immediate
purpose need not. We have already enough to explain the
fact, that a play, which is treated like this, somehow fails to
arouse interest. It is now seldom edited, and hardly ever
read (I speak from observation) except in fragments or for
strictly philological purposes; and we can only wonder, first,
how the poet himself, with the literary power which he
exhibits, not only before and afterwards but in bits of this
very work, can have been blind to the suicidal faults of the
conception and, still more, of the execution; and secondly,
how a piece, which impresses us mainly as 'an unsuccessful
attempt to triumph again with a plot like that of the *Tauric
Iphigenia*'—the summary of a recent critic—should ever
have had sufficient celebrity to find its way, along with that
very *Iphigenia*, into the comparatively small selection of
Euripides which has been preserved.

But it is time to show, what is to be the outcome of these
criticisms. 'What escape,' my reader will ask of me, as
Menelaus asks of Helen in the play, when she proposes that
he shall pretend to bring the news of his own death[2], 'what
escape or remedy does this promise to you and me? For the
notion, as such, is somewhat stale.'

$$\sigma\omega\tau\eta\rho\text{í}\alpha\varsigma \ \delta\grave{\epsilon} \ \tauο\hat{\upsilon}\tau' \ \check{\epsilon}\chi\epsilon\iota \ \tau\text{í} \ \nu\hat{\omega}\nu \ \check{\alpha}\kappa\text{ο}\varsigma \ ;$$
$$\pi\alpha\lambda\alpha\iota\text{ό}\tau\eta\varsigma \ \gamma\grave{\alpha}\rho \ \tau\hat{\omega} \ \lambda\text{ό}\gamma\omega \ \gamma' \ \check{\epsilon}\nu\epsilon\sigma\tau\text{í} \ \tau\iota\varsigma.$$

In a tragedy such candour seems rather crude; but this study
would already be too long, if it were to end in merely
sharpening and accenting a little the common opinion, as
represented by Hermann, that the *Helen* on the whole is
tame.

The traits above indicated, and others of the same kind,
would have a different complexion, if we could suppose, as
I have suggested in the Introduction, that the 'tragedy' was
a jest, a refined and delicate mockery of serious drama,

---

[1] *vv.* 306–329.   [2] *v.* 1055.

differing widely indeed in method, but not differing essentially
in spirit and purpose, from such caricatures as Canning's
imitation of German romance, or *Chrononhotonthologos*, or the
tragedy in the *Critic*.

But it will of course be objected, that such a play,
produced along with other and regular tragedies at the
Athenian Dionysia, must have been unintelligible. ' Is this
meant for a joke?' is a question deadly to leave open.
Now *Helen* is most certainly not a burlesque. There are
indeed touches in it, such as the comment upon Helen's
invention, just cited, which seem so comical that it has been
thought necessary to remove them by emendation[1], touches
of burlesque, fit only, one would suppose, for Aristophanes.
But these are rare. What appears everywhere is only an
exaggeration, mild but deleterious, of maladies natural to
drama, and seldom or never avoided altogether even in the
most strenuous work. It is as if the Muse were poisoned,
or permeated by some parasitic enfeeblement. A reader or
student, when he has collected all the symptoms, may, or
perhaps must, begin to suspect, that the dramatist was not
unaware of them. But not so an unprepared audience. The
most acute spectator must spend some time in mere dissatis-
faction, and an average person could perceive only flatness to
the end. Euripides would have merely courted the criticism
addressed by a certain humorist to a tragic actor, ' Mr ——,
I must see your "Hamlet." I hear that it is really funny,
without being in the least vulgar.' Such must have been
the certain consequence of exhibiting a drama, which was
not serious, on an occasion presupposing the contrary.

But our *Helen* was not originally composed for the theatre,
nor at the theatre was it first heard. I speak positively, and
will justify the assertion. There is ample evidence, internal
and external, that it was composed for a private recitation,
contemporaneous and in some way connected with the festival
of Thesmophoria, the festival kept by women in honour of
Demeter and Koré, the Mother and the Maid. The place
of the recitation was not Athens, but a private residence in

---

[1] ἀπαιόλη for παλαιότης, Hermann.

a remote island. The play was originally addressed, as the connexion with the Thesmophoria would imply and the text shows, especially to women. The purport of it is a playful apology on the part of Euripides to the female sex, for the alleged offence that he 'never exhibited a woman of virtue.' This time at least, as he points out to them, this cannot be said, since he has proved and praised the virtue, not merely of a woman, but of the most notorious scandal to her sex: he has rehabilitated Helen.

The poet Stesichorus had long before apologised, not to the sex but to Helen herself, as a personage by some supposed immortal and divine, for the popular libels upon her character, and had formally contradicted them in a famous poem. That Euripides followed this lead, and borrowed from Stesichorus some part of his idea (we know not how much nor does it matter), is universally and rightly supposed. His reason for doing so was, that he also, in his own humorous way, was making an apology.

The evidence, I have said, is both external and internal. As the internal evidence is of a kind which, so far as I know, has not been observed, and which very likely does not occur, in any other work of Hellenic antiquity, it may be conveniently introduced by a parallel example from our own literature ; where the facts, which might have been inferred, in the absence of other evidence, from the original document, happen to be also given by tradition and notorious. Milton's *Comus* was composed, we know, to be performed by the family of the Earl of Bridgewater, President of Wales, at his residence, Ludlow Castle. Its merit and celebrity have caused and permitted it to be occasionally performed by ordinary companies, in public theatres, and to common audiences ; but it is from the circumstances of the original representation that the piece derives its plan and character. Now those circumstances happen to be recorded for us in extraneous and authentic documents. They are also indicated, though imperfectly, by what we may call the semi-extraneous evidence of the stage-directions. But suppose that we had nothing but a bare text of the spoken parts, such as our

actual text of Euripides; and suppose, as in that case we
may well suppose, that we not only had no record of the
first performance, but did not even know by extraneous
evidence that such a manner of performance was possible.
Should we be condemned to ignorance of the fact that the
original circumstances of production were peculiar, and important to the design? Certainly not. From the bare
text we might have proved this; because the piece contains
things *which are irrelevant to the dramatic story*. These
things, in common fairness to the author, must have been
supposed relevant in some way to the purpose of his work,
and explicable by something; which something, since it is
not the dramatic story, must, from the nature of the case,
have been sought in the circumstances of the production.
For example, the prologue informs us that

> *Neptune, besides the sway*
> *Of every salt flood and each ebbing stream,*
> *Took in by lot 'twixt high and nether Jove*
> *Imperial rule of all the sea-girt iles;...*
> *...but this ile*
> *The greatest and the best of all the main,*
> *He quarters to his blue-hair'd deities;*
> *And all this tract that fronts the falling sun,*
> *A noble peer of mickle trust and power*
> *Has in his charge, with tempered awe to guide*
> *An old and haughty nation, proud in arms:*
> Where his fair off-spring nurst in princely lore
> Are coming to attend their father's *state*
> *And new-entrusted sceptre*; but their way
> Lies through the perplext paths of this drear wood,...
> And here their tender age might suffer peril
> But that by quick command from sovran Jove
> I was dispatcht for their defence and guard;
> And listen why....

which brings us to the true matter of the story, to Comus and
his enchantments, the Lady, and so on. Now to this story
all the statements here distinguished by italics are irrelevant.
It is nothing to the story that the home of the wanderers
is on an *island*: the scene might be laid, as far as the story
is concerned, in the middle of Asia; it is nothing, that the

place is situated towards the *west* of that island; or that the master of the house is a *noble peer*, and governs with *entrusted sceptre* an *old nation*. All this is concerned with Ludlow Castle, the Earl of Bridgewater, and the Presidency of Wales, with none of which conceptions the dramatic story, as such, has any concern whatever. And from this and other like phenomena a careful student of the bare text might have inferred in substance everything about the original production which is significant for the proper appreciation of the work as a whole.

The *Helen* is a parallel case, where the external evidence is equally strong (for Aristophanes is a witness not less authentic than Lawes) and the internal evidence, if not stronger, is much more salient and striking.

First then, the original production of the play was associated not with the theatrical contest at all, but with the Thesmophoria, the festival of the Mother and the Maid (Demeter and Koré) celebrated by women in the autumn, about the end of October. There are in the play many minor indications of this circumstance, to which we will return hereafter; but the principal mark is this. One of the choric odes[1], one only, instead of treating, like the odes in tragedies generally and like all the other odes in this, topics arising out of the story and the dramatic situation, is occupied entirely with narrating the legend of the Mother and the Maid, and commending the religious performances based upon that legend. It is an exquisite poem, the literary gem of the piece; but it makes no pretence of arising out of the dramatic situation, and is, at least in *prima facie* appearance, so absolutely irrelevant to the story, that some readers have actually supposed it to be an interpolation, a piece from elsewhere, imported by some accident into the text. Not an incident of the story is mentioned in it, nor (by name at least and in an intelligible way) any one of the dramatic personages. It appears in short to be frankly extraneous. The attempt has of course been made to trace a connexion[2]; but if this attempt were more successful than is commonly

[1] *vv.* 1301 foll.   [2] See the note on this ode in the Appendix.

thought, it would be nothing to the present argument ; it would prove at most that the poet has found a pretext for importing into his play a topic which no one could expect. Pretext or no pretext, the thing is a manifest importation. It surprises and perplexes all readers, and must *a fortiori* have surprised and bewildered an audience, unless they were in some way provided with a reason for it.

Now this phenomenon is without a parallel, so far as I am aware, in extant Greek drama. But, wherever it may occur, there is but one way of accounting for it. The topic of the ode, since it is not naturally suggested by the story, must have been suggested, *and imperatively required*, by the only other condition with which the author could have any concern, that is to say, the circumstances of the representation. It must have been *necessary*, for some plain reason which every spectator could instantly understand, that Euripides on this occasion should pay homage to the legend and worship of the Mother and Maid. Let us only imagine what we should feel, as spectators, if, when we were expecting the usual dramatic or semi-dramatic ode, the Chorus went off upon an elaborate narrative for which we had no conceivable cue !

We should perhaps note, since the relation between chorus and drama is sometimes discussed rather loosely, that we have here no concern with the question, how much part and what kind of part the Chorus as actors should have in the action. The Chorus in *Helen* has at least as much part in the action as usual, perhaps not less than in any extant drama, except of course those of Aeschylus. Nor are we concerned with the use of irrelevant interludes *as a system*. This, which has been practised, would be a defensible and perhaps inevitable expedient, if we were to suppose that interludes of some sort were a permanent necessity of the dramatic form. But the question is, whether, in a system of relevant interludes, a playwright would abruptly introduce *one* not relevant. Why should he ? And how, if he did, could he expect the comprehension of his audience ?

We should assume then, *prima facie*, in fairness to

Euripides, that his play, as a performance, had some close and obvious connexion with the worship of Demeter and Koré. The season of the Thesmophoria, the great Athenian festival of these deities, would suggest itself, I think, as the most probable occasion, though of course without external testimony we should not be justified in fixing on this particular feast.

We may note however at once, that the purport of the play, in its largest aspect, is very well suited to a festival of women, an occasion specially devoted to the honour of that sex; and further, that the dramatist makes a point of this. In bidding farewell to his audience, he takes credit with them, *and especially with the women,* for the benefit conferred upon them by his defence of Helen. Helen was the notorious 'scandal of her sex[1]'; but Euripides, developing the paradoxical hints of the poet Stesichorus, here presents her as a supreme example of conjugal fidelity. And he claims credit for this with the women. 'May ye be happy,' says the last speaker, addressing the women of the Chorus and the company generally, 'May ye be happy in the excellent discretion of Helen, *a thing which for many women is not possible[2]!*' Impossible it is, as the humorous modesty of the expression signifies, for most women, indeed for all, and for all men too, for everybody except the spectators, as such, of this particular play. To find happiness in the virtue of Helen is a pleasure reserved for those who will accept the paradox which the dramatist here defends. For these indeed, the pleasure would be common to all; and since the dramatist lays stress upon the happiness and advantage accruing to women, and indeed, if we take him strictly, would appear to speak of this only,

---

[1] Eur. *Orest.* 1153, *Andr.* 218, 229, etc.

[2] *Hel.* 1686 καὶ χαίρεθ᾽ Ἑλένης οὕνεκ᾽ εὐγενεστάτης | γνώμης, ὃ πολλαῖς ἐν γυναιξὶν οὐκ ἔνι. That the address is general, not restricted, like what precedes, to the Twin Brethren, appears by the abrupt change of number: the Twins are addressed (1684) in the dual. And indeed, as addressed to them, the reference to women would be pointless; it points to the sex of the Chorus. There is no excuse for translating ὃ...ἔνι as if the neuter ὃ referred to γνώμης: the proper and necessary antecedent is τὸ χαίρειν Ἑλένης οὕνεκα γνώμης.—To the choric 'tag' which follows, and to the connexion of the passage generally, we shall return hereafter.

we must naturally suppose that he had reason for this, and that his business on this occasion lay, for some plain cause, with the interests of the female sex in particular. Such a cause is provided by the association, indicated by the ode, between the play and the worship of the two goddesses, and would be specially obvious if the performance was connected with the festival of which women were the only proper and official celebrants, the festival of the Thesmophoria.

And now comes in Aristophanes. Whenever and where-ever *Helen* may have been first recited, it came, we know, eventually to be exhibited publicly, in the theatre, and at the Dionysia.

Now in the year next after that in which *Helen* was so exhibited to the public, Aristophanes brought out the *Thesmo-phoriazusae*, the *Celebrants of the Thesmophoria*, which refers to *Helen* as recent, and contains two scenes of burlesque, one based upon *Helen* and the other on *Andromeda*, also a Euripidean play of the year before. The subject of the comedy is a profanation of the Thesmophoria by Euripides. Hearing that the women, at their private mystery, intend to devise some punishment for his persistent defamation of the sex by the exhibition of bad women only, Euripides resolves to defend himself against this charge, and, being unfitted for a feminine disguise, employs a kinsman as his advocate. The advocate, whose apology is of course satirical, is detected, and the situation is developed with gusto. That this plot had some basis in fact, we might almost infer from Aristophanes himself; for his Euripides is assisted in the business by the tragedian Agathon, who furnishes advice and properties for the make-up; and this conjunction of the poets savours strongly of some literary enterprise, in which Euripides had been principal and Agathon in some way participant.

How then stands the matter as between the *Helen* and the *Thesmophoriazusae?* On the one hand we have a play of Euripides, which, on the face of it, is associated by some external circumstance with the worship of Demeter and Koré, and which, on the face of it, claims, in a humorous manner, the approval and gratitude of women for the defence (under difficulties) of the female sex, and for the presentation, in a somewhat surprising form, of a singularly virtuous woman. No sooner does this play, by exhibition in the theatre, become generally known, and suitable as a subject for theatric allusion, than Aristophanes, at the first opportunity, produces a burlesque, in which Euripides is represented as misusing the Thesmophoria, the great festival of Demeter and Koré, for the purpose of defending himself against the charge of never exhibiting a virtuous woman ; and in this burlesque he takes conspicuous notice of the *Helen*. Surely, if our observations could be carried no further than this, we should already have reason to suspect that these facts have a connexion, and that the external circumstance, which originally dictated these peculiarities of the *Helen*, was an association with the festival of the Thesmophoria. There are, as we shall see hereafter, other conspiring indications of this in the Euripidean play itself ; but we will proceed for the present to a second external circumstance, for which also we have the confirmation of Aristophanes.

If the play was originally designed for recitation at the season of the Thesmophoria, it would follow, I think, that the recitation was a private affair. So far as I am aware, there is no reason whatever to suppose that the civic theatre, the only theatre, was used at that festival; or that dramatic performances such as the *Helen*, or indeed of any kind, formed part of the Thesmophoria proper, the mysteries officially then celebrated by women as part of the civic religion. The recitation of *Helen*, if designed to take place at the season and in honour of the Thesmophoria, must have been a domestic recitation, given under private patronage and at a private residence. There is nothing in this to surprise us ; on the contrary it would be, as we shall see hereafter, extraordinary and scarcely credible, in the circumstances of the time, that dramatic pieces should not have been often circulated and tried in this way. The best, but only the very best, eventually reached the theatre. In the theatrical form of course they were preserved ; and of the private origin little or nothing can be seen in them, or could be, unless there were a case in which the private circumstances were so essential a part of the work, that it would not bear transformation, but, if the theatre called for it, must go to the theatre essentially as it was first framed. Precisely such a case is the *Helen*, our only extant proof of a process infinitely important to the development of Athenian drama, and without which the line which that process took would not be wholly comprehensible.

Our internal test must still follow the principle which we saw to be valid in the case of *Comus*, and have already applied to the Thesmophorian ode: the principle or axiom that a dramatist, like anyone else, will keep to his subject, and will not put forward things of no conceivable interest either to himself, as narrator of the story, or to those who are to hear it. Anything conspicuous in the piece, which is not accounted for by the story, must have been accounted for by the circumstances of the representation. What else of this kind, besides the ode, is conspicuous in *Helen*? One other thing at least: I mean the contrivance, extravagant and irrational to the highest degree, by which the poet forces into his epilogue a complimentary allusion to the island of Helené.

Along a portion of the east coast of Attica, at a short distance off, extends a ridge of rock or hill, narrow but eight miles long. It has pastures, and is now inhabited, in the summer only, by the herdsmen; the same condition is indicated by geographers and topographers of the Roman empire. Wells however are found in it. The geographers and topographers are apparently the only original authors of antiquity, except Euripides, who ever mention the island[1].

It was called Macris (since Makronisi), and also Helené. The latter name was variously connected with the voyages of the famous heroine to or from Troy: it was said, for instance, that Paris and his paramour (hugging the coast apparently, like the fleet of Xerxes, and making for the Euripus) had rested in Helené for a night[2]. The extant notices of these derivations are much later than Euripides, and the production

---

[1] See Smith's *Dict. of Geography* s.v. Helena, and Pausanias 1. 35. § 1 with Dr Frazer's note.

[2] It was identified by some with the 'Kranae' of Hom. *Il.* 3. 445.

of them may have been stimulated by his successful example; but perhaps, if a Strabo, a Mela, or a Pausanias had written in the fifth century B.C., his notice of the island would have comprised some such note on the name. It did not, so far as we know, give rise to any cult or legend commonly accepted. The stories are mentioned by those, and those only, who are compelled to mention the island.

Now the plot of *Helen*, so far from requiring a reference to this illustrious locality, would naturally and almost necessarily exclude it. According to this play, the Helen who sailed to Troy, the only Helen who could be brought, by any plausible licence of supposition, to Macris, was merely a 'double' of the heroine, a phantasmal imitation, whose separate wanderings, up to the day upon which she arrives in Egypt and vanishes, are, as Euripides himself indicates[1], a topic which his theme does not include. And if it were necessary (but how should it be?) to mention the island and account for its alternative name, the obvious thing was to follow the usual derivation *mutatis mutandis*, and to say that the phantom Helen, with Paris, rested there. But why notice the island at all? Neither the place nor its associations were generally interesting, or commonly noticed. Why not let it alone?

And now let us see what Euripides actually does. In the general blessing, bestowed at the close by the Twin Brethren, Helen receives the promise of divine honours; and then we read this[2]:

'The place to which Hermes removed thee first from Sparta...when he stole thy person to preserve thee from Paris, the long[3] sentinel-isle that flanks the Attic shore, shall henceforth bear among men the name of *Helené*, because it received thee when from thy home so stolen.'

οὗ δ' ὥρισέν σε πρῶτα Μαιάδος τόκος
Σπάρτης......
Ἑλένη τὸ λοιπὸν ἐν βροτοῖς κεκλήσεται.

That is to say, Hermes, when he conveyed the real Helen through the air from Sparta to Egypt, did not make one

---

[1] *vv.* 765–771.   [2] *v.* 1670.   [3] τεταμένην, alluding to *Macris*.

flight of it, but lighted with her first upon Macris *alias* Helené.

To clear the substance, I have omitted in the translation a detail of which the sense is disputed. Completed, it would run thus: 'The place to which Hermes removed thee first from Sparta (his journey began from the mansions of the sky¹), when he stole thy person' etc. The parenthesis explains, I take it, what (heaven knows) requires an explanation, why the god did not fly straight on from Sparta to Egypt, why there was any 'first stage' in the journey at all. He had already flown (we are reminded) from the top of heaven to Sparta, before he picked up Helen, so that the flight thence to the island, with the woman, made altogether enough for one stretch ; to Egypt direct would have been too far! The extravagance of such an explanation, and the light tone of it, are quite in keeping with the rest, and suitable, as we shall see hereafter, to the general purpose. But the parenthesis is at all events a detail ; let us consider the substance of the story.

And *first*, the statement comes as an utter surprise. The journey from Sparta to Egypt has been already described by Helen in the prologue, without hint of divergence or pause : 'Hermes took me, hidden in ethereal folds of cloud, and set me here in the house of Proteus².' *Next*, the story is nonsense, not coherent or acceptable even as a fable: the island is not on the way to Egypt, not nearer than Sparta itself. *Thirdly*, between the heroine and the island it makes no appreciable link : Helen was once in it for a few minutes ; therefore it (rather than Pharos, say, where she lived, according to the play, seventeen years) shall henceforth bear her name !

To account for this fantastic excursion there is but one fair way. It must have been *necessary*, for some plain, broad, imperative reason which all the audience would comprehend, that Euripides on this occasion should do or pretend to do, what in general no one did, that is, pay some regard to the insignificant island and its apocryphal story. The island

---

¹ ἀπάρας τῶν κατ᾽ οὐρανὸν δόμων.   ² v. 44. See also vv. 241 foll.

must have been a datum, as Ludlow Castle was for Milton when he composed *Comus*, though of course not necessarily for the same reason.   The island, and a special interest of the audience in the island, must have been an axis, as the season of the Thesmophoria was another, by which the lines of his composition were regulated.   Upon that supposition we can understand him.   The conjunction of ideas was not promising. The island bore a name infamous to womankind, and was thought of, when thought of at all, as the scene of the most notorious of adulteries.   The festival was sacred to the sex and to marriage.   To exhibit the historic Helen at such a time would have been to commit really the offence of which Euripides was falsely accused, a preference for the portraiture of feminine vice.   The dilemma prompted the happy and witty expedient of improving on the apology of Stesichorus. The real Helen was not vicious, but a paragon of wifely virtue. The vicious woman was no woman, but a mere phantom. But only the vicious phantom then can have visited the island ? Not at all, says the dramatist cheerfully.   A poet is no more bound by logic, than miracles by reason.   The true Helen did come to Helené, was brought there by Hermes ; one scarcely knows why, but so it was.

Why the island, though not in the least interesting, so far as appears, to people in general, should have been interesting to the special audience of *Helen*, this allusion would not tell us.   Many causes of such interest would be conceivable. It would be enough, for example, if the patron or patrons of the occasion were proprietors of the island.   But an obvious hypothesis, and one which we should properly test before seeking any other, is that the island, a house on the island, was the place of the original recitation.   The season of the Thesmophoria, about the end of October, the perfection of the southern autumn, when worshippers in the open air could keep up their ceremonies through the day-bright hours of the full-moon[1], was a time when a house in the island might well be occupied.   We should enquire then next, whether the

---

[1] *Hel.* 1365 foll., with note in the Appendix.   For the official ceremonies see Miss Harrison, *Prolegomena to Greek Religion*, pp. 120 foll.

play exhibits any evidence that an island, and a house on an island, was specially concerned in the composition and production of it. We shall not have to look far. The prologue, spoken by Helen, opens thus : ' This place is Nile, river of fair maidens, which, instead of heaven's rain, moistens, when the white snow melts, the soil and fields of Egypt. Proteus, while he lived, was king of this land, having his dwelling in the island of Pharos, though lord of Egypt[1]. He married one of the sea-maidens, Psamathe, when she quitted the couch of Aeacus, and begat two children to this house, a boy, whom he (because he[2] had lived piously all his days) named (but in vain) " Theoclymenus," and a happily-born maiden, named Eido (Beauty)[3], as her mother's jewel, when she was a babe ; but since she came to age mature for marriage, they have called her Theonoe, because she had the divine knowledge of all things that are and that are to be, having received this privilege from her grandsire Nereus. And I myself come of a country not without fame, Sparta,...' and so we proceed to the history of the heroine and the foundation of the play.

Now this passage, like that which was cited above from the prologue to *Comus*, bristles with points and statements for which the dramatic story furnishes no reason or explanation whatever. We will take here only two of them. Why does the dramatist suggest that the house of Proteus, the house of his play, lies in the island of Pharos[4]? And why does he choose for his king of Egypt the name of Proteus? Let us not only ask these questions, but insist on finding plain and satisfactory answers. The scenes of the drama do

[1] v. 5 Φάρον μὲν οἰκῶν νῆσον, Αἰγύπτου δ' ἄναξ.
[2] v. 9 Θεοκλύμενον ἄρσεν', ὅτι δὴ θεοὺς σέβων βίον διήνεγκε.
The subject of διήνεγκε is the father, Proteus: the conduct of the boy could not be yet known. δή signifies that, according to Helen, the hopes of the pious father were disappointed. ὅτι, *because*, is explained by Θεοκλύμενον, which is to be read as in inverted commas, and construed as equivalent to ὃν ὠνόμασε Θεοκλύμενον.— The metre of v. 9 is rough, but should not be suspected. See notes on the play in the Appendix.
[3] Or *Eidos*, as the MS.: Εἰδώ, Matthiae.
[4] v. 5, compared with vv. 8, 46, 68, 460. See also the Appendix.

not take place on the island-rock of Pharos, nor in any island at all. The scene is laid and the king's house stands, as the first line of the play implies, *by the Nile*, that is to say, on the mainland of Egypt, miles away from Pharos. The single line of the prologue which says that the deceased monarch, 'though lord of Egypt, dwelt in the island of Pharos,' is, I believe, the sole reference to 'Pharos' or 'island' which the play contains. That a king of Egypt should live on Pharos, would be, as the turn of the phrase suggests, sufficiently surprising, even if we suppose, which we shall hardly do, that Euripides foresaw and anticipated the foundation of Alexandria. That the palace of this play is not there, is abundantly and consistently proved. One visitor arrives at 'the fields of Nile[1]'; others, before they arrive, have wandered 'all about the country[2],' without suspecting that the sea surrounds them, or that they have landed on a mere rock. The royal docks of Egypt are close to the palace[3], as assuredly (unless Euripides anticipated Alexander) they were not to Pharos. The cave, it is true, in which a whole ship's company of more than fifty persons find perfect concealment so long as they choose[4], would scarcely be found, we may doubt, in Egypt proper ; but neither would it be found in Pharos or any where else. It is a mere freak of imagination, but indispensable to the story, and needing no other excuse. The circumstances generally agree with the opening in laying the scene *in Egypt, by the Nile* ; and the island, as such, has no more to do with the story than England, *qua* island, with the story of Comus. Only the inconsistency of Euripides is far greater than that of Milton ; for in *Comus*, though to the story it makes no difference that the enchanter's wood is on an island, at least there is no reason why it should not be ; whereas in *Helen*, if we really try to place ourselves on Pharos, the story becomes unworkable. Why then, when Euripides has first placed his scene where it really lies, on the mainland of Egypt and beside the Nile, does he not leave

---

[1] *v.* 89 Νείλου τοῦσδε γύας.

[2] *vv.* 597—598, 408—432.

[3] *vv.* 1526 foll.

[4] *vv.* 424, 1532, 1537 foll.

it there? Why insert a verse by which, for the first and last time, it is suggested that the house of Proteus, the house of the drama, is on the rock or island of Pharos?

If we say that Pharos is wanted because in the *Odyssey* it is the home of Proteus, we only go from *ignotum* to *ignotius*. For why again, in the name of common sense, should Euripides pretend that the personage of his story is a Proteus? The Proteus of Homer, and of other poets, is a miraculous or divine personage, a wizard of the sea, who pastures a flock of seals, and transforms himself at pleasure. Menelaus in the *Odyssey* consults him as a wizard; and the marvellous encounter is laid in Pharos because, as the epic story notes[1], it was a day's sail away from 'Egypt'; and probably it had little traffic, until it was transformed by the Macedonian engineers. All which are excellent reasons why Euripides should name his personage not Proteus, but anything rather. Neither in the person, nor the place, nor the incidents of the story, is there the least resemblance. The Proteus of Euripides, the late king, was apparently not a prophet, even when he lived; for we are expressly told, as if to prohibit any such notion, that the supernatural wisdom of his daughter Theonoe came not from her father but from her maternal grandfather[2]. Menelaus in Euripides does not come to Egypt for the purpose of consulting Proteus, or of consulting anybody. The whole scenery, circumstances, and facts of the Homeric episode are not merely irrelevant to the drama of Euripides, but incompatible. Apart from the name Proteus, the play makes no allusion to the epic; and should we import into it reminiscences of Homer, we should make nonsense. Why then did not Euripides call the king by some other name, any other, and dismiss both the Homeric wizard and the Homeric island from a work which has nothing to do with them?

The truth is that this prologue betrays, like the prologue to *Comus*, but much more manifestly, the influence of inconsistent requirements. The dramatist, for some reason or

---

[1] *Od.* 4. 354 foll., where 'Egypt' apparently means the Nile (*Dict. Geog.*, s. v. Pharos). [2] *vv.* 7, 15, 1003.

other, is not free to consult only the requirements of his story. Milton was bound to place his enchanted wood near the seat of an English nobleman and vice-gerent, near Ludlow Castle, though in truth it is not there and nothing in the story would lead us to suppose so. Euripides, though his scene is not laid on an island, must hint, at all events once, that it is, and though his king of Egypt is not Proteus, must give him that name. In the case of Milton we know the reason; in that of Euripides, if we would understand him, we must find it out. Why he must have a Proteus, we shall see hereafter; why an island, we may already guess. If his play was designed for recitation in Macris, at a particular house in Macris, if it not only contains domestic allusions, but in two most important personages represents the successive house-holders, if the whole work, in some of its most significant aspects, is related not to Egypt at all but to Macris, and if it requires that we figure ourselves to be, not only for some purposes in Egypt and at the palace of the Egyptian king, but also for other purposes in Macris and at the house of the representation—then we can understand why the prologue should hover, as it does, between two incongruous conceptions, and in particular why Pharos, here and here only, should make its irrelevant appearance. The story takes place by the banks of the Nile; but no sooner has the author said so than he retracts it, adding that nevertheless we are in an island, the island of Pharos. Why? Because in an island somehow we are to be; and Pharos (besides opening the way to another innuendo which we shall understand presently) was at least an island, an Egyptian island, and offered, as such, a link of translation between the two pictures of the place, which the author must in some way combine.

And now comes in again Aristophanes. The *Celebrants of the Thesmophoria* not only bases its plot upon the original occasion of *Helen*, but contains a scene of parody[1], in which the personages of the comedy temporarily assume the parts and speak, in travesty, the language of the Euripidean play.

---

[1] *Thesm.* 855–919.

The scene opens thus[1]: 'This place is Nile, river of fair maidens, which, instead of heaven's rain, gives moisture to Egypt's white soil, a stone (people)[2] as black as a black dose.' Now what is Aristophanes here about? What is his point, and why, to make fun of the *Helen*, does he raise this pother about the colour and consistency of the Egyptian soil? Of course it is neither white nor stony, but black and soft, *nigra harena*, as the literature of antiquity frequently describes it. But why insist upon the fact? Who controverted it, and what has it to do with the Euripidean play, which never once, so far as I can discover, alludes to the subject? Without the *Helen*, we could not answer these questions fully; but this we could say, that in the play, and in the opening of the play, Euripides must in some way have assumed an 'Egypt' which had or should have a rocky and a light-coloured soil; that he must have identified Egypt with such a place; that the identification must have been necessary to him; that it must have embarrassed him; and that he must have betrayed his embarrassment in some conspicuous way. Unless all this were true, the parody of Aristophanes would be pointless and unintelligible. Given this, it is witty. Aristophanes, by stopping his quotation at the right place, contrives to construe Euripides as if, though he had not called the soil of his Egypt stony, he actually had called it *white*. He pretends to think, though the contrary is obvious, that this is

---

[1] Νείλου μὲν αἵδε καλλιπάρθενοι ῥοαί,
ὃς ἀντὶ δίας ψακάδος Αἰγύπτου πέδον
λευκῆς νοτίζει μελανοσύρμαιον λεών—

imitating Euripides,

Νείλου μὲν αἵδε καλλιπάρθενοι ῥοαί,
ὃς ἀντὶ δίας ψακάδος Αἰγύπτου πέδον
λευκῆς τακείσης χιόνος ὑγραίνει γύας.

[2] That λεών here means primarily *stone*, a by-form of λᾶς as in the adjective κραταίλεως, I infer from its apposition to πέδον (cf. κραταίλεων πέδον in Eur. *El.* 534), from the fact that it replaces the Euripidean γύας, and from the antithesis of λευκός and μέλας. The translation *people* certainly does not give the whole or the chief part of the sense; there may be a pun on the proper sense of λεώς; but as this introduces both a puzzling idea and an odd construction, I am not sure that we ought to suppose so. The συρμαία was an Egyptian medicine. The reason why it is mentioned will appear hereafter.

what Euripides meant. An excellent point, if there was reason
to ascribe the idea, though not the language, to Euripides, but
otherwise pointless and irrelevant. The Euripidean play and
prologue explain it. Euripides does, for his purpose, identify
the land of Nile with the island of Macris ; his scene is both
at once ; and therefore, says Aristophanes, he might as well
have told us that his 'Egypt' was composed of a *not* black
rock ; nay, may we not say that he actually has told us so ?

We turn then with interest to the plot and personages of
Euripides, to see whether and where they show trace of an
allusive purpose. Of the plot, the confiding of a wife to the
care of a pious householder, his long protection of her, the
wooing of her by his unworthy son, the defeat of his son and
restitution of the wife by the piety and fidelity of his daughter,
we may say with apparent certainty that it has no domestic
reference. Apart from the improbability of such a coincidence
between a story attributable to Helen and that of a house
where, as it happened, a *Helen* was to be represented, the
story is in some respects such, that the mere possibility of
a domestic reference would have been enough, one would
suppose, to forbid the choice of it. But we cannot say the
same of the persons, or not of all.

Theoclymenus indeed, the son, and Menelaus, and even
Helen, are no vehicles for compliment ; but Theonoe, the
prophetic daughter, seems made for it. Her 'divine intelligence' governs all the action, and yet she stands in a
manner outside of it. She appears once, in almost superhuman dignity[1], to receive homage and dispense fates, and
then 'withdraws into silence[2],' while the rest continue, as
before, to work out their destiny within the limits of her
permission. She is the real queen of the place, the true
representative of her father, the mistress for whom her slaves
are ready to die[3], and who overrules as she pleases the will of
the so-called master[4]. A woman of intellect, admired for her
virtue but specially for her wisdom, wealthy, unmarried, and
resolved to maintain her independence, in short, a 'Virgin-

---

[1] *v.* 865.   [2] *v.* 1023.
[3] *v.* 1640.   [4] *vv.* 998 foll., 1627 foll.

Queen'—such is Theonoe; and a more suitable president
for the performance of *Helen* one cannot imagine. Her
declaration that 'she will, if possible'—that is, of course, if
her besiegers will by any means let her—'keep her maiden
condition for ever[1],' has perplexed modern readers, who have
proposed to omit it, as indeed they have conveniently sig-
nalled, by similar proposals, several of the most significant,
because extra-dramatic, passages in the piece. Her resolve
not to wed has certainly nothing to do with the story ; but to
the authority of the real woman it was vital. Now it is just
Theonoe of whom the prologue speaks as if she were really
not the dramatic figure, but somebody else. We are told that
though 'they call her' Theonoe for her wisdom, that was not
her name. Her name was *Eidŏs* (or *Eidō*)[2], chosen because of
her infant beauty. Why are we told this? Nothing comes
of it. It does not illustrate either the story or the alleged
relations of the dramatic family. So far as these are concerned, it would have been natural to suppose that the
grand-daughter of a prophetic deity, the destined recipient
of his gift[3], had the properest of names from the first. Yet
the statement must surely have some purpose. We must
accept it then, we cannot but accept it, in its plain meaning,
that Eido she was. That she had been a lovely baby was
doubtless certified by tradition ; and we are left to presume,
though her personal appearance is of no importance to the
play, that she had not, at any rate noticeably, belied her
infant promise. Her position as mistress of the house and
successor to her father is of first-rate importance to the play,
as we shall see. It is quite possible that the part of Theonoe
was recited by the mistress herself.

If 'Theonoe' has a personal application, so has 'Proteus.'
She is essentially his representative. The spirit of the dead
father, the domestic worship of him, his piety and loyalty, the
security of his promises, and his daughter's fidelity to their
utmost obligation[4], are not important only to the plot, but

---

[1] *v.* 1008 πειράσομαι δὲ παρθένος μένειν ἀεί, omitted by Dindorf and others.
[2] *v.* 11 εἶδος MSS., Εἰδώ Matthiae and later texts.   [3] *v.* 15.
[4] See the part of Theonoe, especially *vv.* 1003—1016, and the play *passim*.

are honoured by a notice which has received, like other extra-dramatic touches, the significant stamp of critical excision[1]. Helen has entreated Theonoe to honour her father's pledge, by restoring the wife of Menelaus to the lawful claimant. Helen has appealed to the father's grave. Theonoe confirms this appeal; her father in a sense is *there*, and the tomb would be insulted, if she refused to do what he would have done. Then, looking up, she adds with startling solemnity,

'Ay indeed, payment of such a bond is possible for *all* of mankind, both for those which are below and those which are above. The *mind* of the dead, though it lives not, hath yet a conscience immortal, when into immortal ether it hath passed.'

καὶ γὰρ τίσις τῶνδ' ἔστι[2] τοῖς τε νερτέροις
καὶ τοῖς ἄνωθεν πᾶσιν ἀνθρώποις· ὁ νοῦς
τῶν κατθανόντων ζῇ μὲν οὐ, γνώμην δ' ἔχει
ἀθάνατον, εἰς ἀθάνατον αἰθέρ' ἐμπεσών.

This 'very remarkable passage' (Paley) arrests the attention of every reader; and 'why it should be considered an interpolation by Dindorf' is, with all respect to Paley, perfectly clear. The thrilling note of genuine religious feeling is discordant with the tone of the drama, and specially with the light, irreverent way in which the established deities, Aphrodite and Hera, are treated in this very scene and by the same speaker[3]. If the Theonoe of the stage were alone concerned, Dindorf would be right in his excision. But it is Eido who here speaks, the friend of Euripides, who had indeed a religion, not that of Hera and Aphrodite, but the cult of her father 'Proteus' and the belief in the immortal soul.

The father's name was *Proteas*, and with the Proteus of the *Odyssey*, the sea-god, he had perhaps this slight but real connexion, that the resemblance of the names may have led him to take a name for his pretty daughter out of the same epic chapter; for the sea-god had a daughter called Eidothoe[4], of which 'Eidos' was the applicable part. He had been a practitioner in medicine, and a dealer in drugs, herbs, etc., in short an apothecary, and his wealth was probably acquired in this way. This fact, about which Euripides is naturally silent, is supplied by Aristophanes, whose parody of *Helen* in the *Thesmophoriazusae*[1] turns almost entirely on the name and profession of 'Proteus.' Mnesilochus, the detected advocate of Euripides at the Thesmophoria, is a captive in the hands of the women. Euripides attempts a rescue, to cover which enterprise Mnesilochus assumes the part of Helen and the poet that of Menelaus. Mnesilochus, as we have seen, gives the opening of the *Helen*, but with a variant reading:

'This place is Nile, river of fair maidens, which, instead of heaven's rain, gives moisture to Egypt's white soil, a stone as black *as a black dose.*'

The women are for the moment mystified. But presently comes Menelaus, shipwrecked, as in the real play, but also *sea-sick, and with a headache*:

'A solid house! Might the possessor of it be such a one as should receive voyagers *weak from the rocking of the sea* in storm and shipwreck[2]?'

'To Proteus it belongs,' replies Mnesilochus-Helen.

'*Proteus*?' says Euripides-Menelaus with surprise.

'Ah poor unhappy man,' puts in one of the women, 'he is telling you false, that he is. *Proteas* has been dead these ten years.'

Menelaus however persists; he learns from Helen with amazement, as in the play[3], that he has reached Egypt, and then asks whether *Proteus* (*sic*) is 'at home or abroad.'

'The sickness,' says the interrupter of the dialogue, 'must be still in your head! You have been told that *Proteas* (*sic*) is dead, and you ask whether he is "at home or abroad"!'

All this fencing over Proteus and Proteas is warranted, as indeed, to have any point, it must be, by the play itself[3]. The doubt about the true appellation, which the Aristophanic

---

[1] *vv.* 850–924. See above, p. 77.

[2] Cf. *Hel.* 68. It need scarcely be said that neither the Teucer nor the Menelaus of Euripides offers a model for ποντίῳ σάλῳ κάμνοντας.

[3] *Hel.* 460–465.

Menelaus expresses broadly and farcically, is hinted delicately by his Euripidean prototype. 'Proteus it is that dwells here,' says the keeper of the door. But presently Menelaus asks, 'And this King...*what you call him*, is he within the house?', ἔστ' οὖν ἐν οἴκοις...ὄντιν' ὀνομάζεις ἄναξ; (And it is worth notice that, in the scene where 'Theonoe' appears[1], her father, though mentioned incessantly, is not once named by any of the interlocutors; nor is she. The pseudonyms, common else-where[2], would there have been discordant with the respectful allusions to the real man and the sentiments attributed to the real daughter.) The reference to 'black doses,' and the suggestion that Menelaus is seeking a doctor, reveal the profession of the householder; and it is noticed again, when Menelaus and Helen recognize one another: 'One more like Helen than you, lady, I never saw.'—'Nor I one more like than you to Menelaus—*at least out of a herb-shop*[3].' The suggestion is (it is probably true and may have been known) that the actors at the original performance of *Helen*, dependants of 'Theonoe,' had some of them served in the dispensary. They did very well, it seems, considering[4].

The burlesque Helen tells the burlesque Menelaus, that 'the old woman,' the celebrant of the official Thesmophoria, who keeps interrupting, is 'Theonoe, daughter of Proteus.'

---

[1] *vv.* 865–1029.

[2] *vv.* 152, 460, 542, 787, 1166, 1370; 859 and *passim*.

[3] *Thesm.* 910 (*Hel.* 564) ἐγὼ δὲ Μενέλεῳ σ'—ὅσα γ' ἐκ τῶν ἰφύων. The ἴφυον was a herb: τὰ ἴφυα means the place where it is sold.

[4] I cannot think that we should be content to see here an allusion to the fact or allegation that the mother of Euripides, who is made by the comedian to personate Menelaus, sold vegetables (*schol. ad loc.*). What has that to do with the *Helen*? Unless Euripides really played Menelaus, a supposition forbidden (to say nothing more) by his age, it is poor fun to suggest that he would not make a good one. And why should a man make a worse Menelaus, because his mother sold vegetables? Besides *ex hypothesi* Aristophanes' actor is not here masked as Euripides. He is got up to look like 'a Menelaus out of a herb-shop,' a chemist's assistant with a taste for theatricals. The *scholia* (and we too) sometimes suppose Aristophanes to be very dull. It should be observed that the authors of the *scholia* had not here, and do not pretend to have, any tradition: 'Proteas was an Athenian who had been dead a long time' is their note on τέθνηκε Πρωτέας ἔτη δέκα.

The anger with which the Athenian lady rejects this insinuation, and proclaims her full title, including the deme, 'Critylla, daughter of Antitheus, of Gargēttus,' suggests, what the silence of the prologue to *Helen* confirms, that Proteas and his family had no pretensions to birth[1]. His pride, and the pride of his daughter after him, was that his word was his bond, that he 'paid his promise,' the pride of an honest tradesman[2]. Hence the spirited encomium which Helen, when she would move the daughter to keep the promise of the father by restoring her to Menelaus, pronounces upon *honesty in the acquisition of wealth*: 'For God hateth violence, and biddeth all to take what may be taken lawfully, but not in the way of plunder. Wealth not honest is not to be touched. For as heaven is common to all mankind, so is earth, wherein they should so fill their houses, as that they neither keep nor seize what belongs to another.'[3] All this obviously exceeds the dramatic situation, *and has accordingly been marked for excision*. The truth is that, like the doctrine of Theonoe on the obligations of the dead[4], it properly refers not to Proteus but to the real Proteas, the man of business. He was a merchant of Athens, but we have no reason to suppose him a citizen; his art of medicine, both as science and trade, he would have studied abroad, in Egypt probably for one place. Aristophanes would have called the whole set Egyptians, and tells us so: 'Are you a Greek, lady, or a woman of this country (Egypt)?'—'A Greek. But I too would ask, are you?' The lines are Euripides, word for word[5], but among the 'doses' and 'herbs' they have a different effect.

About the mother of Eido the prologue says little; but as all that little is superfluous to the story, which has nothing to do with her, we must suppose it to represent the true facts, and to be inserted for the sake of the real woman. Her

---

[1] The word εὐγενής, as used in *Hel.* 10, has nothing to do with pedigree. It denotes merely a satisfactory child.

[2] *Hel.* 939 foll., 1009 foll., and the plot of the play *passim*.

[3] *vv.* 903–908, omitted by Dindorf.   [4] *vv.* 1013 foll. See above, p. 80.

[5] *Hel.* 561–562.

name, Psamathé, was inconvenient ; for the nymph of that name, according to the grave testimony of Hesiod[1], was united not to Proteus but to Aeacus. Euripides explains *pro forma* that she married 'Proteus' afterwards[2]. The only thing we hear about her—but this is worth notice—is that her daughter's wisdom, that is to say, her intellectual gifts and literary tastes, is expressly traced to the mother's side. She was probably an accomplished *hetaera*, a word for which we may be content to have no English equivalent, but which described a condition perfectly honest according to the notions of the fifth century B.C., the condition indeed of most women who took part in what we call 'society.' Theoclymenus the son, a ridiculous personage and indispensable to the story, is presumably a mere fiction.

More about the real persons and external situation might probably be seen in Aristophanes or in Euripides, if we knew it, as the original audiences did, beforehand ; but we will not now attempt anything beyond the outline. I will note only one strangely perplexing place in *Helen*, where the possibility of an extra-dramatic reference should be considered. When the Egyptian oarsmen, who take the galley out to sea for the pretended funeral of Menelaus, discover that he and his companions are really bound for Argos, one of them exclaims: 'The expedition is a trick! Let us go back to Axia. You (*to the keleustēs*) call the directions, and you (*to the helmsman*) turn the tiller.'

$$\kappa\alpha\acute{\iota} \ \tau\iota\varsigma \ \tau\acute{o}\delta' \ e\mathring{\iota}\pi\epsilon, \ \text{'}\delta\acute{o}\lambda\iota o\varsigma \ \mathring{\eta} \ \nu\alpha\upsilon\kappa\lambda\eta\rho\acute{\iota}\alpha\cdot$$
$$\pi\acute{\alpha}\lambda\iota\nu \ \pi\lambda\acute{\epsilon}\omega\mu\epsilon\nu \ \text{'}A\xi\acute{\iota}\alpha\nu\cdot \ \kappa\acute{\epsilon}\lambda\epsilon\upsilon\epsilon \ \sigma\acute{\upsilon},$$
$$\sigma\grave{\upsilon} \ \delta\grave{\epsilon} \ \sigma\tau\rho\acute{\epsilon}\phi' \ o\mathring{\iota}\alpha\kappa\alpha[3].\text{'}$$

Now about this *Axia* the puzzle is, not merely that the particular word offers no meaning, but that apparently no conceivable word would fit in. It cannot well form a clause by itself[4]; the following clause (κέλευε σύ) refuses any

---

[1] *Theog.* 1002, cited by Musgrave.
[2] *v.* 7. Αἰακοῦ Musgrave, αἰόλου MS.
[3] *Hel.* 1590. ἀξίαν (*va*) is reported as the reading of the MS.
[4] So Hermann, πάλιν πλέωμεν, ἀξιῶ, but plainly this will not do.

addition ; the preceding words 'let us go back,' though they might stand alone, will bear no natural addition except the place whither, which should be ' Pharos.' Neither *Axia* nor *Naxia*, the conjecture added by our copyist, seems to be known in such a sense, nor indeed would they serve the purpose if they were, since the introduction of an obscure synonym at this point would be absurd. No interpretation even plausible has been proposed, nor, so far as I see, can be proposed, if we look only to the dramatic requirements. We are compelled, it would seem, to look beyond.

Now it may be observed, that the dramatist, on the lines that we have been following, has here reached the most difficult point in his scheme. The tragedy, though it has some serious parts or touches, is throughout essentially playful. The apology of Euripides to women, if offered gravely, would have been an act of gratuitous self-accusation. This being so, it was a necessity, the bare requirement of good taste, not to include in the story, and above all within the limits of the action, anything horrible or distressing to the imagination. Everywhere else but here, this requirement is easily and scrupulously fulfilled. Nothing is done before us, or even reported, which calls for a painful compassion. The imprisonment of Helen, the shipwreck of Menelaus, are seen not to distress even the sufferers. Helen walks in and out of her sanctuary ; Menelaus jests about his clothes. But here we come inevitably to an incident which, if seriously pictured, would be horrid. The Egyptian sailors are without shadow of offence ; they are doing a work of charity and piety. The sailors of Menelaus are posted over them, 'man to man,' with concealed cutlasses ; and at the word of command the poor fellows, defending themselves with 'bits of wood,' are slaughtered or chased overboard. And this is narrated by the sole survivor, so it would appear, of the fifty. Euripides, and any audience fit for Euripides, would feel this to be hideous, a thing intolerable, unless, in some extreme circumstances, it might perhaps be presented as a stern necessity. In the *Iphigenia* for instance it might conceivably have figured, though in fact the incident there corresponding is nothing like this in cold-blooded cruelty[1]. Yet no attempt is made, nor on the lines of the *Helen* could be made, to present it as such a necessity. The deceiving of Theoclymenus, sole cause of the massacre, is a mockery, and a needless pretence. The sailor's own narrative, as we have seen and shall see again, has traits, both preceding and following the massacre, at which we are compelled to laugh. But nevertheless, there stands the massacre itself, the violent slaughter of fifty innocent men. And to carry out the notion of an escape, to imitate in appearance the *Iphigenia in Taurica*, something of the kind must occur.

The dramatist had then, so it seems to me, the most powerful motive conceivable for making us remember just here, just when the massacre is to be related, that this, between him and us, is like all the rest, not serious; that we are not really and truly to imagine any such thing. He owed this absolutely to himself, his audience, and his art.

Yet how could it be done? In one way only: by dropping altogether for a moment the dramatic fiction, by inserting a touch of pure burlesque. We expect 'to Pharos.' Now for the extra-dramatic aspect of this play, 'Pharos' is Helené; it signifies Helené, and nothing else, in the only place where it occurs[2], and the house on 'Pharos' is the house, not of Theonoe, but of Eido. I believe that Euripides deliberately put in here the name either of the house itself, or of the place, some knot of cabins, where it lay; and that therefore we have no reason for rejecting 'Axia.' Of course the effect would be purely comic, but nothing short of this would save the situation, and justify the importation of such an incident as the massacre. For this purpose the false, or rather true, name would naturally be brought in with pause and emphasis; after which the massacre might proceed without danger of offence to the most susceptible.

Let us now sum up briefly the principal facts in the external circumstances of *Helen*. Among the women of the Euripidean circle, the rare but not unknown votaresses of literature who are marked in the *Medea*[3], was a wealthy maiden

---

[1] *Iph. T.* 1327–1378.   [2] *v.* 5; see above, pp. 75–78.   [3] *Med.* 1084.

lady, named Eido. Her father Proteas, a respectable and successful man in a line which was then both profession and trade, died in the early part of the decade 421—411 B.C.[1], and she inherited his fortune. She owned property and had a residence, which she occupied at the favourable season, in the island of Macris or Helené; and she was pleased to discover, or to imagine, that her island had a romantic association with Helen the heroine. Being, as a woman, specially interested in the Thesmophoria, she proposed to celebrate that festival by a dramatic performance or recitation, to be then given at her island-home. Euripides was to compose the play. He had the felicitous thought to combine these data by adopting, from the apology of Stesichorus, the paradox that Helen had been a model of chastity, and presenting this picture, in a sort of mock-tragedy, half sport and half earnest, as a playful defence, addressed to the sex, against the ridiculous charge of his detractors, that he 'never exhibited a good woman.' A kinsman of his, Mnesilochus, and the tragedian Agathon, aided, or were in some way concerned, in the production. The date may be put between 420 and 415. The *Iphigenia in Taurica* was already written, and known in private circles; and that play, with the *Andromache*, supplied the chief features for imitation. When the *Iphigenia* had been produced publicly at the theatre, the *Helen*, already notorious, though 'new' in the official sense, followed it, probably in the year 412, accompanied by other plays, presumably of the usual tragic stamp. In the next year (411) Aristophanes burlesqued the whole proceeding in the *Celebrants of the Thesmophoria*.

Originated thus, the *Helen* not only admitted a playful treatment, but admitted no other. To the false and perverse charge in question, Euripides would not have made any serious answer, nor would his friends, women or others, have borne that he should. The very title, when considered with reference to the occasion, carried with it the significance of a paradoxical purpose; and if any more preparation were desirable, in a private circle it could be supplied. Before

[1] Aristoph. *Thesm.* 876. Of course we cannot press the 'ten years' exactly.

the piece reached the theatre, its literary character was for literary people already fixed; and the probable or certain ignorance of the many, to whom all plays were merely shows, was in this case, as in all cases, unimportant.

The conception of a drama serious in form, but in reality delicately self-critical throughout, was one thoroughly congenial, if a proper occasion could be found, to Euripides' natural bent. He occasionally succumbed, as we know, to the temptation of putting criticism into grave works, the *Electra* for instance and the *Phoenissae*, and shows everywhere a great interest in technique. The *Helen*, in point of structure, is a subtle exhibition of bad technique, designed to amuse a literary society familiar with a century of drama and steeped in critical judgments, the same judgments of common sense which were summed and formulated long afterwards by Aristotle. Everything is irregular and just wrong. The myth is extravagant; the fabulous element is made prominent, and put into the very heart of the action. The sentiment is spurious, the moral is twisted. The pathos smiles, the motives flag, the machinery halts, and the situations just never come off. It does not follow, and is not the fact, that the play, which, like *A Midsummer Night's Dream*, is full of loose and careless beauties, contains nothing grave. The praise of conjugal fidelity, for example, is none the less genuine because to take Helen as an illustration of it is paradoxical and absurd. The denunciations of war[1] are wholly without irony. But of solemnity there is nothing, except a few touches visibly extra-dramatic and domestic[2], and of horror or tragic pity not the faintest trace whatever. The whole piece imitates tragedy closely, but by compact between author and audience never attains the line.

To understand or explain such a work completely is for us now plainly impossible. Our materials and our faculties must be insufficient. To take but one point: we have no plays of Agathon. A special relation between this poet and the apology of Euripides is indicated, though not explained,

---

[1] *e.g. vv.* 1151 foll.
[2] Principally *vv.* 903 foll., 1013 foll., as already noticed.

by Aristophanes[1]. We may take it as certain that the *Helen* contains allusions, complimentary or critical, to his principles, manner, and works; but all are beyond our reach. And other like helps we must want, without even knowing what it is that we miss. And beyond all this lies the language, in which the best modern scholar conceivable could not be equipped as the case requires. A phrase too hackneyed, or too artificial, or bringing the wrong instead of the right associations from literary reminiscence—such things are all-important to the purpose. No one will pretend that he has in these necessary matters a skill comparable to that of the contemporary audience. None will have it again.

But it is still possible to discuss some of the interesting questions, which the turns of the dialogue would naturally suggest to the Euripidean circle. One, which goes to the very heart of drama, we will here consider briefly.

Twice in the play it is debated whether Theoclymenus, the so-called despot, may be attacked by Menelaus and put to death; once, when Helen first describes to her husband her position in the house and her (alleged) danger from the master's desire to marry her[2]; and again when Theonoe has given her consent to the escape, and the husband and wife are left to devise the means. 'How would it be, if I were to hide in the house, and give him the edge of the sword?' is one of his simple and elegant suggestions[3]. It is explained to him, on the first occasion, that surprise is impossible, that nothing can be done but by permission of the all-seeing sister[4]; and permission to escape is solemnly obtained from her accordingly, by the joint urgency, though in fact she needs no urging, of Helen and of Menelaus himself[5]. His recurrence in these circumstances to the proposal of a treacherous murder is the very acme of brutality and stupidity. It is of course pointed out to him by Helen that the connivence of the sister would scarcely extend so far; if it came to killing her brother in the house, she would certainly speak[6]!

[1] *Thesm.* 29–264. [2] *vv.* 808 foll. At *v.* 808, I think, he draws his sword. [3] *v.* 1043. [4] *vv.* 809–829. [5] *vv.* 894–1023. [6] *v.* 1045.

Now why is this absurd passage introduced? There is no dramatic point in exhibiting Menelaus as a brute, nor is that design pursued generally in the play: he is a mere stage-puppet, without any definite character at all. Or why should it be explained with such emphasis, that Theonoe will not allow violence? Of course she will not, but why bring it out?

The passage reflects a criticism, a view which must have been widely held, *and supported by* '*Theonoe*,' respecting the *Iphigenia in Taurica*. All this part of *Helen*, including these scenes, runs parallel with the *Iphigenia*. It is *Iphigenia* repeated, with all sorts of amusing or suggestive differences. Now the *Iphigenia* presents a problem of aesthetic not unlike the familiar question about *King Lear*, 'whether Cordelia might not have been suffered to escape death,' whether the whole tragedy would not have been dreadful enough without the cumulative accident by which she perishes. Sentiment has often said yes; sound judges, I believe, say no. The Euripidean question was, and is, 'whether Iphigenia might not, and should not, have been made *to forbid the murder of Thoas.*'

The *Iphigenia*[1] is perhaps the most ghastly story imaginable, not so much for the facts, though these are hideous, as because there is no one, no one at all among the principal characters, with whom one can fully sympathize. Of the three victims two, Orestes and Pylades, have been guilty of a revolting and (as Euripides paints it) an inexcusable murder. One is crazy, the other stupid and obstinate. Their enterprise is an act of superstitious robbery, a sort of piratical pilgrimage; and it is moreover, as they might have known it to be, hopeless from the first. Each of them has fine qualities, but pity for their fate is embittered by disgust and contempt. There remains Iphigenia, a beautiful, most pitiable, and in many respects loveable figure. But the business through which she is dragged is so bad, that the loyalty of the spectator is sorely tried. And she nearly kills it, as I have remarked elsewhere[2], when she has the chance to forbid the murder of Thoas,

---

[1] See *Euripides the Rationalist*, p. 166.　　　[2] *ib.* p. 194.

and...pauses upon it, and...rejects it only as not practicable[1].
Thoas is a savage, in every sense of the word. But the Greeks
of the play are savages too, and are the aggressors. To kill
Thoas could serve no purpose ; and the proposal to do it is
stupid, brutal, and only too like the puzzle-headed proposal
of Menelaus to kill Theoclymenus, saving that in the mad
and miserable Orestes we cannot laugh at it. To Iphigenia
the barbarian king has been much kinder than her own people ;
he regards her, and she professes to regard him, with something like affection. Merely as a woman, she might be
expected to abominate a futile assassination. But the tension
of her brother's peril, and all the appalling terrors of the
moment, mislead her heart and her judgment. Orestes asks
if the murder be practicable. And Iphigenia shudders, but
says only that it is too great a risk. It is, I think, natural ;
it is perhaps necessary to the truth of the picture. But it is
heart-rending, horrible ; and sentiment cries to the dramatist,
'For pity's sake, let her say that *the thing must not be*! In
this welter of crime and folly, give us at least one glimpse
of sensibility and sense.' Now it may be assumed that
'Theonoe,' the real woman, held, as a woman, with this
sentiment ; and that is why Euripides insists on the point,
that in a plot controlled by Theonoe there cannot be a
murder of King Theoclymenus. About Iphigenia and King
Thoas he probably adhered to his own view.

Other such observations will occur upon a comparison
of the two plays, and may be followed up with profit. But
how uncertain must be our investigation, how many clues
we must miss, even with the help of the *Iphigenia*, and how
many more, because we have lost the indispensable apparatus!
And moreover, such things need to be comprehended *instanter* :
they are half-spoiled if they must be explained. A commentary on *Helen*, such as could now be made, would be very
long, and I fear it might be very dull. But taken superficially, the 'tragedy,' if we start on the right line, is even now
full of interest. We must be content here to note without
system some scattered points in the order of their occurrence.

For marking the connexion of the performance with the

[1] *Iph. T.* 1020–1023.

Thesmophoria, the author relied chiefly on the independent
ode ; and indeed no other efficient way was open, the story
as such having not the remotest affinity to that festival.   But
in the semi-dramatic parts of the work there are minor
allusions, especially in the prologue.   Aristophanes, in the
prayer with which his *Celebrants* open their proceedings[1],
names the deities of the festival as follows : 'Demeter and
the Maid, Plutus, Kalligeneia, Kourotrophos, Hermes, and
the Charites or Graces.'   The five subordinate ˌpowers, as
here grouped, make a transparent allegory, comprising what
mothers would desire for happiness in their daughters, wealth,
happy birth, rearing, and education, and finally a fortunate
courtship, denoted probably by the conjunction of Hermes
and the Graces[2].   All of them are introduced by Euripides.
The play proper begins[3] with a comparison of the house of
King Proteus to that of 'Plutus,' a compliment to the actual
house of the recitation.   The prologue begins with an allusion
to Kalligeneia, *Fair-birth*, an important Thesmophorian personage, a double, as it would seem, of Koré the Maid.   This
word offered difficulties to a composer of iambics, but is
suggested by an ingenious turn.   The Nile in the first verse
is described as *kalliparthenos*, river of fair maidens, an epithet
which has naturally provoked question[4], being neither usual
nor significant to the story.   The explanation, I think, is this.
All waters as such are κουροτρόφοι, breeders of the children
whom they feed.   Euripides would, if he could, have called
his river καλλιγενῶν παρθένων τροφόν or the like.   This being
inadmissible, he has put half the important epithet, *kalligenēs*,
here, and completed it by *eu-genēs parthenos* (*v.* 10), bringing
in another *parthenos* (*v.* 6) as a link to the ear.   To a
Thesmophorian audience all would be perfectly clear.   It is
of course arranged, in the circumstances of the house, that
the girl of the family, Eido, shall have all the compliment.
The son, Theoclymenus, having no real prototype, is disowned
as unsatisfactory.

---

[1] *Thesm.* 295.
[2] Cf. Plutarch, *Coniugalia Praec.*, *prooemium*, cited by Orelli, on Horace,
Odes I. 30. 8.
[3] *v.* 69 Πλούτου γὰρ οἶκος ἄξιος προσεικάσαι.   [4] See Paley *ad loc.*

For the like reason, Eido being unmarried and averse to marriage, we have no conjunction of Hermes and the Graces; but both are mentioned. Hermes (under Zeus) is the deity who chose the house as the place where Helen should reside for the preservation of her conjugal fidelity[1]. The Graces (under Zeus) took the lead, as we hear in the Thesmophorian ode[2], in consoling the Mother for the carrying away of the Maid on the original occasion of the Thesmophoria.

As to the secrets of the festival, the things which only women might behold[3], Euripides, if he knew anything, would of course on such an occasion be scrupulously silent. But he perhaps alludes, discreetly and with confession of ignorance, to the existence of secrets. From our informants, all men, we know that the ritual performances, or some of them, were called *pursuits* (diōgmata)[4]; this much, and no more, seems to have been public property. Now the prologue has a passage[5], superfluous to the story, in which the name Helen is derived, '*if the account is true*,' from a pursuit or *diōgma*[5].

'There is a doubtful account, that Zeus visited my mother Leda as a bird, in the form of a swan, which won to her arms by pretending to fly the *pursuit* (if this account is true) of an eagle; and I received the name of Helené.' The purpose of this may be to bring in with emphasis (note the place in the verse) the mysterious word, and to give the women of the audience the opportunity of remarking with a smile, that the poet's notion of a *diōgma* was, as he presumes it may be, not true but utterly wrong[6].

We may also note here in passing that Menelaus, at his

[1] *vv.* 44–48.
[2] *vv.* 1339–1344.
[3] Aristoph. *Thesm.* 626.
[4] Hesychius and Suidas *s.v.*
[5] *v.* 18
ἔστιν δὲ δὴ
λόγος τις, ὡς Ζεὺς μητέρ' ἔπτατ' εἰς ἐμὴν
Λήδαν, κύκνου μορφώματ' ὄρνιθος λαβών,
ὃς δόλιον εὐνὴν ἐξέπραξ' ὑπ' αἰετοῦ
δίωγμα φεύγων, εἰ σαφὴς οὗτος λόγος·
Ἑλένη δ' ἐκλήθην,
as if from ἔλε νηδύν apparently. But the word δίωγμα also occurs at *v.* 354 and *v.* 1623, and not, it seems, with any special meaning. See note in Appendix, *v.* 22.

[6] For a more probable account of these performances, which had analogies in other rites, see Miss Harrison, *Prolegomena to Greek Religion*, Chap. IV.

first appearance, introduces himself with a superfluous
reference to the history of his grandfather Pelops, into which
is imported, still more artificially, an obscure legend which
seems to have been connected in some way with Deo or
Demeter[1]. The irrelevance is so manifest, that some have
proposed excision; but what was the motive of the interpolation? The passage indicates rather that the author had
reason for hitching his work, upon however slight a pretext,
on to the legend of the Earth-Mother.

In the prologue (*v.* 36) we are told that the Trojan war
was engrafted by Zeus on to the quarrel of Hera and
Aphrodite with a double purpose, to relieve 'mother earth' of
excessive population, and to make known 'the mightiest in
Hellas.' The fables are commonplaces, but not relevant to
this drama; and the fact is that both have a new turn here.
The first is thrown in for the sake of the Thesmophoria, to
which the prologue makes other allusions. The second
prepares us for an amusing twist later on. 'The mightiest in
Hellas,' whose fame the war was to serve, was, in common
acceptance, Achilles. But neither prologue nor play has
praise for this hero[2]; and Helen here proceeds (*v.* 49) as if the
compliment were intended for her 'unfortunate husband,'
as general of the Hellenic host. Presently (*v.* 393) Menelaus
caps this, by appropriating, 'without boast,' all the glory
to himself and Agamemnon, especially himself, on the ground
that 'beyond question my force was the largest'!

The episode of Teucer (*vv.* 68—163), who arrives on this
particular day, but independently of Menelaus, to consult
Theonoe, as an oracle, on the project of founding the colony
of Salamis in Cyprus, is mainly a compliment to the wise
queen of the house, but also serves the mechanical function of
informing Helen upon Greek affairs, and thus providing topics

---

[1] *vv.* 386–389, with the remarks of Hermann, cited by Paley. Hermann
would correct the passage so as to name Demeter, but this is not clearly
necessary. As it stands, it imports that Pelops, not Tantalus, gave the famous
banquet to the gods, and was advised to do so by some one not named, whom we
should suspect, from other forms of the story, to be Demeter. The avoiding of
the name may be intentional, a mystic discretion. Nauck omits ἡνίκα...ἐποίεις.

[2] And see the slighting reference in *vv.* 98–99.

for the musical lamentations which follow, as well as an occasion for the preposterous appeal of Helen to the lady within for the completion of Teucer's report[1]. The impudent carelessness of the incident as a dramatic device, its utter unlikelihood and irrelevance, must be intentional, and is pointed probably at something beyond our knowledge. But we can appreciate the climax, when Teucer, having done what he is wanted for, is told by Helen (*v.* 151) that, as for getting to Cyprus, *solvitur navigando* (πλοῦς αὐτὸς σημανεῖ); and that he had best go at once, for the king of Egypt is by way of putting all Greek visitors, when he catches them, to death, for reasons 'which I do not explain, as it would be of no service to you.' Teucer thanks her kindly (καλῶς ἔλεξας), gives her his blessing, and takes himself off.

At *v.* 255, we have an oration from Helen which must perplex us, if we suppose that the audience were intended to keep their gravity. 'Women my friends,' she begins, 'what a fate has been mine! Was I not from my mother's womb a wonder to mankind? *Never did woman of Hellas, or of the world, put forth her offspring in a white shell; yet so, they say, did Leda conceive me of Zeus.* A wonder indeed is my life, and such have my fortunes been.' We correct this (after Badham) by omitting the sentence in italics, which goes certainly to the very edge of burlesque. But that is the purpose. Euripides does but exaggerate, delicately and humorously, a flaw inherent in drama based, like the Greek, upon myths. The matter will scarcely bear the strain of exhibition to the eye. When Deianira in the prologue to the *Trachiniae*, as a visible woman, tells us how the river-god, her suitor, beset her father's house in changing form of bull and snake and man, we are already near to danger; nearer still, when Creon informs Oedipus that the Sphinx, with her riddle and depredations, so absorbed the attention of Thebes, that the murder of the king was disregarded[2]. Keep such things in the background, says Aristotle, registering the practice of common sense; and Euripides, as well as Sophocles, did so with rigour and vigour. But in *Helen* we

[1] See above, p. 59. [2] Soph. *O.T.* 130.

have broken with common sense, and may enjoy the singular spectacle of a woman deploring to her companions the prodigious fatality—that she was born in an egg!

At the close of the same speech, tragedy demands another correction[1]. To die well or nobly (καλῶς θανεῖν) is a tragic desire; but not quite so *to die like a beauty*, the sense preferred by Helen, who, as we noticed once before, is more conscious of her charms than in this play any one else is. What suicide, she asks, is most fit for her? Hanging is ugly; and then she is (as she chooses to argue) 'a slave,' and for slaves to hang themselves is thought not proper. She inclines to the sword, —and does nothing.

This speech contains the famous verse[2] τὰ βαρβάρων γὰρ δοῦλα πάντα πλὴν ἑνός, *Outside of Hellas, all are slaves but the one master.* It is pointed here at the tyrannical power of Theoclymenus, about which we know what to think; and I suspect that it is quoted from some other play, where it was really appropriate. Helen's impossible wish, that her face could be 'painted out like a picture, and drawn again less fair[3],' should be compared with that of the calumniated Hippolytus[4], conscious of innocence but bound by his promise not to prove it, that he could look into his own eyes. Nothing will better show what sort of a 'tragedy' this is. Hippolytus touches the very spring of tears; but what man or woman, having any sense of humour, could weep with such a Helen? When she laments[5] that her jewel, her infant Hermione, must be getting to 'grey hairs, and still *no husband*,' how are we to forget, though she chooses to ignore, what sort of a marriage she has found herself? If her story were real, and she had a real sense of it, she ought to pray that her child might never marry at all. The situation is a satire on the words, and such is the intention. In the house of 'Theonoe,' grey hairs and no husband would not pass for a description of misery[6]. The whole speech is a thing to smile over, and doubtless has

---

[1] *vv.* 299-302 are omitted by Dindorf, after Hartung.
[2] *v.* 276.   [3] *v.* 262.   [4] *Hipp.* 1077.
[5] *v.* 282.   [6] See *v.* 1008, and *supra* pp. 78-87.

many humorous points, in the way of parody, which we
cannot now perceive.

With the entrance of Menelaus we come to new and
broader effects of the same sort. Indeed there is little to be
said about the soliloquies of the great captain, or his interview
with the portress, which has not been said by followers of
Schlegel or, with much more insight into the nature of the
business, by Paley. These ridiculous things are not blunders,
nor even 'comic elements' (whatever that may mean) in
a picture professedly serious. They are just parts, harmonious
parts, of the quasi-tragedy. The crown of the royal
wanderer's misfortunes, towering over the Trojan war and
other minor miseries, is that in the recent shipwreck he has
lost his wardrobe ;

> as may well be guessed
> From what I wear, this refuse of the ship.
> My former robes, my gorgeous draperies,
> My luxury, sea-swallowed[1]!

Of course the poverty or even the discomfort of a prince may,
in a proper way and proper place, be treated as a theme for
compassion; and we gather from Aristophanes that in the
Telephus and elsewhere it was so treated by Euripides. Here
he is serving a dish like that of Aristophanes, differently
flavoured indeed, but of the same meat ; and the burlesque
of this scene in the *Thesmophoriazusae*, so far as concerns
the dramatic personages, is scarcely an exaggeration of the
original. It is out of the Euripidean company, the dramatist,
actors and audience as such, out of the celebrants of the
Thesmophoria, 'Theonoe,' her family, and her household, that
Aristophanes this time gets his fun ; and very good fun it is.
As for the dramatic picture, it hardly leaves caricature any
room. Here are some specimens :

'In a deep cave I have hidden the woman who to me has
been the origin of all misfortune ; and the remnant of my

---

[1] *v.* 421
$$αὐτὰ δ' εἰκάσαι$$
πάρεστι ναὸς ἔκβολ' οἷς ἀμπίσχομαι.
πέπλους δὲ τοὺς πρὶν λαμπρά τ' ἀμφιβλήματα
χλιδάς τε πόντος ἥρπασε.

companions are guarding, *under compulsion*, my marital rights'—

> ἐν δ' ἄντρου μυχοῖς
> κρύψας γυναῖκα τὴν κακῶν πάντων ἐμοὶ
> ἄρξασαν ἥκω, τούς τε περιλελειμμένους
> φίλων φυλάσσειν τἄμ' ἀναγκάσας λέχη[1].

The crew were apparently of opinion that the captain's anxiety to keep his lady was a mistake, and that another Paris would best put an end to their difficulties.

'Ever since I took Troy Town, I have been wanting to get home....On the Libyan coast there is not a place so lonely and unvisited, but my ship has been there. And every time I approach home, I am blown off again, and not once have had the wind that would bring me to Sparta[2].' Such is the simple explanation which accounts for seven years! Tales of adventure, really designed and fit to excite interest, do often make demands upon our belief, which in the aggregate would startle us; but it is not usual for the narrator, in this candid manner, to present the addition.

But the cream of the scene, from the contemporary point of view, would be the passage[3] in which Menelaus, having learned that there is in the house a Helen, daughter of Zeus, formerly of Sparta, but resident here since the expedition to Troy, puzzles over the possibility of reconciling these facts with the existence of his phantom companion. 'Two Troys and two Spartas—perhaps; two Helens very likely; but another Zeus? *An Egyptian of that name??* Well, never mind; there is surely but one *Menelaus*, and *this* name will be a sure passport to charity.' It is the very image of that mechanical rationalism, the translation of legend into commonplace by supposed coincidences of name, through which the better minds had passed and passed out: the juggling with κρῖος-Κρῖος, βορέας-Βορέας, ταῦρος-Ταῦρος, βρόχος-βραχίων[4], men called Hermes, women called Sphinx,

---

[1] *v.* 424.   [2] *v.* 400.
[3] *vv.* 483 foll. Paley strikes the right note.
[4] See *Heracles* 153, and the essay on that play hereafter.

and ships called Pegasus. Euripides had made use of it himself for by-ends[1]; but as a system, to one who had thought
out his *Heracles*, it was detestable in its irrational pedantry,
and he tramples cheerfully upon the fallacy of the whole
method. There are people still to be found who do not
understand the weight of cumulative coincidences, and who
might profitably meditate with Menelaus.

The re-entrance of the Chorus and Helen[2] takes us back
to the oracular function of Theonoe, whose response is reported.
Menelaus is not dead ; he is wandering still, but will arrive—
'when he attains the end of his troubles[3].' The oracle is
guarded, as an oracle should be. But certainly we need not
suppose in this case any defect of knowledge. The intelligence of Theonoe, as a human intelligence, is sound, which is
necessary and sufficient for the complimentary purpose of the
character ; but her supernatural quality is, as for the same
purpose it ought to be, a pretence and a caricature. Up to
this point the drama, while assuming that she must have
known all the past, shows also that in fact she did not. She
now is found to know of the present exactly what any one
might know, who was not bound to respect the flimsy
hypotheses of the play. Menelaus is coming ; of course he
is. Nowhere else but in this Egypt could his presence, with
his remarkable wife and his fifty companions concealed in
a cave, be a secret. And what of the future? Will he get
safely out of Egypt? Helen was 'so pleased to know him
safe at present that she abstained from pressing that point[4].'
Most convenient for the oracle, and, strangely enough, exactly
how Xuthus behaves when consulting the Pythian oracle in
Ion. Having learned that he is father of a son, 'for the joy
of that, he did not ask who was the mother[5].' He would have
posed the prophetess if he had, not (in that instance) because
she did not know, but because she did[6]. But in a general
way, such an emotional disturbance in the consultant, and

---

[1] *Hippol.* 338. See Prof. Murray's text.
[2] *v.* 528.   [3] *v.* 534 ἥξειν—ὅταν δὴ πημάτων λάβῃ τέλος.
[4] *vv.* 535-537.   [5] *Ion* 541, τερφθεὶς τοῦτο κεῖν' οὐκ ἠρόμην.
[6] See *Euripides the Rationalist*, and my edition of the play.

arrest of the enquiry at a suitable point, was useful to oracles, especially so in stories and plays; and we may assume that the audience of *Helen* were not unfamiliar with the phenomenon. The supernatural powers of Theonoe receive one other illustration, perhaps still more impressive. When the mutual recognition of the spouses, with various loud and long developments, has taken place in front of the house, and when Menelaus has received a sketch of the family and its infallible mistress,—the door is at last opened[1]. 'Ah!,' shrieks Helen, 'all is lost: Theonoe comes....Fly, Menelaus, fly—but what avail? Present or not present, *she knows that you have arrived.*' After all that has passed, if we may so say, on the door-steps, this proof of supersensuous perception must convince the most sceptical! But the truth is, that, on the Attic stage, the fore-court of a house does sometimes seem almost sacred from human observation. In the *Electra* of Sophocles[2], the raptures of the recognition between Orestes and Electra, passing as it does in full view of Clytaemnestra's palace, are silenced, by 'sounds from the doorway,' certainly not too soon for probability. Between this moderate and effective employment of the theatrical *data*, and the gross abuse of them in *Helen*, lay doubtless, in the dramatic repertory, a many-shaded scale of non-observation, quite sufficient to test and illustrate the superhuman acuteness of Theonoe. Theoclymenus, when undeceived at the last, sums up on this point very justly[3]: 'She saw Menelaus in the house, and she never told me! Never again shall she impose on a man with her divination.'

With the entrance of Theonoe (*v.* 865), we strike into a scene different from all that precede and follow it in this respect, that the main sentiment of it is serious, but extra-dramatic, pertinent not only, or principally, to the persons of the drama, but to the real history and real feelings of the mistress of the house, who is represented (or represents herself) upon the stage. The respect of *Proteus'* daughter for the memory of *Proteus*, the fidelity of *Proteus* to his

---

[1] *v.* 857.   [2] *vv.* 1322 foll.

[3] *v.* 1625   ...ἥτις ἐν δόμοις ὁρῶσα Μενέλεων οὐκ εἶπέ μοι.
τοιγὰρ οὔποτ' ἄλλον ἄνδρα ψεύσεται μαντεύμασιν.

engagements, and the duty and desire of *Theonoe* to perform those engagements no less strictly than her revered predecessor would have done—this is the motive to which Helen and Menelaus appeal, and which Theonoe promptly obeys. The key-notes of the scene, the most significant passages, are precisely those which, as we noticed before, have been excised by critics, endeavouring to bring the text into conformity with the dramatic hypothesis, because both in substance and in solemnity of tone they manifestly exceed the situation—the digression of Helen in praise of commercial probity[1], and the digression of Theonoe on the consciousness of the dead, as importing the permanence of their obligations[2]. These, and the whole scene so far as it is serious, were composed not for the imaginary daughter of sea-gods, but for the real heiress of Proteas, the faithful representative of a name honoured in business. A ray of genuine feeling, not tragic but grave, is shot here and there across the humorous phantasmagoria of the story.

Apart from this, the scene sustains the dominant key of graceful, quasi-tragic, pretence. The triumph of Theonoe in the vindication of her supernatural powers[3] is the purest irony. She knows what has been shouted in her hearing, that and no more. Menelaus, she says, is so unhappy as not to know even now whether he will get safe home. Nor, we are sure, does she, except so far as the immediate future, the next step, depends obviously upon her permission. This it does, without reference to the question whether or not, as she lightly asserts, the gods, such gods as Hera and Aphrodite, have brought their trivial rivalry to an issue which 'rests with her[4].'

In this matter of Menelaus' safe return, his impatience to foresee the event, and the tacit, but unwarranted, assumption that it is foreseen by the oracular virgin, we are again in the track of the *Iphigenia in Taurica*. Euripides is treating with a playful irony things which there are treated with irony fierce and frightful. There Orestes, who has staked his life upon the prescience of Delphi, and who has already proved (though

---

[1] *vv.* 903–908.   [2] *vv.* 1013–1016.
[3] *v.* 873.   [4] *vv.* 877 foll.

he dares not admit it) that the oracle, which sent him to his
doom, was either ignorant or treacherously reticent, strives
with hollow fallacy to convince himself of what has become
his last hope, that it was his 'return' to Hellas, *and only that*,
which was not expressly revealed to him, though the god (of
course) foresaw and implicitly promised it[1]. But the virgin of
Delphi, alas, foresaw nothing but what any one might have
foreseen, that she was sending her consultant to death. The
virgin of Pharos is differently minded, and her limitations are
matter only for smiles; but her scope of vision is exactly
that of Apollo, neither more nor less.

When we come to the pleadings of Helen and Menelaus,
a certain distinction is, I think, to be observed in the tone of
the rhetoric. Unreal indeed the whole affair is in this way,
that the result is a foregone conclusion. Theonoe, by what
we have heard already, is committed to the support of Helen.
Her pretence of an opposite intention[2] gives a cue for entreaty,
but cannot beguile the spectator into anxiety. Nor has the
plea of Helen the note of genuine passion. When she
diverges into the topic of probity in the acquisition of wealth,
we feel indeed that she is going out of her dramatic brief;
but we do *not* feel, as we should if the like occurred in the
great speeches of Medea, Phaedra, Creusa, or Iphigenia, that
the digression is a bathos; on the contrary it rises, and the
sudden sublimity of it[3] is the most impressive thing in the
declamation. The rest is just an imitation of tragedy, but, so
far as I see, it is a graceful imitation. Nothing in it is
apparently meant to be ridiculous, nor should we expect this.
The situation of Helen, as supposed in this play, has an
absurd side, when we think of her Menelaus, but has also
a serious side. Her sense of unmerited obloquy, as such,
is not ridiculous, nor even, as such, her conjugal affection;

---

[1] *Iph. T.* 1015   ἅπαντα γὰρ

ξυνθεὶς τάδ' εἰς ἓν νόστον ἐλπίζω λαθεῖν.

See *Euripides the Rationalist*, p. 180, note. The parallel with *Hel.* 877, οὐδ'
οἶσθα νόστον οἴκαδ' εἶτ' αὐτοῦ μενεῖς, is in favour of the variant λαθεῖν in *Iph. T.*
l. c., though if λαβεῖν be read, the purport of that passage, and the relation of the
other to it, is still substantially the same.

[2] *v.* 892. See Paley's note.   [3] *vv.* 906–908.

and these topics, especially the first and the better, are here handled with a pleasing but not agitating tenderness:

> For there is none but hateth Helen now,
> Through Hellas called forsaker of my lord
> To dwell in gold-abounding Phrygian halls.
> But if to Greece I come, in Sparta stand,
> Then hearing, seeing, that by heaven's device
> They died, nor was I traitress to my friends,
> They shall restore me unto virtue's ranks ;
> I shall betroth the child none now will wed ;
> And, leaving this my bitter homelessness,
> Shall I *enjoy the treasures in my home*[1].

Euripides is more musical than this, but such is the substance ; and manifestly it is not the genuine language of a human creature ground between the millstones of a malicious Fate. Indeed one must not affirm without reserve that it is not ridiculous ; the end of our quotation is bathos, and can hardly be meant for anything else. This much we may say : Helen is gravity itself, if we compare her with Menelaus.

He rises to the occasion like a man and a soldier, and delivers an exquisite tirade. To make the effect quite sure, Theonoe (or the Chorus[2]) is made to express curiosity as to how he will come off; and he himself at the conclusion appeals for applause, explaining the rhetorical principles of his success :

> *How's that ?* With tears, taking the womanish line,
> I had been piteous, *but not vigorous.*
> Slay, if thou wilt ; I shall not die disgraced.
> *But rather let my speech persuade ; for so*
> *Shalt thou be just and I shall get my wife*[3].

---

[1] *vv.* 926 foll. (Way).

[2] *vv.* 944–946 are given to the Chorus by the tradition, but Menelaus' opening sounds like a reply to Theonoe herself. See note in the Appendix.

[3] *vv.* 991 foll. (A. W. V.)

τί ταῦτα; δακρύοις ἐς τὸ θῆλυ τρεπόμενος
ἐλεινὸς ἦν ἂν μᾶλλον ἢ δραστήριος.
κτεῖν', εἰ δοκεῖ σοι· δυσκλεῶς γὰρ οὐ κτενεῖς·
μᾶλλόν γε μέντοι τοῖς ἐμοῖς πείθου λόγοις,
ἵν' ἧς δικαία καὶ δάμαρτ' ἐγὼ λάβω.

For τί ταῦτα; *What of that? What do you think of that?* cf. *v.* 873 τί τἀμά, πῶς ἔχει, θεσπίσματα; The rendering *Why (say) this?* is admissible in itself, but does not fit the context.

And the Chorus crown the effect by the appropriate remark

> Thou, lady, art *the umpire of the pleas*,
> And may thy sentence satisfy us all.

With such preface and comment, the most genuine eloquence would not move us. As for that of Menelaus, it is an admirable specimen of the oratory which is not tragic, but has in all ages been proffered and taken for tragic by imperfect taste; in short, it is a rant. This is the way in which the orator raises, as he conceives, the dignity of his appeal to the dead, that is, to the promise of the deceased Proteus:

> O Hades, on thy championship I call,
> Who hast welcomed many dead, for Helen's sake
> Slain by my sword: *thou hast them for thine hire.*
> Or give them back with life's breath filled again,
> Or thou constrain this maid to show her worthy
> Of a good sire, and render back my wife[1].

Here is a grand bold handling of big ideas! Here is something to humble Aeschylus' Clytaemnestra and her cry to the fiends of Hell,

> Full many a sup, mine offering, have ye lapped[2].

Death retained with a fee of corpses to plead the soldier's cause! Dryden, in his dramatic style, would have pounced upon the conception with delight. No Elizabethan, not the greatest, could have been trusted to reject it. There are like things in Hugo. And doubtless there were many like things in Carcinus and in the innumerable young tragedians of whom we hear from Aristophanes[3]; possibly some things not unlike in works of the Three, to which time and chance has been kind. But in Euripides, as we know him, this is the style of a man who is going mad[4]. The big idea, the big words, have no relation to the facts of the case and the natural feelings of the persons concerned; and this might pass for a definition of *rant*. Even better, that is to say, more delicately and exquisitely bad, is the exordium,

---

[1] *vv.* 969 foll. (Way).
[2] *Eum.* 106.
[3] *Frogs* 90.
[4] *Heracles* 565-573.

where the military orator is so anxious to be at once affecting and manly, and considers so carefully the tone and limits of such a part, that one wonders whether he will ever begin. Translation is hopeless; here is the thing itself:

ἐγὼ σὸν οὔτ' ἂν προσπεσεῖν τλαίην γόνυ
οὔτ' ἂν δακρῦσαι βλέφαρα· τὴν Τροίαν γὰρ ἂν
δειλοὶ γενόμενοι πλεῖστον αἰσχύνοιμεν ἄν.—
καίτοι λέγουσιν ὡς πρὸς ἀνδρὸς εὐγενοῦς
ἐν ξυμφοραῖσι δάκρυ' ἀπ' ὀφθαλμῶν βαλεῖν.
ἀλλ' οὐχὶ τοῦτο τὸ καλόν—εἰ καλὸν τόδε—
αἱρήσομαι 'γὼ πρόσθε τῆς εὐψυχίας.
ἀλλ' εἰ μὲν ἄνδρα σοι δοκεῖ σῶσαι ξένον,
ζητοῦντά γ' ὀρθῶς ἀπολαβεῖν δάμαρτ' ἐμήν,
ἀπόδος τε καὶ πρὸς σῶσον. εἰ δὲ μὴ δοκεῖ—
ἐγὼ μὲν οὐ νῦν πρῶτον ἀλλὰ πολλάκις[1]
ἄθλιος ἂν εἴην, σὺ δὲ γυνὴ κακὴ φανεῖ.

Then comes another illustration of how not to do it. From Theonoe he turns to her father in his grave, but not without first telling her that 'now comes what will touch her most.' So begins the invocation; how it ends we have already seen. Next he informs the lady of 'that which Helen has omitted to mention,' the course which he will take, if she and her brother persist in robbing him. First he will fight Theoclymenus; 'and either he or I must die, that is quite plain.' Like Antony in Shakespeare, challenging high-battled Caesar, he forgets that it takes two to make a fight; only, unlike Antony, he does *not* forget it, but explains what will happen 'if he refuse to meet me, foot to foot,' painting the consequence, the determined slaughter of his wife and himself, in what we may best describe as cold gore:

κἄπειτ' ἐμὸν
πρὸς ἧπαρ ὦσαι δίστομον ξίφος τόδε
τύμβου 'πὶ νώτοις τοῦδ', ἵν' αἵματος ῥοαὶ

[1] v. 957, omitted by Nauck and others as a tag from *Medea* 446. It is a tag, and a bad one; but Menelaus is afraid that he is getting too humble. *V.* 960 (*Med.* 1360) is another tag. Probably the speech would be found to be pretty well made of them, if we had a proper view of the materials.

τάφου καταστάζωσι· κεισόμεσθα δὲ
νεκρὼ δύ᾽ ἐξῆς τῷδ᾽ ἐπὶ ξεστῷ τάφῳ,
ἀθάνατον ἄλγος σοί, ψόγος δὲ σῷ πατρί—

where perhaps ἐξῆς, *side by side, in a row*, is the word that
moves us most. But as for 'Theonoe,' what one chiefly
divines is, that the setting of the *Iphigenia in Taurica*, with
its 'blood-stained mouldings' and 'frieze of skulls[1],' had
made her, as it might, a little sick. To the sublimities of
Menelaus, who is not in the least danger, she might listen
quite comfortably :

οὐ γὰρ γαμεῖ τήνδ᾽ οὔτε σύγγονος σέθεν
οὔτ᾽ ἄλλος οὐδείς· ἀλλ᾽ ἐγώ σφ᾽ ἀπάξομαι,
εἰ μὴ πρὸς οἴκους δυνάμεθ᾽, ἀλλὰ πρὸς νεκρούς.—
τί ταῦτα;

> I, I will carry her away,
> If to my home I cannot, then to the dead !—
> *How's that?...*

The brief and obvious decision pronounced by the lady
is noticeable only for the skilful introduction of the extra-
dramatic touches[2], especially the grave and tender lines
before quoted, which, by reproving gently the soulless
philosophy of Menelaus, and reminding us that not all of
the dead, nor his true self, is in his grave, guard the
scene from the possibility of appearing to treat lightly the
relation between Proteas and Eido :

ἃ δ᾽ ἀμφὶ τύμβῳ τῷδ᾽ ὀνειδίζεις πατρί,
ἡμῖν ὅδ᾽ αὐτὸς μῦθος. ἀδικοίην νιν ἄν
εἰ μὴ ἀποδώσω· καὶ γὰρ ἂν κεῖνος βλέπων
ἀπέδωκεν ἄν σοι τήνδ᾽ ἔχειν, ταύτῃ δὲ σέ.
καὶ γὰρ τίσις τῶνδ᾽ ἔστι τοῖς τε νερτέροις
καὶ τοῖς ἄνωθεν πᾶσιν ἀνθρώποις· ὁ νοῦς
τῶν κατθανόντων ζῇ μὲν οὔ, γνώμην δ᾽ ἔχει
ἀθάνατον, εἰς ἀθάνατον αἰθέρ᾽ ἐμπεσών.

This scene, which concludes, after the departure of Theonoe,
with the arrangement of the escape, is separated from the

---

[1] *Iph. T.* 69–75.   [2] *vv.* 1008, 1013–1016.

next by the 'nightingale' ode[1], which may be so entitled from the invocation of the musical bird with which it begins. The three odes of the *Helen* present the same parallel to the *Iphigenia in Taurica*, which governs all the latter and larger part of the play. For the 'nightingale' ode we have there the 'halcyon' ode[2], of which the opening uses similarly the melancholy cry of the sea-bird. Another pair take their subjects from two voyages, one[3] following the ship of Orestes from Greece to Taurica, the other that of Menelaus from Egypt to Greece[4]. The third and most remarkable pair are the Pythian ode in the earlier play[5], and the Thesmophorian ode[6] in the later. In the arrangement of the three respectively there is this difference, that the voyage-ode of the *Iphigenia* refers to the past, and therefore comes first, that of the *Helen* refers to the future and comes last. Otherwise the relation of the parallel odes to the plot will be found in all respects similar. So also the other lyrical portions of the plays pair off, the lamentations of Helen (and Chorus) with those of Iphigenia (and Chorus)[7], and the recognition of Menelaus with the recognition of Orestes[8]. This parallelism grows naturally out of the relation between the works, but has some interest for its bearing on a comparison between the Pythian ode and the Thesmophorian. There are striking resemblances. Both are purely narrative poems, lyric legends complete in themselves and not necessarily dependent upon the scenes among which they are placed. Even in point of actual disconnexion from the drama, the Pythian ode (of which I have given a full study elsewhere[9]) has some analogy, though but little, to the Thesmophorian. This may suggest the question, whether there was in the circumstances of the *Iphigenia* anything to account for a digression into the legend of Delphi. It may be so ; but at present I find no sufficient reason for the supposition. The Pythian ode, though it can be detached from its play, is by no means irrelevant to it.

---

[1] *v.* 1107. [2] *Iph. T.* 1088. [3] *Iph. T.* 392.
[4] *Hel.* 1451. [5] *Iph. T.* 1234. [6] *Hel.* 1301.
[7] *Hel.* 164, *Iph. T.* 123. [8] *Hel.* 625, *Iph. T.* 827.
[9] *Euripides the Rationalist*, p. 217.

Demeter and Koré have no more to do with the *Helen*, in its dramatic aspect, than with *Julius Caesar*. But Apollo and Delphi are the theme of the *Iphigenia*; and though the Pythian ode is not exactly the sort of piece which in its place we should expect, yet, without extra-dramatic help, we may very well understand why it is what it is. Moreover (and this is important) the Pythian ode is not related, at least plainly, to any particular rite, festival, or season in the calendar. It celebrates (in a fashion) the praise of Apollo as possessor of the great oracle, but contains no apparent reference to any particular ceremony. The Thesmophorian ode celebrates not merely the goddesses but their worship, and concludes with a description of rites. Further (and this is almost decisive) *Iphigenia* is a work which could not, unless by way of deliberate insult, have been associated specially with a Pythian ceremony; the story, as shaped and coloured by Euripides, is disgraceful and derogatory to the oracle, more so than enough (one would think) for prudence, without any such exasperation as a Pythian festival would supply. Even the Pythian ode itself, with all its grace, is in substance satirical, and would have scandalized such a person as Aeschylus. But the *Helen*, as a story, is in no way anti-thesmophorian; it is simply non-thesmophorian; and the work is too light and humorous to have, as a whole, any truly religious bearing whatever. The Thesmophorian ode is exactly suitable to such an occasion. There is no real religion in it, no gravity or passion; it is a poet's compliment to the poetry and popular features of the legend and the celebration, that and nothing more. But as such a compliment it is perfect and without drawback, more beautiful even than the Pythian ode, and free from the suspicion of a sneer. All these considerations would yield at once to positive evidence, internal or external, that the occasion of the *Iphigenia* was Pythian. Hitherto I have found no evidence; and I do not consider that the relation of the Pythian ode to the play offers even a *prima facie* ground for suspecting that such was the case.

The resemblance of the two poems is to be viewed rather in this way. The choric ode or *stasimon* has always a non-dramatic as well as a dramatic side, either of which may be the more prominent according to the requirements of the case. Thus in the *Choephori* the second *stasimon*[1] is almost an integral part of the scenes with which it is connected, while the first[2] is almost pure interlude, and the third[3] combines both characters. In composing the *Iphigenia*, the poet was led, perhaps by nothing more than the desire to place effectively a brilliant poem, to introduce one interlude a little more independent than dramatic considerations might have suggested. In the general imitation of *Iphigenia* which rules the composition of *Helen*, this precedent proved highly convenient, because the latter occasion required the use of an interlude independent altogether. The two external data, the island Helené and the Festival of the Two Goddesses, have no connexion, except the artificial one created by the poet's apology to the female sex, which itself extends only to the celebrants of the festival, and not to the divinities. Thus, since the island gets the honour of the story, the most and least that could be done for the Mother and Maid was to give them an ode to themselves,—which however, since the given ode is perhaps not inferior to any poem of the kind which the world possesses, may be accepted as sufficient, even now, when the Corn-Maiden has so many and such devoted adherents. In performance, care would of course be taken to mark off this interlude by suitable interruption ; which, since the ode distracts us from nothing more serious than the business of fooling the fool Theoclymenus, the situation will very well bear.

In general, the musical parts of *Helen* have the usual tone of choric poetry, but naturally without much elevation. Next to the Thesmophorian ode, but far below, may be ranked the voyage of Helen[4], where again the comparison with the parallel ode is significant, for that haunting poem includes a curse upon the genuine Helen of legend[5], of which the remembrance adds piquancy to the paradoxical epithalamium of its counterpart. Between the 'halcyon' ode and the

---

[1] *Cho.* 783 (Dindorf). [2] *Cho.* 585. [3] *Cho.* 935.
[4] *Hel.* 1451. [5] *Iph. T.* 439.

'nightingale' ode there is just the external resemblance of the openings, but no more. The piercing pathos of home-sickness in the 'halcyon' ode belongs naturally to the Chorus of the *Iphigenia*, Greek captives who really feel their exile, and whose fate is not the least tragic part of that terrible drama. The Chorus of *Helen*, though formally similar in position, are of course not allowed to feel anything in particular; and the 'nightingale' ode, a slight tissue of myths and moralities, may be regarded as little more than a vehicle for the music. One point in it may be noticed as a proof of finish in workmanship. The singers relate, briefly but with the assumption of full knowledge, the wrecking of the Greek fleet on the way from Troy, by a false beacon malignantly lighted on the rocks of the Capherides[1]. Now not only is it impossible, according to the presuppositions of the play, that they should know any incident of the Greeks' return, but we have actually been reminded that they do *not* know this particular incident; for it is mentioned, but not related, by Menelaus[2], when he declines generally, and doubtless with discretion, to relate to his wife his adventures during the period when her place was supplied. 'Your answer,' says Helen herself with opportune recollection, 'is better than my question.' So it is; but the effect is that neither she nor her companions get information about 'the beacons of Euboea.' In some writers this contradiction might pass for an oversight, though the accident in that case would be odd. But Euri-pides was, as the nature of his work required, punctilious about such things[3]. If he had wanted his ode to agree with the play, it would not have conspicuously disagreed. As a fact, he wishes to detach it, and to show that the Chorus here are mere singers, performers of an interlude, whose dramatic personality, so far as they have any, is irrelevant. The de-tachment is preparatory to their complete and necessary independence in the next ode, the Thesmophorian. It is however probable that the obvious device of an independent *stasimon* had been used before, when the private recitation

---

[1] *Hel.* 1126–1131.   [2] *Hel.* 767.
[3] See especially the *Heracles*, discussed hereafter.

of plays was connected with some special occasion or circumstances ; and we shall presently notice a trace of this, which survives in the public version of the *Medea*.

With the departure of Theonoe, and the commencement of the plot for escape, the story loses all trace of gravity, and proceeds with accumulating extravagance through the 'deception' of Theoclymenus to the foreseen end. The discussion of plans between Menelaus and Helen[1] is closely similar to that between Orestes and Iphigenia[2], with this difference, that the one situation is desperate, the other dangerous only in pretence. The very form betrays the opposition, the sharp alternation of verse and verse being exchanged for leisurely couplets. The wild and savage proposals of Orestes, offspring of his crazy mind and tortured nerves, make one shiver, but have, as we saw[3], quite another effect when propounded with calm stupidity by Menelaus. We have noticed too before[4], though it deserves to be noticed again, the sheer farce of his contemptuous comment on the originality of Helen's device, that he should pretend to be the reporter of his own death. ' But will *that* bring us off ? ' says he. ' The story, as such, is somewhat stale[5].' It was indeed, having been classical in tragedy at least since the *Choephori*, near fifty years, and we know not how long before, and having been repeated doubtless dozens of times with less excuse and skill than in the *Electra* of Sophocles. In the Tauric drama this *cliché* is carefully avoided. Iphigenia has, or supposes herself to have, reasons for believing Orestes dead, until she learns from himself that he is alive; and it is this true intelligence which, with some false addition, she communicates in the deception to King Thoas[6]. But in *Helen*, what we want and get is the most threadbare imposture which the repertory supplied, resuscitated in circumstances which make it positively ridiculous. All Helen's inventions, with their assumption of limitless credulity in the deceived, have the same transparent candour, and are accepted by

[1] *vv.* 1032 foll.   [2] *Iph. T.* 1017 foll.
[3] p. 89.   [4] p. 60.
[5] *v.* 1055.   [6] *Iph. T.* 1183 foll.

Menelaus with the same sneering acquiescence[1]. She has her revenge, however, when Menelaus carries his affectation of dulness so far as to ask, *who* is to be the pretended reporter of his death. ' *You!*' she replies[2], with pardonable sharpness, for this point, though not explicitly mentioned at the outset, is plainly implied, and Menelaus has shown already that he thinks it only too obvious[3]. ' *You!*—And you must say, that you were the only one of Menelaus' shipmates to escape, and that you saw him die.' Though it is nevertheless assumed[4] that the plot is to include somehow the whole of his crew, and indeed it must do so in order to succeed. But through this and through everything the gods of the topsy-turvy pantheon are justly relied upon to pull the machine.

But the best point in the dialogue, the best which with existing lights is appreciable, is the confidence of Menelaus in *the wind*. Helen is naturally anxious about this: 'If only we have a speeding wind to our sail, and the ship may run!' '*It will;*' says he, 'for the Powers will end my troubles[5]'; and doubtless he speaks with knowledge. The geography of Greece and the framework of Greek legend were such, that 'the speeding wind,' which announces that the *Hecuba* has reached its close[6], must often have favoured at the destined hour the personages of tragedy, who, however their adventures might be varied by the composer of the moment, had generally an inexorable appointment with Fate for the ultimate accomplishment of their traditional escapes, home-comings, and so forth. We hardly dare conjecture how often this dramatic gale must have blown to order, before, in the Tauric enterprise of Orestes—it failed. There, at the very moment when according to religious expectation the Powers

---

[1] *e.g. v.* 1067 τοῦτ' αὖ κατορθοῖς.

[2] *v.* 1077   σοῦ· καὶ μόνος γε φάσκε διαφυγεῖν μόρον
                  Ἀτρέως πλέων ξὺν παιδί, καὶ θανόνθ' ὁρᾶν.

[3] *v.* 1051 (λέγων), *v.* 1056.   [4] *v.* 1069.

[5] *v.* 1074   ΕΛ.   πόμπιμοι μόνον
            λαίφει πνοαὶ γένοιντο καὶ νεὼς δρόμος.
      ΜΕ.   ἔσται· πόνους γὰρ δαίμονες παύσουσί μου.

[6] *Hec.* 1289; see also Soph. *Phil.* 1465 foll.

should declare for the devotee of Apollo in the natural way, they declare against him, and blow him fiercely back to death. It is the last stroke of the irony which in that tragedy pursues the victims throughout[1]. But in general the Aeolus of the theatre was doubtless more obedient; and Menelaus has reason to suppose that, however strong may be the external resemblance of the *Helen* to the *Iphigenia*, he need not fear disappointment in this respect. It is the just expectation of a hero whose traditional time of wandering is up. The breeze will come, says he; and so it does, punctually[2].

Of Theoclymenus, the pseudo-tyrant, perhaps enough was said before. The whole conception of his part, a personage supposed to be formidable in character and authority, but in fact perpetually deluded and disobeyed, is a caricature of dramatic inconsequence. He scarcely ever speaks or is spoken to without exposing, sometimes crudely and sometimes delicately, the futility of his function. As a tragic figure, he disposes of himself at his very entrance. He comes in, like Hippolytus[3], from the chase, with huntsmen, dogs, and nets, but not like Hippolytus with grateful salutations and offerings to Artemis the patroness of the field. On the contrary he is out of humour with his men, and in dismissing them blames himself for excessive clemency in the article of punishment[4], —in short, we divine, without being told, that he has had no sport. His salutation is offered, as in all his comings and goings (so he tells us)[5], to the tomb of his sainted father, a custom creditable doubtless to both parties, but in this particular connexion not a little incongruous. And anything less like a tyrant in love one cannot imagine. Helen is not in his thoughts; and the manner in which he recalls her is laughable. His guards are no better than his huntsmen: some Hellene or other, he says, has come openly into the country...to spy of course, or perhaps intending to steal....

---

[1] *Iph. T.* 1394; see *Euripides the Rationalist*, p. 196.

[2] *v.* 1612 οἱ δ' ἰστί᾽ ᾖρον, οὔριαι δ' ἦκον πνοαί, where ἦκον almost suggests the keeping of an appointment.

[3] *Hipp.* 58.   [4] *vv.* 1169–1172.   [5] *vv.* 1165–1168.

'*Helen!*' he exclaims, with sudden recollection[1], 'He shall die!...that is, if he can but be caught.' He looks into the sanctuary, which is apparently now closed, but proves to be empty! So the grooms are called out again for pursuit, and there are a few minutes of confusion[2], terminated by Helen herself, walking quietly out of the house, but elaborately got up, according to her agreement with Menelaus[3], as a mourner for Menelaus deceased. The whole business is undignified and comical.

A propos of the comparison between the entrance of Theoclymenus and that of Hippolytus, we should note that it is actually indicated by a simple but significant feature in the scene. As in the *Hippolytus*, so here, the two goddesses, upon whose contention the plot turns or is supposed to turn, are represented by images. There the opposition is between Aphrodite and Artemis, here between Aphrodite and Hera, the first opposing and the latter promoting the return of Helen to Hellas. That Aphrodite and Hera are actually represented, appears from the direction of Theonoe that the escape shall commence with prayers addressed to them, and the contrasted prayers which Helen addresses accordingly; in the words which precede her prayers she speaks of the two opposed inclinations as visible[4]. Theonoe is made to disparage Aphrodite, in comparison with Hera, in words[5] of which the respectful irony strongly recalls that of Hippolytus

---

[1] *v.* 1173   καὶ νῦν πέπυσμαι φανερὸν Ἑλλήνων τινὰ
ἐς γῆν ἀφῖχθαι καὶ λεληθέναι σκοπούς,...
ἤτοι κατόπτην...ἢ κλοπαῖς θηρώμενον...
Ἑλένην. θανεῖται δ', ἤν γε δὴ ληφθῇ μόνον.—
ἔα·
ἀλλ' ὡς ἔοικε, πάντα διαπεπραγμένα
εὕρηκα. τύμβου γὰρ κενὰς λιποῦσ' ἕδρας κ.τ.λ.

[2] *vv.* 1180–1183.   [3] *v.* 1087.

[4] *vv.* 878 foll., 1024 foll., 1090–1106. The last passage, I think, makes the point clear. Note τῶν in *v.* 1024, and βλέπω in *v.* 1090.

[5] *Hel.* 1006   ἡ Κύπρις δέ μοι
ἵλεως μὲν εἴη, συμβέβηκε δ' οὐδαμοῦ.

Compare the whole scene in *Hippolytus vv.* 58–120, especially *v.* 113 τὴν σὴν δὲ Κύπριν πόλλ' ἐγὼ χαίρειν λέγω, noting that ἵλεως εἴη is, for a god, equivalent to λέγω χαίρειν.

in comparing her with Artemis under similar circumstances. The absence of Artemis therefore could not fail to strike spectators familiar with the *Hippolytus*, and lends point to the return of the unsuccessful sportsman. The two visible goddesses, Aphrodite and Hera, are of course the chosen patrons not of Theonoe but of Theoclymenus, the nominal master of the house, who as a lover hopes for their support in his wooing of Helen.

All this leads up excellently to the deception, with its trailing facilities and transparent conundrums. Nothing in the friendly satire, directed in this play upon the weaknesses of Athenian tragedy, is better deserved. All Athenian compositions are penetrated by the Greek and specially Athenian taste for dexterous verbal ambiguity. In tragedy the habit of irony, of making points imperceptible (*ex hypothesi*) to the auditors on the stage but intelligible to the audience, was fortified by the almost superhuman faculty of Aeschylus, not only for managing ambiguous language, but for maintaining that impression of solemnity, which prevents the spectator from consulting his experience, and raising the question, whether the dialogue would actually work as supposed. Both his great successors, and doubtless others, profited by the lesson in their own ways[1]. But such irony is a perilous trick; and all the Three, in my opinion and, I suppose, that of most readers, sometimes run it fine. For instance, when Amphitryon is directing the tyrant Lycus into the house where Heracles, whom Lycus believes to be dead, is waiting to slay him, the deceiver is made twice to insist ironically on the certainty that Heracles cannot have come to life again[2]. The audience are supposed to enjoy their superiority of knowledge, and perhaps they might; but is it certain that none of them would ask himself, why a deceiver should sound this warning, and what would be its natural effect upon the deceived? What the thing came to in the hands of bunglers we see in the deception of Theoclymenus. The situation

---

[1] See *e.g.* the ambiguity of ψυχῆς ('*their* life,' '*my* life') in *Med.* 968; but the subject is too familiar for illustration.

[2] *H. F.* 717–719.

is such that any ambiguity whatever in the behaviour of
Helen must betray the secret of her unnatural and fantastic
proposals.   To preserve appearances absolutely would be her
only chance, if chance there were.   And yet at every turn she
must be letting us *see* that Theoclymenus does *not* see that
she says that Menelaus 'has not perished,' 'has not been
buried,' 'is here present,' 'is to go where she would have him,'
'has the garb of her husband,' 'was the only *Achaean* among
the Greeks of her husband's ship[1]'!   And when she has
invited Theoclymenus to 'make her his wife now and here,'
and when he, by an embrace, has in a manner done so, we
can work off a fresh set of ironies[2] about 'burying her husband,'
without the least apprehension of his doubting, any more than
we do, whether we mean the old husband or the new!   The
high-water mark of this foolery is her mysterious declaration
about the 'dead' Menelaus :

$$\phi\acute{\iota}\lambda o\varsigma\ \gamma\acute{a}\rho\ \acute{\epsilon}\sigma\tau\iota\nu,\ \ddot{o}\varsigma\ \pi o\tau'\ \acute{\epsilon}\sigma\tau\acute{\iota}\nu,\ \acute{\epsilon}\nu\theta\acute{a}\delta'\ \ddot{\omega}\nu^3.$$

To the audience this means what it says, that she loves him,
whoever he is, for being here.   But what should it mean
to Theoclymenus?   One can strain out some other sense or
senses which a resolute commentator can put on it.   She gives
it as a reply to the suggestion, that the loss of funeral rites to
her husband is no great matter for lamentation ; and it is
apparently to be accepted by Theoclymenus in the sense that
the dead ' be he what he may, is dear to her *so long as he is in
this world.*'   Well, since the Greeks did use *here* and *there* for
this world and *the other* respectively, the interpretation is
possible.   But what can be more absurd, as a device for
avoiding suspicion, than such a riddle?   Theoclymenus gives
it up, asking in bewilderment whether 'all is straight about
this mourning '; and though, being a fool, he is promptly

[1] *v.* 1207 Ἕλλην, Ἀχαιῶν εἰς ἐμῷ ξύμπλους πόσει.   'Achaeans' here, if distinguished from 'Hellenes' as the emphasis suggests, denotes the ruling race, the
kingly families, and the verse may signify, with the usual cumbrous simplicity,
that the man present is Menelaus himself.   But it need not.
[2] *vv.* 1231–1232, 1237, 1239, 1276–1278, 1285–1289, 1399–1409.
[3] *v.* 1225.

reassured, that does not justify the puzzle, which only serves to illustrate the clumsiness into which a composer may be led by an intemperate taste for duplicity. We may suspect that it is borrowed or adapted from some notorious failures in this style. The double meaning of the phrase 'dead husband,' signifying Menelaus or Theoclymenus according to speaker and context, after being worried to rags by Helen and the two men, is perhaps used to supply evasions for Theonoe[1]. The ambiguities in this scene are so many, and some of them so extravagant, that it is difficult, especially for a foreign interpreter, to be certain, who is supposed to understand what. And indeed it is probably the intention that the audience shall be sometimes merely bewildered. The deception concludes with some more verbal sparring between Helen and Theoclymenus, each contending which can most plainly say the thing which is not to be understood. The lady gives us again her puzzle about *here* and *there*[2], in a form more puzzling than ever ; and finally the lover, not to be beaten, fires off three continuous verses of enigma[3], signifying, though of course the speaker is supposed to be not aware of it, that Menelaus is to take back his wife, convey her home, and live with her happily there henceforward. One can imagine the rounds of applause which saluted his exit after this natural and convincing performance.

The last scene introduces the Egyptian sailor with his

---

[1] *v.* 1371
πόσιν παρόντα τὸν ἐμὸν ἱστορουμένη
οὐκ εἶπ᾽ ἀδελφῷ, κατθανόντα δ᾽ ἐν χθονὶ
οὔ φησιν αὐγὰς εἰσορᾶν ἐμὴν χάριν,
where note the emphasis on πόσιν. The corrupt verse which follows, κάλλιστα δῆτ᾽ ἀνήρπασεν ἐν τύχῃ πόσις, referred, I think, originally to the felicity with which Theonoe apprehended the precious ambiguity of πόσις ; but there is some confusion in the text here. See note in the Appendix.

[2] *v.* 1421   ΘΕ. τὰ τῶν θανόντων οὐδέν, ἀλλ᾽ ἄλλως πόνος.
ΕΛ. ἔστιν τι κἀκεῖ κἀνθάδ᾽ ὧν ἐγὼ λέγω.

[3] Or perhaps five, *vv.* 1436–1440. Note the use of the metaphorical term *sea-embrace* (πελαγίους ἀγκάλας) for *waves* (cf. *v.* 1062). Here it may be construed with ἐλθών, and mean, to the audience, the embracing of Helen on the sea. The word οἴκους is ambiguous throughout, signifying either the home of Menelaus or that of the speaker, at pleasure.

sensational report. Here the text has sustained some injury,
the nature of which is worth consideration. The scene opens
abruptly with a couplet,

> ἄναξ, τὰ κάκιστ᾽ ἐν δόμοις εὑρήκαμεν.
> ὡς καίν᾽ ἀκούσῃ πήματ᾽ ἐξ ἐμοῦ τάχα¹,

of which the first verse is a false and very late insertion². The
supposition³ that it fills the place of a genuine passage omitted
by accident does not seem probable. How should such an
accident hit exactly the beginning of a scene, leaving intact
to the last verse the ode which precedes? What is wanting
is not verses but stage-directions. The arrival of the sailor,
the emotion of the Chorus, the entrance and amazement of
the king, are all exhibited only by action or inarticulate
exclamations, from which fact we should infer that there
is something very startling about the man's appearance. And
this is likely. According to his story, he has barely escaped
first from the sword and then from the sea, and must be
in a most woeful plight. Now we have already remarked
that his story, so much of it as is horrible, would be incongruous and offensive, unless the audience were sufficiently
assured that it is not seriously meant⁴. Nothing could serve
this purpose better than a touch of caricature in the make-up,
a thing the more easy because the Greek stage was not so
familiar as that of modern tragedy and melodrama with objects
visibly hideous. One such effect we have had already; for the
ghastly toilette of Helen the mourner, exhibited in the midst
of the king's hunt, could not fail to be grotesque⁵. Another,
I think, we have here. The sailor must be the grimmest
of figures, battered and bruised and livid. To make such
a figure pathetic would perhaps be not impossible, but easier,
and here more proper, to make it a little ridiculous. Let it
come on abruptly; let the women first and then the king
salute it in appropriate tones; let it address the prince in the
true style of a tragic apparition, after a solemn pause but

¹ *v.* 1512.
² The false quantity betrays a writer accustomed to scan by accent.
³ Dindorf.   ⁴ p. 84.   ⁵ *vv.* 1087, 1184–1190.

without any invocation, 'How strange a tale of woe thou art
to hear!'—and we shall have the best possible introduction
to the humours and horrors of the narrative. As usual,
comparison is challenged, and a standard for estimating the
effect is furnished, by the *Iphigenia*, where the corresponding
personage, the narrator of the parallel story, is marked with
ugly and formidable wounds, to which he calls attention[1],
a circumstance which, however proper to that play, must have
provoked criticism in Athenian audiences. Here also the
Helen appears to have pursued its purpose, to convert into
extravagance, by exaggeration, whatever in the technique of
drama current opinion had noted for dangerous. Of the
narrative we have already said enough[2]. Every part of it is
humorous and absurd, except the massacre, which by its
nature does not admit such treatment. This, being nevertheless indispensable, is summarily reduced to the proper level
of unreality by the preliminary allusion to 'Axia.'

As for the Divine Twins, who appear at the close, they
have this disadvantage, as compared with the human personages, that the gods of the Euripidean finale are, as a rule,
beyond the reach of parody. To be more futile and unreal
than the Athena of the *Iphigenia* would be impossible. But
there is humour in the Twins nevertheless. Very candid and
satisfactory is their confession, that their promotion by Zeus
to the rank of gods has not enabled them to interfere with
fate, or with the superior deities who 'were pleased that the
thing should be as it was[3].' Such was the simple philosophy
of the Greek pantheon. The peculiar occasion of *Helen* gives
to the epilogizing deities (who doubtless dispensed for the
nonce with a machine) the unusual opportunity of referring
to the external circumstances of the representation, as when
they explain the new name of the island Macris. The '*island
of the blest*'—singular not plural[4]—which is promised as
a habitation to the 'travelled' Menelaus, is Macris *alias*
Helené itself, to which 'Menelaus,' being one of the dependants
of 'Theonoe,' and having come, as Aristophanes says, out of

---

[1] *Iph. T.* 1366.
[2] pp. 54, 57, 84, 113.
[3] *vv.* 1658–1661.
[4] *v.* 1677 μακάρων νῆσον.

the herb-shop, had apparently then retired. He had probably travelled, especially to Egypt, in his commercial as well as in his heroic capacity. So also the libations and entertainment, which Helen, having finished her (dramatic) life, is to share with her divine brothers, are nothing else but the festivity which followed the performance and included the more dignified performers[1]. The less gifted members of the company and household would wait upon the feasters as usual:

τοὺς εὐγενεῖς γὰρ οὐ στυγοῦσι δαίμονες,
τῶν δ' ἀναριθμήτων μᾶλλόν εἰσιν οἱ πόνοι.

Great ones the gods mislike not ; toils belong,
As more appropriate, to the unreckoned throng.

But the best laugh is reserved for the end, when the Chorus, left alone upon the scene, deliver, with a new and witty application, the Euripidean play-end, or tag, πολλαὶ μορφαὶ τῶν δαιμονίων and so forth. 'Many a shape has fate, and many a surprise the gods decree ; expectation is not accomplished, and for the unexpected Heaven finds a way. And so has this action ended!' The full history of this formula, which occurs several times[2] in our collection, we cannot trace ; but it surely refers, with a certain shameless sarcasm, to the huddled expedients which in all ages have been permitted or practised in the theatrical wind-up, and specially to the peculiar treatment of a miraculous intervention, which was required by the position and purposes of Euripides[3]. In the *Medea* for instance, the tag anticipates the remark of Aristotle, that nothing in the plot of that play justifies or prepares us for the final rescue of the heroine by an aerial chariot ; it is a 'divine surprise.' But in *Helen*, by the peculiar character of the play, the poet is enabled to produce a new kind of surprise, and one particularly adverse to certain expectations which have been raised in the minds of the Chorus. The play compares at all points, as we have seen, with the *Iphigenia in Taurica*, which also has its surprise, but one different from that of the *Medea*. It consists[4], as in the

[1] *Zeus* (v. 1659 and v. 1669) is Euripides.
[2] *Alcestis, Medea, Andromache, Helen, Bacchae*, with slight variations.
[3] See *Euripides the Rationalist*, p. 77.   [4] *ib.* p. 168.

Orestes[1], in a reversal, by the intervening deity, of the proper and inevitable conclusion to which the story has actually been carried. Iphigenia and her companions are saved from destruction by a simple order, given by Athena, without pretence of reason, to the king of Taurica; and the deliverance is extended, by a freak, the extravagance of which is expressly emphasized, to the Greek slave-women who compose the Chorus[2]. They also are to be sent back to their country. No reader of the *Iphigenia* could forget either their heroism or their reward; for the one is the most beautiful thing in the story, the other the wittiest thing in the epilogue. Now the Chorus of the *Helen*, in sex, position, function, part, are precisely similar to that of the *Iphigenia*; and we have in the play an explicit promise that the parallel shall extend to their ultimate fate. Helen, like Iphigenia, requires their secrecy, and offers, in language almost identical, the prospect of their escape[3]. Nothing indeed can be less like than the effect of the two scenes and the two offers, the one desperate, the other impudent; but the formal resemblance is exact. We expect therefore, and the Chorus expect, betraying doubtless their expectation by joyful acquiescence, that their release and restoration to Hellas will be ordered in due course by the intervening deity. But Castor, alas, forgets this part of his duty. His speech, which the handmaidens follow, we must presume, from point to point with signs of eager anticipation, concludes without mention of them, does not demand their enfranchisement, does not even include them in the invitation to the banquet; and his final words (above cited[4]) seem to refer them to their ordinary tasks! There is yet one chance; for Theoclymenus has to speak, and will surely repair the omission. But from him also they get nothing, except their share, as women, in the happiness of contemplating a virtuous Helen! We can

---

[1] See essay on that play hereafter.

[2] *Iph. T.* 1467, *Euripides the Rationalist*, l.c.

[3] *Iph. T.* 1067 σωθεῖσα δ', ὡς ἂν καὶ σὺ κοινωνῇς τύχης,
σώσω σ' ἐς Ἑλλάδα.

Hel. 1388   ἦν δυνώμεθα
σωθέντες αὐτοὶ καὶ σὲ συσσῶσαί ποτε.

[4] *v.* 1679.

imagine therefore, when 'the great ones' have passed into the house, with what melancholy gestures, and amid what merriment, their inferiors prepare to follow, intoning in a minor key (or whatever was the Greek equivalent) the familiar words, 'Many a surprise the gods decree; expectation is not accomplished, and for the unexpected Heaven finds a way. And so has this action ended!'

On the whole, and much as we inevitably miss, we can perceive, in most of the play, a conformity to the humorous purpose of the Euripidean apology. The portions least apparently suitable are the musical, especially the *commos*, that is to say the lyrical part of the mutual lamentations between Helen and the handmaidens upon their first entrance[1]. At least I do not here find in the words generally anything inconsistent with gravity. But the spirit of the piece by no means requires that the sorrows of the heroine should be altogether ridiculous. Possibly there was a touch of parody in the music. And even the words present at all events one passage which is not offered for admiration. Here is a not unfair translation of it. Helen sings:

> Ah, maiden of Arcady, happy, Kallisto, art thou,
>   O fourfoot-pacing thing who wast Zeus's bride!
> Better by far than my mother's is thy lot now,
>   Who hast cast the burden of human sorrow aside,
>   And only now for the shaggy limb
>   Of the brute with tears are thy fierce eyes dim.
> Yea, happier she whom Artemis drave from her choir,
>   A stag gold-antlered, Merops' Titanian daughter,
> Because of her beauty,—but mine with the brands of desire
> Hath enkindled Dardanian Pergamus' ruin-pyre,
>   And hath given the Achaeans to slaughter[2].

This is Alexandrian poetry, not Attic, learned, frigid, and hollow at the heart. The priestess of Taurica in the parallel passages does not thus illustrate her miseries by miscellaneous mythology[3]. The appearance of such a passage, as a sequel to the absurd conversation with Teucer, and a preliminary to

---

[1] *vv.* 179–251 and 330–385.   [2] *vv.* 375–385 (Way).
[3] *Iph. T.* 143–235.

the preposterous consultation of Theonoe, signifies (and one is glad to know it) that Euripides was alive to the peculiar dangers besetting drama based upon minstrelsy. It was not for every one, as he saw, to follow Aeschylus with success in his

ἰὼ λιγείας μόρον ἀηδόνος·
περέβαλον γάρ οἱ πτεροφόρον δέμας
θεοὶ γλυκύν τ᾽ ἀγῶνα κλαυμάτων ἄτερ·
ἐμοὶ δὲ μίμνει σχισμὸς ἀμφήκει δορί[1].

This is perfect, but poised in its perfection upon a slippery verge. Euripides may have thought that, even in some plays of high note and passages of singular beauty, the alliance of pathos with erudition had gone quite far enough[2]. The private origin and private recitation of the *Helen* is a fact which should not surprise us. It was probably not even exceptional. It would have been strange, and scarcely credible, in the circumstances of the age, that such recitations should not have been common. The number of plays composed about this time at Athens was enormous. Aristophanes can scarcely find a figure sufficient: 'more than ten thousand,' that is, than infinity, is his phrase for the tragedies which the young men were at work upon[3]. The opportunities of public exhibition were infinitesimal. What then became of these fashionable compositions? We can scarcely suppose that all of them were written to be kept in the desk. Reading, silent and solitary reading, was but a recent habit, and readers still few. Recitation had been and was still the normal manner in which literature circulated among all but professed students. In these circumstances it would have been strange indeed, if tragedies had not been privately performed or recited. Even for the very few composers who could reach the theatre and

---

[1] *Agam.* 1146 (Dindorf). Cassandra speaks: 'Alas, for the fate of the musical nightingale! Her did the gods clothe in a winged form, and gave her a sweet and a tearless passage of death. But I must be cleft in twain by the steel's sharp edge.'

[2] See Soph. *Ant.* 823.

[3] *Frogs* 89
μειρακύλλια
τραγῳδίας ποιοῦντα πλεῖν ἢ μυριάς.

theatrical festivals, private performance of some kind was an obvious method of experiment; and one would suppose rather that many or most tragedies passed through it.   One tragedy of the time we have (attributed, perhaps wrongly, to Euripides) which cannot have been intended, one would suppose, for the theatre—I mean the *Rhesus*.   The Greek preface to that play speaks indeed of its being 'recorded as genuine in the *didascaliae*'; but if this means (though perhaps it need not) that an exhibition of it in the theatre was recorded, one would almost doubt the fact.   The action passes in the night; and that it was performed in such circumstances as those of the civic theatre and festival is scarcely believable; at all events this cannot have been the original intention.   Nor is it likely, in that age, that the composer thought only of readers.   For private recitation or performance a suitable time and arrangement could be chosen; and it would be interesting as a variety.   But apart from this exception there is much in extant tragedy, especially that of Euripides, which suggests the influence of domestic recitation.   For many, perhaps a majority, of his plays, the forecourt of a house, or the space in front of it, would be a scene not merely as good as that of the theatre, but in many ways better.   Of course a play, which 'obtained a Chorus' and reached the dignity of exhibition, would generally need some recasting or retouching to fit it for the peculiar conditions of the Athenian theatre; and in this process those features, if any there were, which the piece derived from the circumstances of its origin, would disappear; as they seem to have disappeared for the most part, but, as we shall presently see, not completely, from the public versions preserved to us, in all cases except that of *Helen*.

But it is a fortunate or a judicious choice which has preserved to us one play of Euripides which, by the nature of the case, could not undergo any material change in being transferred from private performance to the publicity of the Dionysia.   The *Helen* is so intimately connected with the house of 'Theonoe,' that it could not be disengaged from its origin, but, when demanded by the general curiosity, had to be given as it was made.   We are thus reminded of the important

aid which private performance must have rendered to the
general development of the Euripidean drama out of the
Aeschylean. It is not too much to say that, without the help
of some external frame more suitable than the theatre of
Dionysus, nothing less than a miracle could have created such
types of art as the *Alcestis*, the *Phoenissae*, the *Hippolytus*,
the *Andromache*, and above all the *Medea*. We naturally have
received these works, and are thankful so to have them, in
their public shape. But that is not the original nor the most
appropriate shape. One of them at least, the most celebrated
(which is not to say the best) of the poet's extant plays, has
been deplorably injured, as the poet himself indicates[1], in the
vain, though doubtless inevitable, attempt to fit it for the
incongruous conditions of a civic spectacle, and retains in its
perversion many traces of the better mould.

The story of Medea, as treated by Euripides, though
admirably fitted for exposition by monologue and dialogue,
is one which, to a delicate taste, must lose on the whole rather
than gain by performance of any kind, and is painfully
unsuitable for presentation to a huge mass of people. The
finest parts of the play are thoughts, private thoughts, so secret
and so terrible that the thinking mind must struggle to
disguise them even from itself, and that even to write and
read them is already to do some violence to nature. All the
rest consists of colloquies essentially private and intimate.
For pomp there is neither need nor opportunity. Not a single
situation requires or even admits that sort of illustration
which a great stage and large company can supply. The
best acting and delivery would be the simplest. Indeed it is
not easy to imagine what skill in the enunciation of κακῶς
πέπρακται[2] or ὢ τέκνα τέκνα[3] could perfectly compensate for
the impropriety of having such things *spoken* at all. Is it
likely that they were imagined and composed for the purpose
of being declaimed with professional effects to the assembled
population of a great city? Moreover the plot is such that
a Chorus, the necessary condition of public performance

---

[1] See below, p. 127. [2] *Med.* 364 foll. [3] *ib.* 1021 foll.

at Athens, is an exasperating absurdity. For a Medea,
murderess of her children, one single confidant would be
too much ; and the co-operation of fifteen casual visitors is
not a whit the less outrageous because, tempted or forced by
the conditions of his time, Euripides consented to authorize
it, and to introduce, for the sake of the theatre, other elements
not less unfortunate.

The play will bear no Chorus; and for a domestic performance none would be necessary. For this purpose, an
empty stage would be a sufficient separation between the
scenes ; or if an interlude were desired, it might be best
delivered by a single voice. One such interlude, unique in
the extant literature, actually survives[1]. Instead of an ode
bearing upon the action and designed for a band of performers nominally engaged in the action, we have an unbroken recitation, totally non-dramatic in theme and manner,
and, though connected remotely with the subject of the play,
not even affecting to have any relation to the plot. It was
not for fifteen voices, nor for the leader of fifteen, that the
poet wrote

πολλάκις ἤδη
διὰ λεπτοτέρων μύθων ἔμολον
καὶ πρὸς ἁμίλλας ἦλθον μείζους
ἢ χρὴ γενεὰν θῆλυν ἐρευνᾶν·
ἀλλὰ γὰρ ἔστιν μοῦσα καὶ ἡμῖν,
ἢ προσομιλεῖ σοφίας ἕνεκεν—
πάσαισι μὲν οὔ, παῦρον δὲ γένος,
μίαν ἐν πολλαῖς, εὕροις ἂν ἴσως—
κοὐκ ἀπόμουσον τὸ γυναικῶν.
καί φημι βροτῶν οἵτινές εἰσιν
πάμπαν ἄπειροι μηδ᾽ ἐφύτευσαν
παῖδας, προφέρειν εἰς εὐτυχίαν
τῶν γειναμένων....

and the rest of this simple and tender meditation. Would
one desire to sit with twenty thousand strangers, while trained
and hired vocalists shouted this ?—

[1] *Med.* 1081 foll.

HELEN

καὶ δὴ γὰρ ἅλις βίοτόν θ' ηὗρον,
σῶμά τ' ἐς ἥβην ἦλυθε τέκνων,
χρηστοί τ' ἐγένοντ'· εἰ δὲ κυρῆσαι
δαίμων οὕτως, φροῦδος ἐς "Αιδην
θάνατος προφέρων σώματα τέκνων—

words made, one would think, to be written in a locked volume, and shown, rather than read, to a dear companion. To the twenty thousand the thing did come, as many things have a strange fortune in the process of life; but never for such a use was it planned. The odes of the *Medea*, the real odes, are some of them admirable compositions; but the consignment of them all to oblivion would have been a small price to pay for the expulsion of the Chorus, and the restoration of the drama to a cast and setting which would make the story conceivable.

Equally unfortunate, though necessary, was the change which, as the existing text betrays, was made, when the play was prepared for the theatre, in the substance and form of the finale. The *dénouement* of the *Medea*, the aerial chariot in which the murderess departs, has been a commonplace of critical condemnation ever since Aristotle, and doubtless before. The poet himself appends on this occasion his critical tag, which confesses that 'the end is not what was expected[1]'; and in truth it is utterly inappropriate. The Medea of the play, the injured woman, is not and cannot be conceived as a supernatural person, or the possessor of supernatural powers. Nothing in the action requires the supposition[2], and the tone and colouring exclude it. With the miracles of Argonautic legend the story has no real connexion. The play scarcely touches on them[3], and to be consistent should not touch at all. Again and again the forsaken mistress is represented as helpless for every purpose but

[1] *Med.* 1415; see above p. 120.
[2] The deaths of the princess and her father assume nothing which may not be conceived as the natural effect of an unknown poison.
[3] *Med.* 478-482. Every reader feels these reminiscences to be out of keeping. They, and some other slight touches, are probably interpolated, though doubtless by Euripides.

revenge. So far is she from commanding the resources of heaven, that she cannot even secure a refuge upon earth but by negotiation with a scrupulous visitor, whose consent to receive her is purchased by the promise of medicinal aid to his virility[1]. This personage offers the protection of Athens, on the condition that, without his aid, she can get out of Corinth; and it is necessary, for the proper defeat of her betrayer, that she should get out. But that in these circumstances she should fly away through the air, receiving, as a thing of course, a yoke of serpents from her grandsire the Sun, is a 'surprise' which the unanimous judgment of cultivated persons has condemned, and which Euripides himself has condemned in advance.

To justify it is impossible; but there is this excuse for it, that the narrow and peculiar conditions of public performance at Athens were not consistent with a proper conclusion, any more than they were with the working of the plot as a whole. The play had once a conclusion not inappropriate, and the lines of it are visible in the altered form. In the final dialogue with Jason, as we still read it, Medea *proposes to bargain with him*: she asks how she is to *purchase a separation*, whereupon he demands that the bodies of the children should be given to him for burial[2]. Nothing comes of this negotiation, nor could anything come of it as the situation is now represented. Medea, speaking from the security of her chariot, of course refuses the demand, and has in fact no reason for inviting it. That she does invite it is proof that, as the scene was originally conceived, she was in a position not of absolute but of temporary safety, not yet able to escape, but able either to grant or refuse decent burial to the children of the traitor. That the father should

---

[1] See the play *passim*, and specially the strange interview with Aegeus (*vv.* 662 foll.).

[2] *Med.* 1373

MH.　στύγει· πικρὰν δὲ βάξιν ἐχθαίρω σέθεν.

IA.　καὶ μὴν ἐγὼ σήν· ῥᾴδιον δ' ἀπαλλαγαί.

MH.　πῶς οὖν; τί δράσω; κάρτα γὰρ κἀγὼ θέλω.

IA.　θάψαι νεκρούς μοι τούσδε καὶ κλαῦσαι πάρες.

MH.　οὐ δῆτ', ἐπεί σφας τῇδ' ἐγὼ θάψω χερί κ.τ.λ.

concede anything, rather than forego the rite, would, I conceive, be perfectly intelligible to the Hellenic mind. Moreover Medea explains that the burial of the children is to be the means or occasion of religious benefit to Corinth[1]. In the present scene this is nothing to the purpose, since, with the dragon-chariot, it matters not at all whether Corinth is contented or not; but it was important and necessary, when the consent of the Corinthians was required to confirm the transaction and permit the departure of the murderess. The inconsistent conduct of the scene, as it stands, is just such a flaw as is likely to appear in the most skilful patchwork, and indicates that the play originally ended, *as we should expect*, in a negotiation by Medea, completing her arrangement with Aegeus, for leave to retire from Corinth. To the same conception of the story belongs the notice in the prologue[2], that Medea was popular among the citizens in her place of exile. That this notice now comes in oddly, is`irrelevant, and is awkwardly worded, is the universal opinion of readers. But something of the kind, now represented by a remnant and a patch, was indispensable for the original *dénouement* by means of a bargain. Such a bargain, grim and sordid, required no miraculous intervention, and terminated the miserable story in a manner not indeed pleasant (how should such a story have a pleasant termination?) but at all events consistent with its colour and sentiment. Why then was it altered? Because a popular audience, eager to amuse their holiday with a spectacle, would find such an ending flat, and for the pleasure of admiring a mechanical surprise would cheerfully sacrifice considerations of propriety and harmony, which the majority would not even perceive. All this is no justification for the scene as it is. But the mistake lay not in adopting this particular method of fitting the *Medea* to be a civic spectacle, but in attempting such a process at all. The temptation, in

---

[1] *Med.* 1381–1383.
[2] *Med.* 11   ἀνδάνουσα μὲν
φυγῇ πολιτῶν ὧν ἀφίκετο χθόνα
αὐτή τε πάντα συμφέρουσ' Ἰάσονι,
where see the commentaries. We should perhaps read αὐτῷ (Earle) for αὐτή.

the conditions of art at Athens, was naturally great ; and this way of doing it was perhaps as good as another. But the *Medea* could in no way be really adjusted to the conditions of the Dionysia ; and if Euripides had known no other conditions than those of the Dionysia, no *Medea* would ever have been written. It is a picture conceived and fitted for private exhibition, but distorted, as we have it, by violent extension to the frame of the Aeschylean company and theatre.

No other extant tragedy (the *Rhesus* and of course the *Helen* excepted) exhibits this quality of origin so strongly as the *Medea*, though there is much in Euripidean drama generally, for which the civic theatre does not account, and the domestic theatre, if we may so call it, does. The passage of plays through the preliminary period of private recitation is generally important for the history and comprehension of Euripides. It accounts for the existence of plays like the *Ion*, the *Alcestis*, and the *Heracles*, plays which, in their existing shape and as performed at the public festival, have the air of a puzzle. Most readers experience the impression that the *Ion* does not work itself out, and that the end of the piece, with a great parade of elucidation, leaves us nevertheless discontented and doubtful. This phenomenon, when examined, is seen to have a simple cause, in the fact that the play propounds and presses an enquiry, which the conclusion does not answer. The story turns upon a question deeply affecting the honour and veracity of the oracle of Delphi. The tone and the trend of events appear throughout to be hostile to the oracle. But at the last moment a conclusion favourable to the oracle is abruptly imposed, without, as it would seem, any real explanation whatever[1]. Such a method ceases to be mysterious, when we consider that we have no reason to figure the *Ion* as composed with original and exclusive regard to the Dionysia. It must have been easy in that age and at Athens to collect private audiences, who would listen with perfect composure and satisfaction, while such a play as the *Ion*, a satire upon the pretensions of Delphi, was played out to the end which is all but visible in

---

[1] See my edition, and *Euripides the Rationalist*, p. 129.

the extant form. Had this not been so, no play such as the *Ion* now is could have been admitted to the civic theatre, and no author, taking that line of hostility to the public religion, which was openly attributed to Euripides, would have been heard there. To such private audiences, the *Ion*, with its proper ending, and without any 'Athena' in the machine to convert its natural import into nonsense, was first recited; and so it was probably recited for some time, before the diffusion of curiosity, and the desire of the author for the only existing method of wide advertisement, led to the production of it before the civic assembly. Here it was necessarily produced with a slight disguise, just enough to avoid legal danger and to content the uncritical masses. The few who looked for more than a spectacle were already enlightened by report, or, if they were not, could satisfy themselves by enquiry. Some there doubtless were, intelligent enough to be dissatisfied, and yet not so situated as to command information. For this reason the method, however necessary in the circumstances, was disadvantageous; and the remains of Euripides show, if we may suppose them to be representative, that it was exceptional. To no other times, and to no other society, would it have been applicable; and this is one of the reasons why the works of Euripides, which have been transmitted to us by public authority and in their public form, present, as attentive readers generally feel, certain difficulties of a unique and peculiar type.

Even in plays which did not require disguise, we are sometimes reminded that the author did not always or habitually think, if we may so put it, in the forms established by Aeschylus. The phenomenon is notorious, and so widely diffused that its weight will be rather diminished than increased by particular illustration. But let the reader turn to the scene of the *Phoenissae*[1], where Jocasta in maternal ecstasy caresses and fondles and strokes and dances round her recovered son; and let him say whether it seems likely that such a vision would have presented itself to a mind occupied by the forms of Aeschylus and the setting of the Dionysia, the

---

[1] *vv.* 301–354, especially *vv.* 312 foll.

cothurnus and mask, the stately robe, the enormous throng, the political sentiment,—all the things which made the only proper atmosphere for the *Orestea*, and were congenial, though not perhaps necessary, to the *Antigone* and the *Oedipus Tyrannus.*

Even modern literature and society, though we have nothing analogous to the theatre of Athens, offer examples of the dangerous and sometimes disastrous pressure of circumstances upon the forms of artistic creation, by which we may help ourselves to comprehend how the *Ion* or the *Medea* came into the extant shape. Instances recent or contemporary will occur to every reader, which prove that a work of imagination may be deliberately perverted and mutilated by the author, both before and after publication, in order to catch the taste or command the attention of a wider and a less competent audience. It was Scott himself who, murmuring and protesting, but yielding to his publisher and the certain demand of the vulgar novel-reader, irreparably damaged what should have been a figure not inferior in tragic interest to the bride of Lammermoor, by recasting *St Ronan's Well* so as to spare the honour of Clara Mowbray; and it was not for want of urging that he refrained from crowning the suicide by actually marrying the maniac, in a happy conclusion, to her lover. It was not to please himself that Mr Kipling patched on a bright ending to *The Light That Failed.* And it is still the miscellaneous mob of the public theatre, which, with its stupid though inevitable demand for a smart finish, produces the worst distortions. If the reader was ever present at a performance of *Mademoiselle de la Seiglière*, as converted from novel to drama, this recollection, or if not this, some other like it, will suggest, with what scarcely suppressed exclamations of displeasure and contempt the chariot of Medea must have been received by the few, the comparatively few, who are aware that not every story is susceptible of a neat and satisfactory wind-up. And if we had only one theatre, a national and official theatre, dedicated (let us say) to St George, we should not be long without a parallel to the Athena of the *Ion*, who bestows a pompous and fatuous blessing upon the conclusion of a piece which, if it means anything, means that Athena never existed.

It is · to be regretted, that we do not possess more information about such private performances or recitations of dramatic works, as can be proved for the *Helen*, and through the *Helen* for the *Iphigenia in Taurica*, without a previous knowledge of which play the *Helen* would not be intelligible. Doubtless they were in apparatus exceedingly simple: no buskin and mask, no machinery, no scenery, or scarcely any, but the yard, the house, and the door, nothing much in the way of costume. The splendour of the Dionysia has covered them with an obscurity all but complete. But just by reason of their simplicity, and of the domestic atmosphere, they must have been incomparably important to the development of such a drama as that of Euripides out of a drama like that of Phrynichus and Aeschylus. Plays of Euripides there are, the *Suppliants* and the *Children of Heracles*, which are designed, like the *Eumenides* or the *Antigone*, as civic spectacles, and apart from the theatre could scarcely exist; but these are not his best, nor his characteristic work. Aristophanes testifies not only to the fact, but to the interest, of the private representations. He criticizes the private performers of *Helen*, and would appear to have somewhere seen them. It is not impossible that he was himself present, as a guest of 'Theonoe,' at the original celebration in the island. It is worth notice (if, as I think, it is true) that the *Celebrants of the Thesmophoria*, and particularly the scene which burlesques *Helen*, contains nothing personally unpleasant for the virgin-queen, no reference, for example, to πειράσομαι δὲ παρθένος μένειν ἀεί or other like points, out of which the comedian might certainly have made capital, if he had chosen. The treatment of the affair is such as, allowing for the tone of the age, would give almost unqualified pleasure to a woman of intelligence and humour; and the patroness of Helené cannot have been without those qualities. She deserves not to be altogether forgotten.

A SOUL'S TRAGEDY.

(*HERACLES.*)

Frantic, he as truth received
What of his birth the crowd believed.   SCOTT.

My life has crept so long on a broken wing.
                                                            TENNYSON.

THE tragedy of *Heracles* or, as it is commonly and
conveniently called, *The Madness of Heracles*, presents with
singular sharpness the fundamental question, which more than
once confronts the student of Euripides:—What are the
supposed facts of the drama? In what sort of world and
amid what kind of experiences are the personages supposed
to have lived, and in particular how, if at all, do these
experiences differ from what Euripides himself, or the average
of his educated contemporaries, would have recognized as
normal or as possible? What in the play is the part, if any,
of miracle?

It may be, and indeed is, a strange thing, that this point
should be open to doubt. With Heracles for the hero, we
might expect to find the miraculous facts of the story given
as plainly and unmistakeably as any other part of it, given as
they are in the *Trachiniae* of Sophocles. There we are
introduced at once to a woman, who has herself been wooed
by a river-god capable of miraculous transformation, who has
herself been carried over a ford by a Centaur[1], who discoursed
with the Centaur while he died, who gathered the blood of his
death-wound, and narrates these experiences without the

---

[1] *Trach.* 555, and the prologue.

least suggestion that they are surprising or abnormal. And the whole story proceeds of course accordingly. We do not find Deianira observing incidentally, that the notion of twy-formed or multiform creatures, the belief that such exist or ever have existed, has always appeared to her to be a pernicious absurdity. What should we say if we did? We should of course eject the remark as the ill-placed jest of an interpolator. We should not for an instant accept both the criticism and the experience as conceivable parts of the same dramatic character, and erect upon this unimaginable basis a so-called interpretation of the so-called play. Nor should we allow ourselves to be put off with the observation, though it might well appear true, that the criticism represented the opinion of Sophocles. The opinion of Sophocles, we should say, has nothing to do with the question, which relates wholly to the opinion of the imaginary Deianira. Given her experiences as related by her, she did *ex hypothesi* know twy-formed animals to exist; and to suppose otherwise would be to make the story and the drama a thing of naught, inconceivable, unintelligible, and null. Yet it is precisely in this fashion that we are told to interpret (if the word is deserved) the *Heracles* of Euripides.

'For my part,' says Heracles, the hero of this play,

> For my part I dó not hold that the gods know unlawful love; and that they should make prisoners one of another I never did think fit nor will believe...*For deity, if deity indeed, is without all needs whatsoever.* These things are poets' miserable tales[1].

Nothing can be plainer. The speaker rejects absolutely, and once for all, such man-like superhuman beings, such deities with the passions of men, as the common legend of Heracles, with its battles of giants and invasions of Hades, requires us to assume as part of the world and of possible human experience. The circumstances, in which he makes this profession of faith, are such (we shall see) as to exclude the possibility of self-deception, delusion, or pretence. We must understand, and no one has ever attempted to prove the

---

[1] *v.* 1341.

contrary, that it is given for the real opinion of the dramatic character presented, a part and an essential part of his mind. It follows therefore, if the story is to be a story, if the play is a play, if it has, as a whole, any sense whatsoever, that the experiences of the hero, as presented and supposed in it, are and have been consistent with the belief which he professes, that he has not had knowledge of any such creatures or persons as Zeus and Typhoeus, as Pluto or Cerberus, that, in short, *the legend of Heracles, as commonly told, is not to be supposed as part of the story, but replaced by some totally different conception of Heracles, and of his mental and physical history.*

To refuse this inference, to evade this necessity, is to be led straight to the conclusion formulated (by Mr Swinburne, if I am not mistaken), with refreshing sincerity and clearness, in the statement that this work, *The Madness of Heracles*, is 'a grotesque abortion,' a monster, a chaos, in which incommunicable parts are joined or mixed without disguise and without attempt (for it need hardly be said that there is no trace of such an attempt) at reconciliation. The statement is bracing in its frankness, and I remember to have received from it a salutary shock. But it would be the same thing in substance, and in form, all things considered, not less decent, to say that Euripides is here not comprehensible to us,—and to study the drama no more. Nor indeed do the modern interpreters escape this practical result. It is usual to praise the play; but those who will examine the laudatory references and allusions to it may satisfy themselves, that what is meant by 'the play' is in reality a small part of it, less than a third[1], which can, without much violence, be read as consistent with the legend of Heracles, the story of Zeus and Hera, the giants, Hades, Cerberus and so forth, assumed as part of the facts. All the rest of the play, the first half and the last fourth or some such fractions, is ignored, is treated as non-existent, and this without any attempt to show that those portions are intended by the author to be separable and non-dramatic, an attempt which, if it were made, would certainly

[1] *vv.* 763–1162, and a few fragments elsewhere.

be foredoomed to failure. Surely it would be simpler and less invidious to say, that what the author meant we do not understand.

To the same effect leads the remark, a commonplace of modern criticism, that the play is 'deficient in unity.' What is signified or covered by this polite expression, is the undeniable truth, that if, as we commonly suppose, the action of the play in its central part depends upon the superhuman quality and history of Heracles, assumed for the purpose of the story as matter of fact, there is irrelevance, and worse than irrelevance, in an enormous prefatory act or scene, in which that superhuman quality is debated, and not merely debated but, to any common apprehension, discredited and disproved.

In these circumstances it would seem imperative, as the next step, at least to attempt the interpretation of the play upon the hypothesis that the hero is *not* a superhuman personage, nor his story supernatural, but he a man, however great, like other men, and the scene of his action, however remote in time and different in circumstances from the age of Euripides or from our own, nevertheless no other in its physical laws than that same world which the Athenians knew and we know. Not only is this the truth, but upon the perception of it depends all the coherence of the play, all its meaning to the intelligence, and the better part of its appeal to the emotions.

It is no matter for surprise, that a play based upon this supposition should have been presented on the tragic stage of the fifth century, no more so than that the contrary supposition should be the basis, for example, of the *Trachiniae*. Both hypotheses were then familiar to the literary world. A legend like that of Heracles, which allowed that the hero, whatever more he was, was certainly a man, lay peculiarly open to rationalistic treatment; and though we have lost almost all the controversial and popular literature of those days, we happen still to have evidence that the legend of Heracles actually was so treated. The early rationalists encountered indeed in this case, as in others, an objection with which they were ill prepared to deal. If Heracles, as they contended was no more than a man, and his career nothing beyond the limits of nature, how did the miraculous story come to exist? And generally, how did any such stories come to exist? This was the embarrassing problem for such writers as Herodorus[1], and for all those whom we may call mechanical rationalists. A legend, they said, is an exaggerated and mistaken version of real but commonplace events, a falsehood evolved out of true facts by rumour, credulity, and ignorance. Taken generally, this theory had in it elements of truth, and probably carried the assent of the better instructed in the fifth century. But the rationalistic interpreters, as is the way of all theorists in the first stage of a controversy, not only worked the method to death, but applied it in detail with a poverty of imagination and puerility of expedient, which became in the aggregate self-refuting.   People of common sense, however willing to doubt whether the maiden Oreithyia had really been carried off by a superhuman lover wielding the power of a *Boreas* with capital B, became, after many repetitions of like devices, as little inclined to believe that she had been blown over a cliff by an ordinary *boreas* or north wind.   The example is cited as typical by Plato in the next generation, and is dismissed with merited irony[2].   Nor was this type of expedient the worst or the most abused.   Equivocations, puns upon words and especially upon names, were adopted, in tracing the generation of the miraculous, with a wearisome and incredible profusion.   Heracles did not strangle the Nemean lion in his arms (ἐν βραχίοσιν).   No, but he did actually capture it in a snare (ἐν βρόχοις).   The legend arose (as in the game of 'Russian scandal') out of a mis-hearing. The ram of Helle was a boatman called *Krios*, the bull of Pasiphae a gallant called *Tauros*.   A little of this sort would be more than enough.   The instance of the Nemean lion is noted and stigmatized by Euripides himself, who attributes it to the villain of our play[3].

But however objectionable or excessive may have been the methods of the rationalizers, it is certain that, at Athens

[1] Murray, *Hist. of Ancient Greek Literature*, p. 127.
[2] *Phaedrus*, p. 229.   [3] *Heracles* 153.

in the fifth century, educated opinion was with them on the main issue. The historical reality indeed of Heracles, for example, was for all Greeks of that age an axiom ; and for the matter of that, it is still, I suppose, the better opinion, that his legend, whatever other elements it may embody, is founded in parts upon the career of an actual hero. But the reality of the gigantic combat at Phlegra, or of the hell-hound Cerberus, exhibited as a prisoner in broad daylight at the Argolic town of Hermione, would hardly have found more defenders, in the circles to whose suffrage Euripides appealed, than among ourselves. This being so, the desire for variety, to say nothing of other motives, would prompt a dramatic author to exhibit the hero in a naturalistic guise. Nor could any valid objection be made in the name of art; unless it is held that fortitude and beneficence, devoted to the service of man, are admirable only if exercised upon a snake with a hundred necks, or that unmerited agony ceases to be pathetic, when it is not inflicted by the revenge of a man-headed horse.

Even the actual speculations of Herodorus and his kind were not without value to a tragedian pursuing, in his own way, essentially the same purpose. To trace pedantically the development of a natural incident into a supernatural was none of his business; but it suited him well enough to present such natural facts, as would suggest to prepared minds the origin of the legendary translation; or again, to touch upon legendary and miraculous incidents, by way of allusion, in such a manner as to suggest and leave room for the current version of the rationalists. Euripides frequently does both. Of the first we shall see an instance in the *Orestes*[1], where a miraculous anecdote from the *Odyssey* is retold and retouched with persuasive dexterity; of the other we have many examples in the play before us.

But among the conceivable factors of legend, among the many ways in which things might come to be believed, though they never happened at all, or at any rate not as they were related, there was one upon which Euripides, whether guided or not by any predecessor, had meditated, as a tragedian, with

---

[1] *vv.* 360 foll. See also *Euripides the Rationalist*, pp. 182–188.

special and specially justifiable interest. That the topic of madness and mental aberration was attractive to him, is noted by ancient critics, and is indeed obvious. Primarily no doubt he was drawn to it, like Aeschylus, Sophocles, and tragic poets in general, as a means of pathos. But standing in such relation as he did to the speculative and critical thought of his time, he could not easily miss the reflexion, that the imagination of insane and irregular minds, accepted by the superstitious as a channel of inspired truth, had probably been a fertile source of revered and accredited nonsense. That he did not miss it we have abundant evidence. The legend of the matricide Orestes, for example, is repeatedly so handled in his extant works, as to convey the impression that the miraculous parts of it originated in mere insanity. In one place, the whole story of Aeschylus' *Eumenides* is narrated, through the mouth of Orestes, in such a way and in such circumstances as irresistibly to suggest a doubt, how much, if any, of that Areopagitic tradition was founded on fact, and not upon the invention of a diseased brain[1]. Similarly even the minor degrees of abnormal and unhealthy excitement, the fumes of intoxication[2], the frenzy of pain[3], the transport of victory[4], the shock of sudden grief[5], the confusion of sleep[6], the wildness of terror[7], are each in turn presented as contributors to the stream of mythology, imagining impossibilities, or investing actual facts with the colours of superstitious deceit.

These however were but steps on the road. It is in the *Heracles* that this conception is applied upon the largest scale, with most skill, most insight, and most profoundly tragic effect. For power, for truth, for poignancy, for depth of penetration into the nature and history of man, this picture of the Hellenic hero may be matched against anything in art.

Although both in fact and in fiction madness is most commonly associated with crime, this conjunction is neither the only one in which mental extravagance is actually found,

[1] *Iph. T.* 939 foll.   [2] *Alc.* 837.   [3] *Hec.* 1205.
[4] *Heraclidae* 847.   [5] *Hippol.* 1198 foll.; see 1173–1184.
[6] *Hec.* 92.   [7] *Androm.* 1147.

nor that in which it may with most profit be studied and depicted. Great hearts, as well as great wits, are to madness near
allied ; and among the consecrated benefactors of mankind
there are perhaps few, whose intellectual constitution appears
to have been conspicuously sane, while in many the vigour of
delusion has been proportional to the general strength of the
faculties and the character. Euripides needed not to look
beyond the market-place of Athens for a personality scarcely
more distinguished from the mass by acuteness and bene-
volence than by eccentricity of spiritual imagination. Nor
are these higher types of aberration exempt, any more than
the vulgar sort, from fluctuation and intermittence. The
madman of genius or virtue may swing, like another, between
sanity and insanity, and may be great in both. Now let us
suppose (and the supposition is surely entertainable) that in
the dark ages of superstition, in the very dawn of civilized life
and intelligent speculation, there arose a· hero physically,
mentally, and morally far superior to his contemporaries, but
curst from his birth with a taint in his blood, a recurrent and
progressive malady of the brain. Let such an one, in ardent
and solitary meditation, have so far purged his notions of
man and God from the grossness and barbarity around him,
as to grasp at least in vision the hint of philosophies still
unbuilt, and the principles of creeds and religions long after
to be preached and established. All this has been achieved
by many a 'madman,' whose thoughts, by the favour of circumstances, have passed into circulation and are famous to
this day; and doubtless (as Euripides justly divined) it has
also been achieved by many and many another, whose voice
was not heard or not even raised, and whose meditation
effected nothing but the uplifting of his own heart and the
ennobling of his own life. Let our hero have done his duty
faithfully up to and beyond the demand and standard of the
time, loving his home and family, devoted in friendship,
fighting gallantly and victoriously for the little struggling
community to which he belonged. Let him have lent his
services without stint to the largest and most beneficial
enterprises which the state of things presented, to penetrate

as pioneer the uncleared and unknown waste, peopled in reality by savage beasts and men, and supposed to be the haunt of imaginary monsters yet more terrible. By the vulgar herd, nay, even by his nearest and dearest, the source and nature of his greatness will be ignorantly misconceived, and most of all by those who admire most. On all sides he will hear his praises translated into language which he loathes and contemns. His superiority to others will be explained by the fiction of a divine parentage, which to his better thoughts will seem a revolting blasphemy. His genuine achievements will be enlarged and travestied by a huge appendix of incongruous falsehood. And worst of all, because of that taint in his blood, because he is not only inspired, but also, in the plain and gross sense of the word, mad, because he has his hours of darkness as well as his hours of illumination, he himself will sometimes lend his authority to confirm the tales which he abhors, will repeat the abominable nonsense with which his ears are fed, proclaiming himself that which he knows he is not, and painting the good deeds, of which he is proud, with the crude, disgusting colours of folly and misbelief. In process of time he will become aware that he does these things. Long before any one else, he will know how it is with him. Self-hatred and self-suspicion will aggravate the inner mischief from which they spring. And at last, upon the occasion of some special excitement, in a few moments and without any effective warning, the thin partition of his brain will break, and a burst of cruel fury will exhibit the benefactor of humanity, for some horrible hours, in the secondary but not less genuine character of a fiend. Such is the Heracles of Euripides.

The scene, which is laid at Thebes, that is to say in the territory so called and in the immediate neighbourhood of the seven-gated fortress, shows a house with an altar before it, the present home of Heracles and his family, which comprises his father Amphitryon, his wife Megara, daughter of Creon the late king of the country, and three sons of tender age. The situation, which remains practically unaltered during a third part of the play and until the arrival of Heracles himself (*v.* 514), is designed to exhibit the wide and incomprehensible divergence of opinion, which divides the city and even the family, respecting the personality, character, and career of the absent hero. With this topic both dialogue and chorus are almost exclusively occupied, the present and undisputed facts serving only to animate with urgency the interest of the dramatic debate. The facts themselves are set forth partly by Amphitryon in a semi-dramatic prologue of the usual Euripidean type, and partly in the following scenes. Amphitryon, for the murder of a near kinsman, was exiled with his family from his native Argos. Both he and his son Heracles have done good service to Thebes in the little campaigns of a primitive city, now against the neighbouring Minyans of Orchomenus, on another and famous occasion against the island marauders of Aetolia[1]. The son moreover, as warrior and hunter, functions not yet very clearly discriminated, has followed the call of duty and adventure far beyond these limits, beyond all limits of common knowledge or report, and has won immense renown by achievements about which, if we put all the contradictory assertions together, we may say that they have been, at the lowest estimate, uncommon and beneficial[2]. He was rewarded with the hand of the King's daughter, and the wedding was celebrated by Thebes with universal applause[3]. But this prosperity of the house is past. The Argive exiles, Greek-like, still pined for Argos; and to purchase restoration Heracles offered his services, in 'redeeming the earth from savagery,' to the Argive king Eurystheus[4]. Of his past exploits in the Argolid and Peloponnese, which to the Thebans of this play and the age supposed are distant and partly untravelled regions, his fellow-citizens and others have the same vague, inconsistent notions as of his former enterprises, some portentously extolling them, some reducing them to proportions moderate or even low[2]. The latest report describes him as having

---

[1] *v.* 60, etc., *v.* 50, *v.* 220, etc.

[2] Compare the statements of Amphitryon, Megara, Lycus, and the Chorus, *passim.*

[3] *v.* 10.   [4] *vv.* 17–20.

descended into the cave of Taenarum, in the extreme south, the reputed entrance of the underworld, and not having returned[1]. Meanwhile the fickle Thebans have risen against Creon, have put him and his sons to death, and raised to the tyranny one Lycus, a foreigner from Euboea, pretending an antiquated claim to the throne. The family of Heracles have taken refuge at a public altar in front of the house, where, helpless and starving, they are beleaguered by their enemy[2].

Under these circumstances Megara and Amphitryon, the wife and the father, debate what is best to be done[3]. Megara is for immediate surrender and the dignified acceptance of death; Amphitryon is unwilling to resign hope. We might suspect here[4], and it soon after becomes evident, that there is more in this than a mere difference of temperament. That which upholds Amphitryon is no common calculation of chances. He entertains respecting his son, with a faith pathetically human in its uncertainty[5] and inconsistency, but strong enough on the whole to affect his judgment, a belief, which the wife from first to last significantly ignores, a belief sufficient, if well-founded, to justify even limitless expectations. The career of Heracles, conceived as not merely wonderful but miraculous, is explained by some after a fashion natural to the popular Hellenic theology: he is superhuman, the son of a god, the son of Zeus. This notion, with certain parts of the miraculous biography from which it arises, Amphitryon, while reserving, with strange and characteristic confusion, an unimpaired assurance of his own fatherhood[6], nevertheless accepts, and in this desperate hour tenaciously defends. And for this reason he persists in the hope, that Heracles, *wherever* he has gone, may still return[7], or at all events that in some way Zeus, the 'part-father,' will interfere on behalf of his progeny[8].

Upon the same side of the question, or at least in the same sphere of belief and sentiment, stand the company of

[1] *v.* 23.
[2] *vv.* 26–59.
[3] *vv.* 60–106.
[4] *v.* 92.
[5] *vv.* 20–21, and *passim.*
[6] *vv.* 3, 14, etc.
[7] *vv.* 25, 97, etc.
[8] *vv.* 170 (where note μέρει), 339, 498, and Amphitryon *passim.*

decrepit elders, loyal but alas, unserviceable friends of fallen
royalty, who compose the Chorus. Quitting[1] with unwonted
effort the sheltering roof and restful couch, which beseem
their years, they drag their wearied limbs to the place of
refuge, in order to testify their respect and sympathy. In
situation and character this Chorus recalls that of Aeschylus'
Agamemnon, and indeed the language in which they respectively introduce themselves has a verbal resemblance
pointing to conscious or unconscious imitation[2]. In both
cases we have a state unsettled by faction, and a consequent dethronement of legitimate princes and elevation of
usurpers. In the *Heracles* the revolution is accomplished
when the action begins, in the *Agamemnon* not accomplished,
though from the first foreboded, until the closing scene.
In both the Chorus represent, in mind and person, the
conquered minority, the discredited past, and are filled with
the sense that their day is over, that they walk in the new
world like dreams among actual things[2]. Each band dis-
plays its spirit and impotence by a vain appeal to arms[3].
Each protests that in the decay of the body the mind retains
the faculty of art, that, though they cannot fight, they can
still sing[4]. In short the parallel is as close as may be, and
can hardly be supposed accidental. It deserves notice for an
interesting reason. In the *Agamemnon* the peculiar personality
of the Chorus, their decrepitude, feebleness, bewilderment,
and conscious inefficiency, are dramatically important: if
the king's friends had been other than they are, the plot by
which he perishes, however we conceive the details of it,
would certainly not have taken the course which it does.
When therefore we see that Euripides has borrowed the
conception for his *Heracles*, we may fairly suppose that he
also had a practical use for it, that something not insignificant to the drama depends upon the extreme physical

1 If (with Scaliger) we insert λιπὼν in *v.* 107. The question is of no general
importance, and in the uncertainty of the strophic metre must remain doubtful.
2 Compare *Ag.* 82 (Dindorf) with *Heracles* 112.
3 *Ag.* 1618 foll., *Her.* 252 foll.
4 *Ag.* 104-107, *Her.* 637-641, 673-686.

weakness of these 'mere voices and phantoms[1],' on whose
declining heads the burden of their antiquity lies like the
weight of Aetna on the giant compressed beneath[2]. We
shall see that something does indeed depend upon it, something without which the scheme of the play could not have
been carried out in its actual form, and cannot be properly
understood.

These, the old Amphitryon and the aged Chorus, are
the champions of the banished Heracles, both as man and as
demigod; for the Chorus, although, like Amphitryon but with
a difference, they are ambiguous on the divine parentage,
leaving in the alternative[3] the doctrines which he contrives to
combine, are even more copious and stubborn than Amphitryon himself in maintaining the miraculous account of
the hero's career.

Upon the other side, and in the extreme, stands Lycus
the tyrant, a coarse, vulgar upstart. He comes[4] in insolent
triumph to demand surrender, and mocks the hopes of
Heracles' father and wife, not only by deriding the demigod[5]
but by vilifying and depreciating the man[6]. Heracles, he
says, has gone to Hades, and of course will no more return
than any other man. Son of Zeus! Absurd! Why should
his family expect consideration? What was he? What did
he do? He may have snared a lion or so—asserting falsely
that he slew the beast with his hands; but after all he was a
poor creature. A fellow that fought with bow and arrows,
the weapons of a coward!

In such startling fashion is flung before us the question
and problem of the play. For, brute though Lycus is, and
plain as it is that his rudeness and cruelty are offered for our
reprobation, it is by no means plain, that everything about
Heracles, which Lycus would deny and his opponents assert,
is true. It is difficult, if not impossible, for us to suppose so.

[1] *Her.* 111.   [2] *v.* 639.
[3] *vv.* 353-354. *After the return of Heracles 'from Hades'* they are positive for
the divinity (696) and adopt *as now proved* the harmonizing view of Amphitryon
vv. 798-809.
[4] *v.* 140.   [5] *v.* 149.   [6] *vv.* 157-164.

In the first place, he is supported at the present time by a victorious party, a dominant majority, in Thebes[1], the place where Heracles has long lived in the familiar aspect of a denizen. We may indeed well suppose that the tone of Lycus does not exactly represent his supporters generally; but we must still suppose, from their conduct, that they stand in opinion much further from Amphitryon. They do not, they cannot believe themselves to have risked the vengeance of one who has aided, in battle against giants, the arms and thunder of the supreme Deity[2], and who, to say nothing more, is not yet ascertained to be dead. And this, their practical testimony to the infidel view, is so far from insignificant that it is almost decisive. Rebels and ingrates they may be, prodigals even some of them and beggars, and bent upon robbery[3]; but for all that they are 'many,' they must be hundreds or thousands in number; they have had every natural opportunity of estimating the likelihood that Heracles was or is capable of scattering armies, crushing giants, and capturing dragons; and, beyond all possibility of question, they are not effectively convinced that he is.

And in the next place, upon what, for want of a better term, we must call the theological aspect of the case, upon the question of miracle, Lycus has an ally in the bosom of his enemy. To this extent Megara herself is with him. Admiring her husband to the very height of man, she plainly does not hold him to be a supernatural person; and what is more, for some reason not apparent in the scene now before us but provoking curiosity, she is plainly unwilling that his pretensions to that character should be advanced or discussed. The sharp and simple difference between Megara and Amphitryon is exactly noted by Lycus, upon his entrance, in words which are a compendium of the ensuing dialogue and a key to the position[4]: ' You father and you wife of Heracles,

---

[1] *vv.* 34, 543, 558–561, 588 foll., etc.   [2] *vv.* 177 foll.

[3] *vv.* 569, 588 foll., etc. *vv.* 588–592 are suspected of interpolation, but only because they emphasize a little that aspect of the situation which is too much ignored.

[4] *vv.* 140 foll.

I would ask you, with leave supposed, a certain question...
To what hour do ye seek to prolong your lives? What hope
or help against death have ye in view? Is it the father of
these boys, who lies with Hades, that will, you trust, return?
How you do exaggerate the cause for lament in your approaching death, *both you* (to Amphitryon), *who have spread
through Hellas the vain boast that Zeus had part in your couch
and a share in your child, and you* (to Megara), *who proclaimed
yourself wife to the noblest of mankind!*' And accordingly
to the wife in particular[1] he proceeds to address his attack
upon the merits of Heracles as a man—'What is it to have
killed a lion or a water-snake?' and again, 'What is the
dignity of an archer?'—by which he reduces the rank of the
hero not merely to the level of natural power, but to a low
place in the human scale. All that is spoken by Megara,
and still more what is left unspoken, confirms and proves his
estimate of her sentiments. Without directly contradicting
or criticising, which neither kindness nor decency would permit, the miraculous allegations of Amphitryon, she disowns
them for her part completely, not only by ignoring and
omitting (though this in itself would be enough), but positively.
'The gods shall be my witnesses!' says Amphitryon[2], in
opening what he conceives to be the true and worthy defence
of his son. 'My husband,' says Megara to Amphitryon with
haughty modesty, 'is glorious *without witnesses.*' And she
proceeds consistently to expostulate with the old man, in
terms scarcely distinguishable from those of Lycus himself,
upon the vanity of expecting 'a dead man' to return from
the other world[3]. This she does without once deigning to
notice the allegations which, if true, would obviously take
Heracles out of the common rule, without once considering
what might be expected from a journey to the other world,
if undertaken by such a voyager as 'the son of Zeus.'

Such are the parties to this staggering and enigmatical
controversy. The two most conspicuous features in it are
the tirade of Amphitryon[4], and the encomium or creed[5]—

---

[1] *v.* 151.   [2] *v.* 176.   [3] *vv.* 290, 295 foll.; compare *v.* 145.
[4] *vv.* 170 foll.   [5] *vv.* 348 foll.

for it is something of both—pronounced by the Chorus upon the theme of Heracles and his exploits, when all appears to be lost and while the victims, having quitted sanctuary, are within the house, making their final preparations for death. The speech and the ode together represent the kind and measure of evidence which, according to the conception of Euripides, we might obtain for such a legend as that of Heracles, if we could reach those among whom it arose, if we could hear what would have been said, in reply to a scoffer, by the contemporary believer. Both are masterpieces in their kind and deserve the most careful attention.

In the apology of the father we may notice first, as a point significant though not principal, its excessive length and verbosity. The satire of Lycus upon Heracles covers twenty verses (145—164); Amphitryon, to the admiration of his old acquaintance, who have never before known him so copious[1], contrives to extend his reply to sixty-six verses, of which sixteen, a singularly inept and wordy defence of archery[2], have much exercised the critics and apologists of the poet. We may spare ourselves the choice between various insufficient excuses, if we observe that one purpose of the speaker, and not the least operative, is to fill time, to speak *as long as ever he can*. The key to this, as to his attitude throughout the opening scenes, is his desperate expectation of aid from the almighty partner of his couch and child. To Zeus, now in hope, now in remonstrance, and finally in wrathful and contemptuous reproach, he alludes and appeals repeatedly[3]. 'For the part of Zeus in our son, let Zeus be his aid' are the first words of his answer to Lycus; and if he makes that answer long, if he seizes with ingenuity on every pretext for a fresh topic which the loose tongue of Lycus has afforded, diverging from giants to centaurs, from centaurs to archery, from archery to the innocence of his grandchildren, and thence, after a despairing pause, to the ingratitude of Thebes ('Yes, Thebes too shall have its turn')[4], if he mixes his final invective with fierce laments for the feeble succour of a 'noisy

---

[1] *vv.* 236–237.
[2] *vv.* 188–203.
[3] *vv.* 170, 177, 212, 339, 498.
[4] *v.* 217.

tongue,' which is all that he now can lend[1],—all is respective
to the part of Zeus, and prompted by the implied reflexion,
odd indeed but profoundly true to the working of a bold
yet superstitious mind, that every word which he can utter
gives another second of opportunity to the Almighty.

Such is the outward form of this strange, but strangely
natural oration. When we turn to its substance, and consider
it as an argument for the professed thesis, that Heracles is
notoriously and demonstrably superhuman, we cannot but
see already, what will appear again and more conspicuously
when the Chorus take up the tale, that the defenders of the
miraculous account have, in the way of evidence, nothing of
any value to adduce. They answer the infidel to their own
satisfaction, because they do not understand his demand.
Lycus has taxed the divinity of Heracles as an 'empty
boast[2],' a notion which, like the miraculous stories upon
which it is based, is *believed* and *reported* but *not true*. Now
if it were true, if such things as were rumoured of Heracles
had really occurred, how should such a challenge be answered
by such a person as Heracles' natural father? How (if for
illustration we may suppose the case) would it have been
answered by Deianira, wife to Heracles in the *Trachiniae*
of Sophocles? Easily of course and conclusively, by the
testimony of *her own experience*. With her own eyes she had
seen Heracles wrestle down a horned and monstrous river-
god[3]. And so should Amphitryon answer, so inevitably
must he, if in fact he had any relevant experience; and this
again he could not be without, if indeed the popular stories
had any foundation. One miraculous incident at least, both
famous and convincing, was supposed in after-times by
worshippers of Heracles to have taken place before Amphitryon's eyes. The divine infant had strangled serpents in
his cradle; so it was said in Thebes[4]. Why then do we not
now hear this, and other like facts, from a competent witness,
the father? Because—what other explanation is possible?—
no such things had he ever seen. What we do hear, what

[1] *v.* 229.   [2] *v.* 148.
[3] Soph. *Trach. vv.* 10 foll., 523 foll.   [4] *Heracles* 1266.

Amphitryon, in his honest unsuspecting simplicity, does
actually allege as warrant for his boast, serves only to mark
the absence of genuine testimony and his incapacity to
comprehend that objection—combats with 'outrageous four-
foot centaurs,' for warrant whereof the objector is referred
to the forests of Arcadia and bidden to 'go and enquire of
Pholoé[1],' awful contests with the gigantic offspring of earth,
battles of the gods, of which we are not told so much as the
locality, and which we are to verify by cross-examining such
witnesses as the thunderbolt and chariot of Zeus[2]. No
informants are specified, nor is it even indicated that any
accessible informants exist. Of miraculous events in the
speaker's home, in Thebes, in Boeotia, in any place, time, or
circumstances permitting his personal knowledge, we have
not one word. Yet of this defect he is himself so perfectly
unconscious, as to remark that for the true character of
Lycus one should go—where? Why, where else but to his
native Euboea[3]? The simplicity is admirable and a proof
of good-faith, but sufficient also to show that for evidence,
for grounds, if there be any, to support the miraculous stories
about Heracles as matter of fact, we must go elsewhere than
to Amphitryon.

We go accordingly to the Chorus, who, as was said, console
themselves in the suspense of the supreme moment by a
mournful recital of the meritorious and splendid achievements
now to be so ill repaid, a lyrical canon, as it were, of the
labours of Heracles[4]. This ode is highly esteemed, and
deservedly, as a piece of graceful poetry. But if we take
it for nothing more, if we suppose that Aeschylus, Sophocles,
or any other known poet except Euripides, would have
composed it as it stands, or that it may, without loss of effect,
be detached as a mere hymn from the scenes to which it
relates, we are in error. Like the speech of Amphitryon,
it is not only an encomium but also a defence and a defiance.
Like Amphitryon, the old men are answering Lycus, and
with him all that younger generation[5], who so perversely

[1] *vv.* 181–183.
[2] *vv.* 174 foll. σὺν μάρτυσιν θεοῖς—Διὸς κεραυνόν τ' ἡρόμην τέθριππά τε.
[3] *v.* 185. [4] *vv.* 348 foll. [5] See κάκιστος τῶν νέων in *v.* 257, *v.* 436, etc.

depreciate and so easily forget the services of the departed hero. And the praise of the Chorus, like that of Amphitryon, whatever truth it may contain, is yet, when considered as an answer to Lycus, as evidence, and especially as evidence for the miraculous, liable to the fatal objection that they do not understand the requirement. They are indeed resentfully conscious that their story in its details is disputed, and they even go so far beyond Amphitryon as to produce, for one part of it, evidence undoubtedly probative. 'Also,' they say, 'the riding host of the Amazons, who dwelt about the many rivers of Maeotis, he did assail, passing the Inhospitable Sea, *with company of comrades gathered (were they not?) from all Hellenic lands*, seeking a deadly prize, the golden girdle that Ares' daughter wore ; which famous spoil of the strange maiden *Hellas received, and Mycenae hath it still*[1]*!'* A crowd of witnesses, a visible memorial, what more can the sceptic ask ? Certainly nothing more *upon this particular count*. The expedition against the Amazons is proved up to the hilt—saving indeed the detail, to which the evidence does not go, that their queen was the daughter of Ares. But Lycus would demur, and readers of Euripides in the fifth century would demur, and we must demur, when the narrators assume that, because one reported feat of Heracles is provable, therefore all reported feats, *of whatever kind*, must be taken without proof for true. The narrators prove what is credible, and then, with a logic not unfamiliar to us, demand credence for things which are not. That there have been Amazons is a fact ; that Heracles invaded and defeated the Amazons would have been granted as possible, perhaps even probable, by Thucydides himself, and is, in a certain sense, admitted by history still. But when the narrators assert[2], with the same confidence, that in 'Erytheia' (wherever that was), in the dim and unknown west, Heracles slew a 'keeper of kine with bodies three,' then a scoffer, a Lycus, or any of that multitude who appear to share his opinions, would of course observe that Amazons are one thing and a three-bodied Geryon quite another ; and they will note it for unfortunate

---

[1] *vv.* 408 foll.   [2] *v.* 423.

(such is their malice) that here, where witnesses and memorial
are peculiarly desirable, no witnesses, no memorial, no evidence
of any kind is alleged, and that the same regrettable defect
prevails throughout, except, strangely enough, just in one
case where the thing alleged is natural and probable in itself.
They will even suggest an inference.

The elders therefore, however much we may sympathize
with their generous fidelity, leave the main question, the
speculative question, precisely where it was, and prove only
the facility with which, in the times represented, a marvellous
tale, once generated, would be accepted, expanded, and
diffused. Upon opponents or impartial judges their protest
could produce no effect whatever. The general purport of
their narrative, that Heracles has been a mighty conqueror of
men and slayer of savage beasts, is not in dispute. Even
Lycus grants lions to the hunter, and of the warrior has
nothing worse to say than that he preferred the bow to the
sword. What *is* in dispute is the miraculous detail, and this
remains, as before, unwarranted. Here again, as in the case
of Amphitryon, we observe, that of the supernatural encounters so proudly enumerated, not one has occurred within the
knowledge of the narrators. Thebes and Boeotia, Phocis even
and Attica, furnish not a giant, not a single gold-headed
deer or thousand-headed snake. The shore of Malis and
the river Anaurus supply an anecdote perfectly natural[1]; but
when we go as far as the Hebrus, horses are fed upon human
flesh[2]. The mountains of Thessaly contain 'wild centaurs[3].'
These, by the way, Amphitryon places in Arcadia[4], and
doubtless they might be indigenous to both regions. But it
is a more significant discrepancy, that whereas the centaurs
of Amphitryon are 'four-footed,' that is to say semi-equine
and monstrous, those of the Chorus are a mere 'fierce tribe of
the hills,' who, arming their hands from the pine-forests of
Pelion and Homolé, 'subdued with their ridings' (ἱππείαις

---

[1] *vv.* 389–393, accepting in *v.* 389, with Prof. Murray, ἄν τε Μηλιάδ' for τάν
τε Πηλιάδ' from Musgrave and Hermann. The reading does not affect our point
but makes the geography consistent with itself.
[2] *vv.* 380–388.   [3] *vv.* 364 foll.   [4] *v.* 182.

ἐδάμαζον) the more fertile plain below. Readers in the fifth
century were familiar with both conceptions of the centaur,
and with the theory that the miraculous conception, that of
Amphitryon, was a figment, evolved by wonder-loving
ignorance out of the non-miraculous, that of the Chorus.
The 'golden apple-tree' and 'guardian serpent' are to be
sought near 'the dwelling-place of Atlas,' wherever that was[1];
but the doubters would scarcely accept an account of such
things from persons who do not even profess to have seen
them. Certainly they would not take it from those who, in
affirming that a certain mischievous deer, slain by the hero,
had 'a golden head,' note, as if it were a confirmation, that he
presented that trophy 'as an ornament' to the temple of
Artemis at Oenoe. Such decorations were commonly gilded;
and, before believing that the reported marvel was anything
more than this, the sceptics would here also wait for the
testimony of some one, who had used his reason and his
eyes[2].

But here another and an opposite thought occurs, a
thought for which, as we have seen, many minds in the fifth
century were prepared by the trend of speculation and
controversy. The more it appears that the story of Heracles,
as told by his contemporary admirers, contains a large
proportion of fantasy, exaggeration, and falsehood, the more
we wonder how such uncertainty could arise, how so enormous
a difference of opinion as that between Lycus and the Chorus
could possibly exist, while the hero of the story was living and
familiar. We ask who has seen these things. But there is
one person who must, it should seem, profess to have seen
them all: and that is Heracles himself. Here, in the inception
of a legend, was the very problem with which free enquirers
in the age of Euripides were gravely if not always wisely

---

[1] *vv.* 394–407.

[2] See *vv.* 375 foll., noting that ἀγάλλει θεάν takes its meaning from ἄγαλμα in
the sense of *ornament*. It would appear that the skull was actually shown at
Oenoe, and that the decoration of it had suggested the explanation of the legend to
which Euripides points. Other such allusions would probably be apparent in
the ode, and elsewhere in the play, if we were sufficiently acquainted with contemporary facts and literature.

busy. It was of course open to them to allege deliberate deception, and they did; but the colouring of the scene forbids us easily to suppose that this is to be the solution of the dramatist, that the son of Amphitryon and husband of Megara will be proved a shameless liar. What then is he? We eagerly expect his appearance, which occurs in the following act.

Before we proceed to it, a word should be said about the place of the action, the house of Heracles, which we described above[1] as near but not within the city or fortress of Thebes. The use of the word πόλις (as in *v.* 593 ἐσελθὼν πόλιν) might mislead an English reader as to this, but the alternative χθών (as in *v.* 598 εἰσῆλθον χθόνα) shows that πόλις here, as often, means the γῆ, the *state* or territory of Thebes, not the *city* in our sense. The distinction is trivial, but in this case important. The circumstances attending the arrival of Heracles and death of Lycus[2], and still more the subsequent arrival of Theseus[3], are inconceivable, if the place of action cannot be reached without passing the gates of a city agitated by revolution. The house must be solitary, free from observation; nor is there anything in the drama inconsistent with this necessary supposition.

From this house then Megara, with Amphitryon and the children, now re-enters[4] attired for death[5]. Lycus has been absent during this preparation, and has not yet returned. The pathos of the situation, hitherto almost neglected in the dominant interest of Heracles, is emphasized by Megara in a lament over the children, which however is itself so turned as to keep the father and his enigmatic personality before our attention[6]. We hear how the great exile would solace himself by promising to his boys a magnificent future, when one should have Argos and should 'dwell, sovereign of fair Pelasgia, in the palace of Eurystheus,' the second should be prince of Thebes, possessing the plains of his mother's inheritance, while the youngest would coax from him the promise of Oechalia, captured once on a time by his archery.

---

[1] p. 142. See *v.* 543.   [2] *vv.* 514–762.   [3] *vv.* 1163 foll.
[4] *v.* 451.   [5] *vv.* 327 foll., 525, 562.   [6] *vv.* 451–496.

The touching humanity of the picture pleases at once; but when we know the sequel and the connexion of the whole, we shall remark that these parental imaginations are not more tender than strange. If it be true, as a master has said[1], that the inmost of a man appears in his day-dreams, it is an unquiet and a disquieting soul which this glimpse reveals. To fancy impossibilities is sometimes a perilous pleasure; and the fancies of Heracles are not altogether innocent. Oechalia he might give, or harmlessly play at giving; but Thebes was 'the inheritance' not of Megara but of her brothers[2]; and as for the realm of Argos, the family had no legitimate hope of it whatever[3]. The trait would be insignificant, were it not for the sequel, but we shall presently have reason to remember with pity that Heracles, in his wilder fancies, loved to suppose himself master of the palace of Eurystheus.

While Megara pursues these melancholy remembrances, and Amphitryon yet once more and for the last time importunes the expected Zeus, Heracles presents himself, safe but unguarded. The scene which ensues[4] is the central light of the play, illuminating past and future with the same abrupt and menacing flash. For here we suddenly discover (scarcely with more surprise than some of the actors, though one, we notice, does not express any), that the hero is not master of himself, that his reason is not proof against excitement, that at this critical moment his brain is in a condition of irritability which renders him almost incapable of action, in short, that he is on the very verge of delirium.

He approaches, and his wife flings herself into his arms. In a rapid colloquy she acquaints him with the situation, the massacre of her family, the enemy in possession of the town, the instant peril of herself and the rest. The wrath of Heracles rises with every reply. And when all is told, he bursts, in such a tone and with such looks and action as we may imagine, into this:

[1] Victor Hugo, *Les Misérables*.   [2] *v.* 539.
[3] See, for the relations of Heracles with Argos and Eurystheus, *vv.* 13–21. In the *Heraclidae* and elsewhere they are represented otherwise.
[4] *vv.* 523–636.

Fling off your wreaths, your garniture of Death,
And upward looking hail the sweet exchange
Of sun and daylight for the darksome deep !
For me, I will away (the hour demands
The arm of Heracles), *to level first
The usurper's palace,* lop the villain's head,
And fling for dogs to worry. *Then the false
In Thebes, obliged to me and found ingrate,
All will I crush with this victorious mace,
Or with my wing-swift arrows sweep away,
Till the blood reddens Dirce's water wan.*
Who better claims my succour than a wife,
Children, and...aged man ? No more of feats
Abroad, preferred in vain to these at home !
My life for their defence, who were to die
Because of me ! Else nothing were my praise,
Who on Eurystheus' errand fought the snake
And lion, if I could not wrest from death
Mine offspring. Then let Heracles renounce
His title, and be 'conqueror' no more[1] !

But his hearers are not so confident! Lycus or his
satellites[2] may re-appear at any moment. If he is allowed
to discover the return of his enemy and to rejoin his partizans,
all is lost. The best hope, slight at the best, of escaping from
the occupants of the town, is to surprise and destroy their
leader. This will at least gain time. And here is Heracles,
the expected saviour, wasting the moments in babble about
razing a fortified palace, and wreaking, single-handed, revenge
upon a whole population! The hesitating comment of the
elders[3] is interrupted by Amphitryon, who, scarcely knowing
what to say, entreats his son to be prudent. The partizans of
the tyrant are many and unscrupulous,...Heracles may have

---

[1] *vv.* 562 foll. I give a version of my own, but Mr Way's, or any, would serve
the purpose. In *v.* 575 I keep, as suggested by Prof. Murray in his edition of the
text, the MSS. reading γέροντι: 'τεκόντι Wakefield : sed videtur iam delirans
Hercules mortalem abnuere patrem, tum monitu Chori se comprimere (583 sq.).'
The adoption of τεκόντι would not affect the character of the speech : see πάτερ in
v. 619. What are the opinions of Heracles on the point in question we shall
learn as we proceed.   [2] *vv.* 240, 724.

[3] *vv.* 583–584, where the interruption should be indicated. 'The cause is
just,' they begin ; the 'but,' which this implies, is cut off by Amphitryon.

been seen,…if so, the enemy may assemble, and then…he may be less safe than he thinks[1]. Heracles begins to rave again[2], but less violently, and his father insinuates, with precaution[3], the obvious counsel, that Lycus should be entrapped. The son consents to take the first step in this direction by going into the house, but in a manner which shows that he is still wandering and not awake to reality. Lycus, Thebes, the present danger, have passed out of his thoughts, which are occupied with an inopportune and a startling scruple. He has been long in the under-world, in 'the sunless deeps of Hades and Persephone'; he must not neglect the immediate duty of saluting the domestic gods. Amphitryon can scarcely believe his ears: 'You have been *there*, son! Really and truly?'—'Ay, and brought up to light the three-headed monster too!'—'Did you take him by force, or did the goddess give him to you?'—'Seized him victoriously; I had seen the Holy Mysteries.'—'And he is really now at the house of Erechtheus?'—'No, in the sanctuary of Chthonia[4] at Hermione[5].'—'And Eurystheus has not had news of your coming up again?'—'No; I came here first for news of home.'—'But why were you down there so long?'— 'Theseus was in Hades, father, and I stayed to rescue him.' —'And where is he now? Gone off to his own country?'— 'Gone to Athens, and glad to be out from below.' During these revelations, father and son, the former anxiously leading the way and the rest of the group with backward glances keeping step for step, have drawn near to the door. Having finished the story Heracles now composedly enters, mocking with fond rebukes the scared children and shaking woman who clutch at his dress. Let them come along in with him;

---

[1] *vv.* 588–592 should not be suspected. The lack of continuity between 592 and 593 is the result not of injury to the text, but of the speaker's agitation and the hearer's obstinacy.   [2] *v.* 595.

[3] Note the irrelevance of *vv.* 599–600, πρόσειπε…ἰδεῖν, to what follows, and also that it is to the irrelevant suggestion that Heracles attends, *vv.* 607 foll. Exactly what Amphitryon thinks of Heracles' behaviour, it is difficult to say. He has scarcely time to form an opinion. But he is clearly both surprised and alarmed.

[4] Demeter Chthonia, an equivalent or double of Persephone.

[5] A town at the east end of Argolis. See hereafter.

things are changed for the better (eh[1]?) since they came out; but why tears? there is nothing to cry for now; and why cling so? he has no wings; he is not going to fly away. What, they will not let go; they hold tighter and tighter! It must have been a terrible scare, a very, very near thing indeed. Well, he will be the big ship, and pull the little ships after him. (As a fact, we must suppose that they are pulling him, in an agony of impatient distress.) He is not ashamed to mind his babes. All men (he stays at the last moment to add this reflexion), all men are alike here: great and small, rich and poor, in loving their children all mankind are kin.

In primary meaning and present effect, this scene, it should seem, requires no commentary. It is evident that any man, great or small, who in such circumstances can so behave, is for the moment little short of mad; evident also, that for what is to come, immediately or eventually, the state of such a man is dangerous in the extreme. And at first sight, or first reading, this is perhaps all that we could here distinctly perceive. But more dimly we might already perceive the dawn of a new light upon the past, the first word of a terrible answer to the problem before propounded to us. Why are people found who entertain such extravagant beliefs about Heracles, since from the preponderant disbelief, and the futility of the professed evidence, we must suspect that those beliefs are not justified? We now begin to see why. To the report of his recent adventures, which Heracles has here made, plainly no faith is due or can be given. It cannot be taken seriously. The very manner of it, the off-hand, trivial tone (I have copied it to the best of my ability and invite comparison with the original), so unworthy of the tremendous theme, would justify us in supposing, if the author be presumed to have any sensibility, that the speaker is not fit to be heard. And when we also remark, that this prodigious version of the hero's descent into the cavern of Taenarum is not revealed to us until his mind, whatever was its condition before, has been manifestly disorganized by the shock of astonishment and rage, and that the only allusion which

---

[1] *v.* 623 ἄρα.

precedes that shock[1], has no such colour or suggestion of it,
but is perfectly compatible with such a conception of the
whole adventure as common experience would justify,—when
we see this, we are forced to suppose, as rational and un-
prejudiced spectators, that, upon this occasion at all events,
the reminiscences of Heracles are clouded, fluctuating, and at
present altogether untrustworthy. But what then of those
other reminiscences and reports, with which in times past he
may be presumed to have occasionally nourished the faith of
favourable recipients, such as the doting father and the
venerable as well as venerating friends? What was the
state of his mind, when he related, as sometimes he apparently
did, that the water-snakes of Lerna were all one snake, one
beast with ten thousand necks, that a Thracian chief kept
horses whose mangers were supplied with human flesh, that
there were horse-men in Arcadia, three-bodied men in
Erytheia, and beyond that, if you went far, far towards and
into the setting sun, there were—what was there not? What
part of these travels had he really made, and what things had
he truly found? The doubt, the suspicion, which cover this
last voyage to Taenarum, are seen, when we reflect, to spread
backwards over everything which he may have been led to
say of himself, especially in the unguarded freedom of
intimacy and the domestic circle. How much was mockery,
how much self-delusion? All is uncertain. Even if delusion
was never imputed to him before, and if his miracles have
passed at the worst, as with Lycus, for empty boasts, that
estimate, we see, will now have to be revised. Every one
knows that there is such a thing as latent insanity and a
mind volcanic, whose clouds and mutterings are unheeded or
misinterpreted until the fatal explosion. Is this the case of
Heracles?

Nor must we overlook, what, but for the pathos and tragedy
of the thing, would be ludicrous, the collapse, under a practical
test, of those high convictions, which the faithful so magnifi-

---

[1] *v.* 524, if indeed we can say that this alludes to Taenarum at all. But for the
sequel, the expression ἐς φάος μολών might well be understood as merely metaphorical for 'a joyful return.' See Aesch. *Agam.* 504, 508, 522 (Dindorf).

cently proclaimed. The Amphitryon of this play is a most pathetic figure, but he has a touch, a captivating touch, of the grotesque, and in the present situation this element is strongly apparent. Even before this, from the very first, a judicious observer might have suspected, that, for all his loudness and persistence, his faith in the divinity of his son, perhaps in divinity generally, is not very sound in quality. Men in whom religion has any depth of root, even rude and ill-instructed men, do not treat their deity like a gigantic but negligent policeman, to be called for if things get bad enough, though too probably he will be off duty and out of hearing. Amphitryon is one of that multitude, permanent in all degrees of barbarism and of civilization, whose religion is of this type ; and in his profession of belief in the divine quality and parentage of Heracles there was much more despair than reliance, as is now simply and conclusively proved. Heracles proposes to crush Thebes and its rebel garrison by the sole might of his victorious mace and winged archery. And why not? Towns are not commonly taken with a bow and arrows ; but Heracles so took one, or at least, so we were told[1]. Alone he routed the whole people of Orchomenus, or at least, so his father declared[2]; then why not the people of Thebes? Nay, and these were but little things on the roll of his achievements. What is Thebes or what are the Thebans, against a champion formidable to the assailants, and valuable to the defenders, of high Heaven itself[3]? If he once fought at the side of Zeus, why may it not be expected that, if wanted, Zeus will now fight at his side? The proposal of Heracles, if Amphitryon really and effectively believes what he has been telling us, should be accepted by him with complacent confidence, as a matter of course. Is it so accepted? It is deprecated with alarm as lively as if Heracles were—what Amphitryon in his heart knows him to be—a man and nothing more. Nor does it make any difference, that Heracles confirms the report, which arose upon his prolonged absence, that he had descended 'into Hades.' Amphitryon was sure

---

[1] v. 472.   [2] v. 220.   [3] v. 177.

of this before; but is he sure of it now? If so, what mean his 'really' and 'verily'?[1]

Not less eloquent is the behaviour of Megara. She, who in no extremity could fancy or pretend that her husband was more than ' the greatest of men[2],' hails him indeed nevertheless, in the natural extravagance of relief, as a saviour 'not less than Zeus.' Her trust, her hopes, her speech run before Amphitryon's, until the outbreak of her husband's passion reveals him —not himself[3]. And from that instant she utters not a word, but aids in trembling silence to coax him within the covert of the house[4]. Now as before, if the wife, in judgment of her husband, is more reasonable, quicker, and more far-sighted than the father, that may be partly because she knows more.

The coaxing is at last accomplished, and the Chorus remain alone. They, overcome by unwonted efforts and excitement, are unable to assist, scarcely able even to comprehend, and are conscious chiefly of their own immense weariness. The burden of age! That is the subject of their thoughts. Anything for youth! Cursed, cursed be age! A second youth—if merit could but have been rewarded with that! To age, only one thing is left—memory, a recording voice. Sing then they will, sing, if it were their swan-song, Heracles victorious, Heracles 'son of Zeus,' deadly to monsters dread and protector of human peace[5]. So they are singing, when Lycus with his guards re-enters, and Amphitryon, watching for him from within, issues to direct him into the trap.

In a few minutes[6] the usurper is trapped, and the Chorus are hailing the Restoration. His armed guard[7], the mark of his function, follow him into the house and share his fate. How many they are does not appear; but since Heracles on his side can command, if necessary, the slaves of the house[8], he may be supposed, with the advantage of surprise, to account easily for as many as may be thought convenient. The scene is brief, in due proportion to its momentary interest, and the

[1] *vv.* 610, 614.   [2] *v.* 150, and Megara's part *passim.*
[3] *vv.* 514–561.   [4] *vv.* 583–636, especially *v.* 626.   [5] *vv.* 637–700.
[6] *vv.* 701–733.   [7] *v.* 724. See also note on *v.* 729 in the Appendix.
[8] *vv.* 950 etc.

hymns of the elders[1] bring us back at once to the religious
and speculative question which continues to hold our attention.
Needless to say, the death of the scoffer is for the Chorus a
divine judgment, a manifest intervention of the gods, especially
of Zeus, and proves the utmost of their imaginations[1]: the
visit of Heracles to the lower world, and his escape therefrom, is now an unquestionable fact ('aye, that did he!')[2], and
the legend of the double paternity, in literal crudeness of
detail, rolls forth, with other picturesque and patriotic fictions,
in all the pomp of renewed and triumphant assurance[3]. But
alas, the true gods or true God, the Power of Nature and
fixed connexion of things[4], is otherwise minded, and returns
to these premature jubilations a prompt and withering reply.

The scene which here opens demands the most careful
consideration. More than anything else in the play, it is now
liable to misunderstanding, not from obscurity in the presentation designed by the dramatist, but from an undesigned and
unforeseen defect, with which, in studying ancient drama, we
must perpetually reckon,—the loss of the action and (if such
ever existed) of the equivalent stage-directions. It is easy to
imagine what problems Shakespeare (let us say) would present,
if he were printed like the *Poetae Scenici Graeci*, but not
quite so easy to bear in mind, that such is actually the
condition of Euripides. The scene now before us must appear
to be nonsense, hopelessly inconsistent with all that precedes
and follows it, unless we figure it as accompanied by certain
action, which can indeed be ascertained, by examination
sufficiently careful and comprehensive, from the bare text,
although a modern reader, especially if preoccupied, as he
well may be, by difficulties of another order, will certainly not
divine it without such examination.

Let us first observe (there is no difficulty so far), that what
here passes within the house, the central incident of the play,
is conveyed to us, the audience, twice. First we learn it
in outline (*vv.* 875—908) by cries and other sounds from
within, with comments by the Chorus, or their leader, without.

[1] *vv.* 756-814.   [2] *vv.* 770 (γε), 805 foll.
[3] *vv.* 794 foll., 798 foll.   [4] *Alcestis* 962 foll.

This passage, half-ruined in the MSS. by non-distinction of parts, was elucidated, I believe for the first time, in the edition of Professor U. von Wilamowitz-Möllendorff, and little more, if anything, remained to be suggested[1]. Next (*vv.* 922—1016) it is related to us fully by an eye-witness. The thing itself, in its main outline, though horrible and to the actors in it astounding, should be no surprise to the attentive and undistracted observer of what has passed before. The insane excitement of Heracles, naturally not assuaged but irritated by the slaying of Lycus, breaks out afresh with increased violence in a new direction. Even the direction has been foreshadowed. We have seen that his mind, even in calmer hours of the past, has been visited by the imagination of dethroning and dispossessing the king of Argos[2]. We have seen him, both long ago[3] and recently[4], haunted by the vision of impossible feats, performed or to be performed by his single prowess—fortresses captured by his arrows, and castles razed by his hands. And now in a torrent of delirium these long-gathering delusions unite. After casting the dead enemy out of doors[5], he assembles the household for a rite of purification, a proceeding (be it noted) consistent indeed with his strange obtrusion, when Lycus was still alive and at large, of his desire to salute the domestic gods[6], but proving in itself that he has not come to his senses. The family are still in extreme peril : they must be attacked soon and may be attacked instantly. Even the Chorus realize that the battle of the good cause is still to be fought[7]. To fly or to prepare for resistance is the only alternative ; and the purification of the house is at such a moment preposterous. But, as we have ourselves seen[8], Heracles is beyond control. However, it does cross his mind (and this is perhaps the most subtle touch in the delineation), it does occur to him, as he is about to commence the ceremony, that the performance is premature, that something is to be done and someone to be fought, before the purification can be

[1] See the text of Prof. Murray.   [2] *v.* 462.
[3] *v.* 472.   [4] *vv.* 565 foll.   [5] See the narrative *vv.* 922 foll.
[6] *v.* 609.   [7] *vv.* 811–814.   [8] *vv.* 585–636.

well done and once for all[1]. He pauses, and then—his
countenance changes, his eyes start out, and crying with a
wild laugh 'The death of Eurystheus! That should come
first,' he sets forth in fancy to breach the fortifications of
Mycenae, and to extirpate his imaginary rival. The expedition, conducted within four walls, ends not until his own
wife and three children lie dead by his hand. His father is
barely saved by a chance blow, received by the madman from
the falling ruins of the chamber, which he, by a turn in his
delusion, interprets fortunately[2]. He sinks exhausted, and
sleeps, and the survivors bind him to a pillar lying amid the
wreck.

Such, clear as terrible, is the report from within; but a
new element, and a dubious, has been added to the story by
what has passed without while these things were being done.
Between the close of the triumphal ode and the outbreak of
the hero's delirium, the interval is filled as follows:

The forms of Iris and Madness appear above the palace.

Chorus.　　　Ha see! ha see!
On you, on me, doth this same panic fall?
Old friends, what phantom hovereth o'er the hall?
　　Ah flee! ah flee
With haste of laggard feet!—speed thou away!
　　Healer, to thee,
O King, to avert from me yon bane I pray!
Iris.　　　Fear not: this is the child of Night ye see,
Madness, grey sires: I, handmaid of the Gods,
Iris. We come not for your city's hurt.
Only on one man's house do we make war—
His, whom Zeus' and Alcmena's son they call.
For, till he had ended all his bitter toils
Fate shielded him, and Father Zeus would not
That I, or Hera, wrought him ever harm.
But, now he hath toiled Eurystheus' labours through,
·Hera will stain him with the blood of kin,
That he shall slay his sons: her will is mine.
On then, close up thine heart from touch of ruth,
O thou unwedded child of murky Night:
With madness thrill this man, with soul-turmoil

---

[1] *vv.* 928–938.
[2] *vv.* 1001–1006, compared with *vv.* 900–908; see Prof. Murray's text.

Child-murdering, with wild boundings of the feet :
Goad him ; the sheets of murder's sails let out,
That, when o'er Acheron's ferry his own hand
In blood hath sped his crown of goodly sons,
Then may he learn how dread is Hera's wrath,
And mine, against him : else the Gods must wane
And mortals wax, if he shall not be punished.

Madness.   Of noble sire and mother was I born,
Even of the blood of Uranus and Night,
But not to do despite to friends I hold
My powers, nor love to haunt for murder's sake.
Fain would I plead with Hera and with thee,
E'er she have erred, if ye will heed my words.
This man, against whose house ye thrust me on,
Nor on the earth is fameless, nor in heaven.
The pathless land, the wild sea, hath he tamed,
And the Gods' honours hath alone restored,
When these by impious men were overthrown.
Therefore I plead, devise no monstrous wrong.

But the scruples of the pious fiend are peremptorily
silenced by the divine emissary : the fiend consents, under
protest, to compel Heracles to the slaughter of his family, and
the scene concludes thus :

Madness.   ...See him—lo, his head he tosses in the fearful race begun !
See his gorgon-glaring eyeballs all in silence wildly rolled !
Like a bull in act to charge, with fiery pantings uncontrolled
Awfully he bellows, howling to the fateful fiends of Hell !
Wilder yet shall be thy dance, as peals my pipe's appalling
    knell !
—Ay, unto Olympus soaring, Iris, tread thy path serene !
Mine the task into the halls of Heracles to plunge unseen.
        Iris ascends, and Madness enters the palace[1].

Now what is the meaning of this apparition ? Of what
nature are these personages, the demon or personification of
Frenzy and the mythical maid-servant of Olympus, who
declare themselves to be the immediate authors, and Hera to
be the cause, of the hideous act which ensues ? Upon the
answer to these questions depends the entire drama. The
answer currently accepted is, that these personages are real,
that is to say, real in the same sense in which any part of the

[1] *vv.* 815–873 (Way).

representation is real, real as Heracles or Amphitryon, their actions being really parts of what, for the purpose of the drama, we are to suppose and believe to happen. If so, let us agree (there is no help for it) that the play is 'a grotesque abortion,' and have done with it. For the play (let us recall once more) is to lead us presently to the proposition that *there is not and cannot be any such thing as deity having passions and desires*[1]. This proposition is to be put in the mouth of a man who would have been able, according to Hellenic belief, to disprove it by his own history and experiences. If the dramatist does not mean us to take it as true for the purpose of his story, then he means nothing, and his play is nought. But how can we so take it, or suppose the author to maintain it, if he exhibits, as assumptions essential to his story, the personality of Iris and the existence of a jealous Hera? Are these then deities incapable of passion or desire?

Here therefore, as in almost every case where superhuman or supernatural persons are introduced into tragedy by Euripides[2], we are compelled to suppose them unreal. But the present example differs in one most important respect from those otherwise parallel. The supernatural figures of Euripides are in general so introduced, so placed in the drama, that they can, as the dramatist intends, be dropped off. The ghost of Polydorus, who speaks the prologue of the *Hecuba*, the Apollo, who pronounces the epilogue of the *Orestes*, are superfluous to the real action, which in the *Hecuba* begins with the exit of Polydorus, and in the *Orestes* ends with the entrance of Apollo. In the case of the *Heracles* such treatment is impossible, from the position, unique in the extant works of Euripides[3], which the apparition occupies in the play, imbedded in the centre, and morticed, if the metaphor is permissible, into the action which precedes and follows. The Apollo of the *Orestes* is nothing at all, not even a fiction for dramatic purposes[4]. Iris and Madness must be something; and yet, if the play as

---

[1] *vv.* 1341–1346.
[2] The single certain exception is the phantom in *Helen*, which *probat regulam*. Debateable exceptions are the *Hippolytus* and the *Bacchae*.
[3] The *Rhesus* being doubtful. [4] See the essay on the *Orestes*, hereafter.

a whole is to have meaning, they cannot be real.   What then are they?

To shape the question is already to suggest the answer. They are, they must be, *a vision*, the picture of some one's imagination, presented externally for theatrical convenience, but not supposed to have any reality other than that of the imagining mind.   The device is familiar enough, and occurs, for instance, in Shakespeare's *Richard III*.   That play is such, in its historical foundation and colouring generally, that the introduction into it of a personage like the Ghost in *Hamlet*, conversing and interacting with the human actors, would be felt as a dramatic solecism.   But no such offence is caused, or difficulty raised, when the guilty imaginations of the sleeping Richard are presented by figures that move and speak.   Their motion, speech, and being are for the sleeper ; whether they have any existence external to his dreams, whether he would still see them if he woke, is a question which need not be raised, but which, if it were raised, might be answered in the negative without prejudice to the story and the action.

If then Iris and Madness be, as we are compelled to suppose, a dream, by whom, so to put it, are they dreamed? By the Chorus.   It is expressly indicated[1] (and the indication is surely significant) that Madness is not perceived when she goes within.   Even Heracles in his frenzy never sees, or imagines himself to see, the being by whose terrors, if the supernatural actors are to be credited, that frenzy is actually produced[2]. The question becomes then this : are the Chorus, during the mythical scene, supposed to perceive the mythical personages with the bodily senses, or with the mind and imagination—to see them, or to dream them?   How, in the absence of stage-directions, is this question to be put to the test?   There is at least one test which, according to common sense and common experience, will be decisive.   That which we see, we can

---

[1] *v.* 872–873 ; note ἄφαντοι.

[2] Compare carefully *vv.* 858–873 with the subsequent narrative (*vv.* 922 foll.), and contrast the dramatic treatment in Sophocles *Ajax* 1–133.   If Madness were to be conceived as a reality, independent of a percipient or percipients, the very nature of her function would require that she should at all events be perceived by Heracles.

remember, and, if it be impressive, must remember ; also we believe it. That which we dream, we often cannot remember at all, and seldom with precision ; also we do not take it for fact, none of us, not even, as a general rule, those who are called believers in dreams. Now upon these familiar and obvious premises, *it is certain that Euripides, if he had any care for truth and probability, did not represent the Chorus as seeing the supernatural apparition, because, when it is past, they do not believe or even remember it.* Of this fact we are assured in the only possible way, that is, negatively, by their silence about the apparition, by their not mentioning or alluding to it, and this throughout a series of situations such that reticence, if the thing were in their consciousness, would be inconceivable. From the moment (*v.* 908) when Madness, if as a person she exists, is supposed to have quitted the house, to the end of the play, is one long scene of 500 verses, more than a third of the whole. The Chorus are present throughout. The dialogue turns wholly upon the recent delirium of Heracles ; and its cause, its connexion in particular with the enmity of Hera, is repeatedly mentioned as matter of inference and debate, assumed by Amphitryon and Heracles, accepted by Theseus, and again by Heracles contemptuously ignored[1], when in the passage before mentioned he denies the very existence of such deities. All this the Chorus, though they speak often, allow to pass without a hint that they were witnesses of the divine action, seeing the emissaries of Hera with their eyes and hearing them with their ears. They behave, in short, exactly as if no such thing had occurred, behaviour inexplicable unless we suppose the thing to have utterly passed out of their consciousness, or, in other words, to have been not an experience but a dream.

We infer then necessarily that the theatrical performance, during the supposed presence of the apparitions, must convey this, must show that the Chorus are not, in the common sense of the word, conscious of what passes before their minds. The text confirms this. The entrance of the slave[2], who narrates

---

[1] See *vv.* 1086, 1127, 1135, 1191, 1303–1310, 1311–1312, 1340–1346, 1393 and *passim. vv.* 1311–1312 are probably spoken by the Chorus themselves.

[2] *v.* 909.

the delirium, is the first point, after the apparition, at which the elders take part in a dialogue, and thereby prove themselves to be awake. And here it is plain that they are awakened :

Slave. O eld-white forms of men !
An Elder. Thou call'st ! What is't, O what?
Slave (pointing). The horrors there within !
An Elder. No prophet truer than I !
Slave. Dead...the children...(*The Elders shriek*). Ah, cry, for there is cause !
An Elder. Murder...fell murder...the father's hands...Ah !
Slave. No words can surpass the fact.
An Elder. How went this woeful deed, done, as thou revealest, by the father on his sons? Tell the way of it. Recount this horror, launched on the house by fate, the children's hapless end.

Every sentence here points to the same inference. The very language of the address, *O eld-white forms of men* (ὦ λευκὰ γήρᾳ σώματα), suggests the situation, and the posture of the Chorus at the moment. There is no reason to suppose that this is, or could be, a mere equivalent for γέροντες, or that old men, as such and in all circumstances, could be addressed as 'age-whitened bodies.' But if they are found recumbent, sitting or lying upon the palace-steps, in attitudes of uneasy rest, which expose the feeble frames and the overflowing of long white hair and long white beards, then the address is natural. So also, but not otherwise, is the startled reply, 'Thou call'st ! What is't?' (ἀνακαλεῖς με τίνα βοάν ;). So, above all, is the exclamation of one, that he foreboded some horrible disclosure, was sure of it, sure as any prophet. If we suppose that the action of Iris and Madness has been witnessed by the elders in an ordinary manner, has been perceived by their senses, and that they are, as then they must be, now conscious of having witnessed it, this talk of foreboding, of anticipation, is unintelligible. A foreboding ! What is left to forebode ? A goddess, delegated by the Queen of Heaven, told them in the plainest possible words, that Heracles was to be forthwith driven mad, and compelled to murder his children. They have seen the demon Frenzy enter the house, with the declared purpose of executing this command. They have interpreted the series of cries, voices, and other sounds by which, to persons so informed, the progress of the tragedy is signified in outline without possibility of mistake¹. And now, on hearing of the horrors within, they are to talk of their prophetic souls, and receive as a 'revelation' (ἀμφαίνεις) the news that the children are dead!

Manifestly the elders here have no knowledge whatever, no definite impression, of what has passed, except and until they are told by the slave. Of what they may have dreamed, or half-perceived, they retain no more, as commonly is the case, than the vague sensation, familiar to dreamers, of being sure that *something* has happened. In the fact that one of them, without prompting, describes the involuntary murder as 'fate-sent' or 'heaven-sent,' we may perhaps see a faint trace of the vanished vision, perhaps, but not necessarily, the supposition of a compelling power being in such cases commonplace and instinctive².

From the awakening we turn to the falling asleep, but without expectation of finding a note of it in the dialogue. From the nature of the case there cannot be any such note, for the slumber of the aged men is of course unprepared and involuntary. Their extreme feebleness, marked and accented throughout³ for the purpose of this scene, and recently forced upon our notice by the appropriation of a whole interlude to the subject⁴, accounts naturally for the incident, which is exhibited merely by their action. Accustomed to seclusion and repose, and exhausted by strain of body and mind, upon the first relaxation of the strain they just drop, as people say, where they stand. The reaction is shown in the concluding verses of the preceding ode, by abrupt changes of thought, accompanied doubtless by corresponding changes in

---

¹ *vv.* 875–908.
² According to the common distribution, assumed in the translation of *v.* 914, the Chorus, after being told that the children are dead, do divine, as they very well may, that they have been murdered, and by Heracles. But this distribution is not certain. A possible division would be: XO. δάιοι φόνοι. ΑΓ. δάιοι δὲ τοκέων χέρες. XO. ὤ. ΑΓ. οὐκ ἄν τις εἴποι κ.τ.λ. I think this perhaps preferable, but either way it is equally clear that now, and not till now, they come to the knowledge of what has been done.
³ *vv.* 107 foll., 268 foll., 637 foll. and *passim.*   ⁴ *vv.* 637 foll.

the music and action.   To the proud hymn of praise and thanksgiving succeeds the remark[1], that Heracles is a better lord for Thebes than a base-born ruler such as Lycus, a comparison scarcely complimentary to the hero and strangely deficient in enthusiasm, but explicable, if we allow for the narrow intensity of Greek patriotism, and remember that Heracles is no Theban, but is to rise upon the extinction of the true line, the male heirs of the house of Creon.   And will he rise after all?   Suddenly and somewhat tardily the elders reflect, that the battle with rebellion is yet to be fought: 'That issue points our view to a contest of rival swords, which shall prove whether the good cause hath still the blessing of heaven[2].' They cease; but the music we may suppose to continue, probably throughout the whole scene of the apparition[3], which is to be conceived as operatic, a passage in recitative.   Pondering their doubts, they group themselves near and upon the broad steps which lead up to the house, and sink down here and there in the sudden sleep of old age. Then and not till then, their chief, who plays the dreamer, betrays his inward agitation by a start and a cry, 'See, O see! This fear which throbs through me, do ye feel it too?...Above the house I see...To fly, to fly!...Up, stiffened limbs, away! Apollo save us!'; and overhead the forms of his day-dream roll forth into the air.

That the vision, as acted, is common in its details to many minds, is of course not to be supposed, and would not be suggested by the performance.   One alone[4], the speaker just cited,

---

[1] *v.* 809.

[2] *vv.* 811–814.   The antecedent to the relative ἅ (neuter plural, *which matter*) is the idea of alternative and choice—Heracles or another Lycus—suggested by the preceding comparison.   Whether we read φαίνει (MSS.) here and ἐφάνη (Hermann) in *v.* 794, or, with Prof. Murray, get exact syllabic responsion by retaining ἔφανε there and substituting it here, does not affect the sense.

[3] *vv.* 815–908.

[4] This I think on the whole most probable, but the distribution of the passages (*vv.* 815–821, 874–908) is here, as always, conjectural.   If several *choreutae* speak, the total effect will be still the same.   The action also is of course conjectural in detail, depending on many theatrical arrangements which are open to different supposition.   But all this is of no importance to us now.   The general nature of the situation is the only thing significant to a reader, and that is ascertainable from the text.

reveals by voice and motions an answering impression, first in full sleep[1], and afterwards, during the enactment of the tragedy within, between asleep and awake[2]; and to his mind, so far as to any, the pictured imagination is to be referred. But in truth it is rather a symbol than an actual presentation, showing, as in the similar example cited from Shakespeare, the type and trend of the dreaming, translated into terms of theatrical convention. By the fact that it figures a dream or dreams we are to explain its fantastic wildness and inconsistency—the goddess-messenger with the temper, as has been truly said, of a *dame de compagnie*[3], the so-called Frenzy, who rationally expostulates with her employers upon the folly and cruelty of her errand. Never did any one, with his full mind, entertain conceptions so grotesquely horrible. But they are proper enough to a phantasmagoria. Hera, Iris, and the like, are phantoms (so the dramatist would suggest) such as, with suitable occasion, might arise in feeble minds, unhappily prepared by habit and beyond the control of reason. Nor has he omitted to provide the suitable occasion. If we ask (it is a fair question) why the old men should just now dream after this fashion, the answer is obvious, that their dreams are a disordered reflexion or suggestion from their previous experience when awake. That the mind of Heracles is in the most perilous state, they have had opportunity to observe. Had they been cool and vigorous, they would have observed this fully and consciously, and would have deduced from it a lively and rational apprehension of the consequences to be feared or expected. Being what they are, and situated as they are, they have still observed it in a vague half-conscious manner; and out of their underlying suspicions arises, released by sleep, the horrid travesty of the vision, not a fact, but a sort of theological nightmare.

For in fact, let us finally remark, it is *not* by Hera, by Iris, or by a demon-emissary, that Heracles is now driven mad, because he is not *now*, and for the first time, maddened by any agency whatever. He is mad before; we have been shown that he is so, in a scene which never would have been intro-

---

[1] *vv.* 815–873.   [2] *vv.* 874–908.   [3] von Wilamowitz-Möllendorff.

duced by the author, if he had really intended us to suppose, that the second and fiercer fit of delirium is suddenly inflicted by a supernatural interposition. The true cause of the delirium lies deep in the past, in the inscrutable nature and order of things. It is still to be traced for us a little further than it has been traced as yet; but one thing we know already, that it is *not* attributable to the arbitrary and capricious interference of divine jealousy, to the revenge of Hera. Hera herself is nought, the dream of dotards, and "such things are poets' miserable tales."

It was open however then, it is open still, to a spectator or reader so minded, to put another value upon the dream, to believe, with Clytaemnestra in Aeschylus[1], that the darkening of the eye is the enlightening of the soul, and that what the elders so behold is indeed a glimpse of the spiritual world. The question has been debated from antiquity to this day; the author of the *Heracles* had an opinion upon it, which among other things is expressed in his play. Freedom to take the Aeschylean view he was forced to leave, perhaps by the peril of the law, certainly by the force of truth; for that the gods may be seen in dreams is a fact. What was required for his own freedom, for the sense and possibility of his work, was that the gods of popular imagination should be visible, if at all, by that inner light and no other. And this he is careful to secure. To the tragic effect of this particular scene, the choice of mental interpretation is indifferent. That the best and mightiest of us are liable to such an overthrow as here befalls Heracles, is horrible if we attribute it to the jealousy of Hera, but not less so, if with Euripides we refuse that explanation and all explanations, and leave the first cause an inscrutable mystery. But to this tragedy as a whole, and to the interests of humanity, the choice is so far from indifferent that comparatively no other thing matters at all. To this hour it is in controversy and seems likely so to remain. Euripides had his opinion.

And now—to proceed with the facts—we are shown the

---

[1] *Eum.* 104.

interior of the house[1], the madman asleep and bound, with his dead lying around him. The miserable Amphitryon enters, but dares not approach, until something is known of his son's condition[2]. At length Heracles stirs and wakes, but his senses and memory are still under a cloud. He sees the dead, but without recognition. The sight only suggests to him a passing suspicion that he has descended again into Hades 'as I did erewhile'; for this impression persists. But since there is

> no rock of Sisyphus in view,
> No Pluto, nor his queen, Demeter's Maid,

he concludes to the contrary[3]. The trivial tone and childish reasoning jar painfully with the theme of these imaginary remembrances, and most pathetically with the actual horrors of the scene. At his cry for help, his father and one of the elders[4] draw near and, finding him quiet, venture to release him, and gradually open his eyes and his mind to the truth. His first thought is of suicide; but recognizing, in a figure at this moment approaching, his friend and cousin Theseus, he is diverted to the desire of hiding his shame, and flings himself with covered face upon the ground.

The arrival of the king of Athens brings immediately to a test the question, if it can be supposed to remain open, whether there is any truth in the miraculous story which Héracles has related during his insanity, whether he has or has not recently descended into Hades. In this story Theseus himself, we remember, played a remarkable part, being found in Hades by Heracles, brought back to light, and dismissed to Attica[5]. Here then is a decisive witness for or against. The cause of his arrival is, as we divine even before we are told, the news of the revolution in Thebes.

---

[1] The brief recitative which precedes these changes of scene (*vv.* 1017–1028) is a mere rest for the strained attention of the audience. For such a purpose the mythological and allusive style is perfectly fit. One is scarcely expected even to hear what is said.

[2] *vv.* 1042–1086. [3] *vv.* 1089–1105.

[4] *v.* 1110. Here, as indeed throughout, it is apparent that for this play at all events orchestra and scene were undivided.

[5] *vv.* 618–621.

He has brought to the assistance of his relatives an Athenian army, now encamped in the neighbourhood[1]. This military intervention, we may observe in passing, is for the course of the action an ingenious, because simple and natural, device. The Athenian forces are naturally supposed by the audience to keep the Theban rebels, who hold the fortress but have lost their leader, efficiently in check. The politics of Thebes, no longer required as machinery, drop quietly into the background, and we can attend without distraction to the hero, and to the question of the moment—what, if anything, has Theseus to tell us about the journey to Hades?

And what is the answer? Well, here is the strangest thing in the play, a thing which, though some phenomena more or less similar may be found in Euripides, will scarcely be paralleled from any other author in the world. Here is the thing, and the only thing, which justified us in classing the *Heracles* with the *Ion* and *Alcestis*, as plays which have the appearance of a puzzle. *There is no answer* to our question, none positive and clear, none which could be ascertained by a mere spectator, following the scene as it proceeds, having no previous knowledge, and unable to revise his impressions. The only thing obvious and superficially certain is, that upon this vital question, the participation or non-participation of Theseus in the alleged experiences of Heracles in Hades, the most attentive spectator could not, from the spectacle merely, collect a sure opinion. The more attentive he was, the more certainly would he conceive a doubt, and retain that doubt to the end.

Broadly speaking indeed, all the evidence is on one side, and that the side, which, when we have got and can review the entire drama, when we have heard the final and conclusive opinion of Heracles upon the gods of mythology, we know to be supported by the dramatist. The whole personality and character of Theseus is, as we shall presently see, such as to make unentertainable the notion of his having passed a time of sojourn in the fabled world of the dead. One might as well suppose such a thing of one's next-door neighbour.

[1] *vv.* 1163–1168.

Almost all that he says is *prima facie* inconsistent with any such supposition, and many things which he says are absolutely and finally irreconcilable with it. But nevertheless in a few places he does allude to something, which *might* be the recent rescue from the underworld, described by Heracles in the first attack of his madness. And it is manifest that, if a negative answer to our question were meant to be obvious, these *possible* allusions to the miraculous expedition would not have appeared in the dialogue. Such is in brief the strange state of the case. The testimony of Theseus respecting the journey to Hades is deliberately and carefully left, for a spectator, uncertain. Several times we seem to approach the subject, and *never* do we get any decisive statement about it.

But in truth this very uncertainty is itself evidence, and decisive evidence, for the same conclusion respecting the purport of the entire play, to which everything, except these disputable allusions, consistently points. For if Euripides had meant to adopt the journey to Hades as part of his story, why should there be, and how could there be, any ambiguity about it? What conceivable motive could an author have for throwing a shade of doubt upon a point in his story, if what he meant to allege was a thing generally received as an article of popular faith? Concealment, ambiguity, evasion, about the facts alleged and supposed in a drama, is a thing in itself inartistic, injurious, and absurd. If a question of fact, vital to the story, is left uncertain, that must be because the story really requires, and is meant to signify, such an answer to the question as the author dared not unequivocally express. If Euripides had meant us to suppose that his Heracles and his Theseus have been together in Hades, he would have made them say so in plain terms, and not have allowed them to suggest anything to the contrary. As a fact, they talk and act the negative all the time; and when, once and again, they seem to suggest an affirmative, it is never in plain terms. When we have time to consider this treatment, the conclusion is certain. The negative is the proposition of the drama, and the semblances of affirmation will assuredly, if examined, be found susceptible of some explanation consistent with the general sense.

Let us now look more closely at both sides of the question; and first let us consider the broad, and in truth irrefragable, mass of evidence that the Heracles and Theseus of this play have not been in Hades together, that neither of them has been in Hades at all.

According to the story which we have heard from Heracles[1], he and Theseus, having emerged together from Hades, have recently parted, at some place not specified but apparently in the Peloponnese, to pursue each his journey home, Heracles having for companion the captive Cerberus. As we saw, this story was told in such circumstances as almost to disprove itself, and in a manner which, to cool and fully competent hearers, would certainly disprove it. We may not know much about Hell; but we do know or feel, all of us, that it is not, in the profane phrase of Shelley, 'a city much like London.' And in the Greek world, as in all ages, a man who professed to have travelled beyond the mouth of Hades, and who reported his travels exactly as if they had been made on this side, would simply have proved, to cool and competent hearers, that he had not been there. But suppose for a moment that this monstrous story is fact, what should now be the thought and language of Theseus? What could it be but enquiry about Heracles? What has befallen him? Has he reached Thebes? Has he been heard of? The danger of the family is but an additional reason for such enquiries as to the fate and whereabouts of their natural protector. But what do we find? We find, without surprise, that Theseus knows nothing whatever of his friend's recent absence, but assumes, as a matter of course, that he is with the rest of the family at Thebes. On hearing of the rebellion, 'I came in force,' says he to Amphitryon, '*to the aid of your son*[2].' Not only so, but from the manner in which he speaks of the rumour, about Lycus and his enterprise, which 'came to Athens,' it is impossible to suppose that his own presence at Athens requires any

[1] *vv.* 607–621.   [2] *v.* 1165.

explanation, impossible to suppose that he had arrived there, recently and barely in time, from Hades or anywhere else. In all that he says, it is manifest that he has made no recent journey, and is unaware that Heracles has made any ; so that, merely by his opening words, the miraculous narrative, given by Heracles in his insanity, is instantly and finally exploded. Not having heard it, and not hearing it now (since all are too full of the present to investigate the past), he cannot contradict it ; but he ignores it, here and everywhere, and his ignorance is contradiction enough.

So also is his bearing and his whole personality. To appreciate this fully, one must go to the original ; but as his character is, from this point onwards, an important factor in the effect, we must essay a summary description of it. Though not an extraordinary person, but rather the contrary, he is for this reason well adapted to his function in the drama. Kind, loyal, generous, and chivalrous, he is, with all this and above all, what no one else in the play can be called, emphatically a man, a man in the full vigour of his manhood, but a normal man, of the normal human pattern, neither above nor below. His religion in particular, which the circumstances bring into prominence, is, if one may so say, superlatively commonplace. His conduct and counsels are in reality guided by motives altogether mundane—natural affection, natural sympathy, and that desire of public approval and fear of general censure, which were so strong in the Greeks, *praeter laudem nullius avaris*. In speculation he takes, like the majority of men, little interest, and is properly neither believer nor dissenter[1]. The current notions about the gods he rather supposes to be true ; and he warmly approves those semi-religious observances, more important in the Greek world than they are now, which offer to good men, that is, to men generally esteemed, the prospect of posthumous remembrance. But a personal creed, a passionate hope, a theory of life and death and the Powers above, these things are beyond him. His calm acquiescence in the popular conception of Olympus presents an equal contrast to the wavering faith of Amphitryon on the one

[1] See particularly *vv.* 1313–1339.

hand, and on the other, to the furious irony and the lofty speculation of Heracles. That such a person has been in contact with the unseen world, or has lights from his own experience upon the destiny of man and the problem of the grave, is a notion not to be entertained with gravity; and as for his having been in Hades, and recently, and with Heràcles, his single reference to that abode, as the place where his friend 'will go when he dies[1],' confirms the irresistible inference from his silence.

> No mortal hath escaped misfortune's taint,
> Nor God—if minstrel-legends be not false.
> Have they not linked them in unlawful bonds
> Of wedlock, and with chains, to win them thrones,
> Outraged their fathers? In Olympus still
> They dwell, by their transgressions unabashed.
> What wilt thou plead, if, mortal as thou art,
> Thou chafe against thy fate, and Gods do not?
>   Nay then, leave Thebes, submissive to the law,
> And unto Pallas' fortress come with me.
> There will I cleanse thine hands from taint of blood,
> Give thee a home, and of my substance half.
> The gifts my people gave for children saved
> Twice seven, when I slew the Knossian bull,
> These will I give thee. All throughout the land
> Have I demesnes assigned me : these shall bear
> Thy name henceforth with men while thou shalt live.
> *And when in death thou goest to Hades' halls,*
> With sacrifice and monuments of stone
> Shall all the Athenians' town exalt thy name :
> For a fair crown to win from Greeks is this
> For us, the glory of a hero helped[2].

Is it necessary or possible to discuss, whether this speaker is supposed by the dramatist to have sojourned, a living prisoner, in the world of the dead, and to have escaped therefrom, within the last few days, by the aid of the man to whom he is speaking?

But on the other hand, equally visible, in the speeches of Theseus and in his conversation with Heracles, is the occurrence from time to time of allusions which would be

---

[1] *v.* 1331 ; and see Heracles, *v.* 1247.   [2] *vv.* 1314–1335 (Way).

taken *prima facie* as referring to the deliverance of Theseus by Heracles from the underworld, allusions which certainly would not appear, in their actual form, unless the dramatist had intended to leave on this question a shade of doubt and a loophole of escape from the negative conclusion. There are four such allusions, all very similar. ' I come here,' says Theseus to Amphitryon, ' to requite Heracles for his good deed in rescuing me from underground.'

τίνων δ' ἀμοιβὰς ὧν ὑπῆρξεν Ἡρακλῆς
σώσας με νέρθεν ἦλθον¹.

And again to Heracles himself : ' I reck not if with you I suffer, as once with you I was fortunate. Let this day be set off against that, when you brought me safe to light from among the dead. For a gratitude that wanes with time I detest,' and so on.

οὐδὲν μέλει μοι σύν γε σοὶ πράσσειν κακῶς·
καὶ γάρ ποτ' εὐτύχησ'· ἐκεῖσ' ἀνοιστέον,
ὅτ' ἐξέσωσάς μ' ἐς φάος νεκρῶν πάρα.
χάριν δὲ γηράσκουσαν ἐχθαίρω φίλων²,...

And again, when he offers to Heracles a home in Athens : ' I on my part will thus repay and requite you for my rescue.'

κἀγὼ χάριν σοι τῆς ἐμῆς σωτηρίας
τήνδ' ἀντιδώσω³.

And again at the last, when he would make Heracles summon his courage to part from the corpses of the wife and children : ' If one should see you womanish, he would not praise!' *Heracles.* ' Have I lived to be in your sight low? It was not so once, methinks.' *Theseus.* ' Truly too low. In this weakness, you are not the Heracles of your fame.' *Heracles.* ' What were you like yourself in your trouble underground ?' *Theseus.* ' In point of courage, nothing could be less than I was.'

ΘΗ.   εἴ σ' ὄψεταί τις θῆλυν ὄντ', οὐκ αἰνέσει.
ΗΡ.   ζῶ σοὶ ταπεινός; ἀλλὰ πρόσθεν οὐ δοκῶ.

¹ *v.* 1169.   ² *v.* 1220.   ³ *v.* 1336.

ΘΗ. ἄγαν γ'· ὁ κλεινὸς Ἡρακλῆς οὐκ εἶ νοσῶν.
ΗΡ. σὺ ποῖος ἦσθα νέρθεν ἐν κακοῖσιν ὤν;
ΘΗ. ὡς ἐς τὸ λῆμα παντὸς ἦν ἥσσων ἀνήρ[1].

With these four allusions we might join, as possibly
bearing on the topic, a reference by Heracles, addressing
Theseus, to the supposed Cerberus[2]. But as this does not
mention the rescue, and does not, on the face of it, presuppose
any connexion between the thing mentioned and Theseus,
it will be best considered separately. Let us confine our
attention for the present to the rescue.

As to this, we are presented with a plain alternative.
Either the import of the whole interview between Heracles
and Theseus, and of the whole play, is nonsense ; or these
allusions, however they may appear at first sight, do not
really, according to the intention of the dramatist, refer to
Hades or to the recent expedition of Heracles at all. And
it is visible in the allusions themselves, visible at a second
glance, that they do not.

The mere wording of them proves this. An author who
wrote of Hades, of the unseen world, the habitation of
departed souls, the abode of Sisyphus and Tantalus, the realm
of Pluto and Persephone—an author who meant to indicate
that certain living men of flesh and blood had sojourned
or travelled in that world, who had in his thoughts things
so terribly distinct as these, could scarcely fail, even in a
single allusion, to use some term or turn of phrase which
clearly and indisputably meant what he meant. In the course
of repeated allusions, he could not possibly fail. Four times,
we should have to suppose, does Euripides say, or intend
to say, that his Theseus has been 'in Hades.' And yet not
once does he say it. Not once does he use a word or
expression which is applicable to a world of departed souls
and to nothing else. By mere accident, we should have to
suppose, all the references may, upon the face of them, be
referred to some totally different matter, some incident
mundane, familiar, and commonplace. Such a series of
improbable accidents is perfectly impossible.

---

[1] vv. 1412–1416.　　　　[2] v. 1386.

We may prove this by a direct and simple test. Mr
Way's translation of Euripides is, as we have often seen,
remarkable for a close and almost verbal fidelity, seldom
achieved in the form of verse. Unquestionably he intends
and supposes himself to have represented Euripides, in these
four passages, as exactly as the English language permits.
But Mr Way comes to them with the thought, which he
attributes to Euripides, that they refer to Hades. Now of the
four, one[1] cannot be made explicit in this reference without
great and voluntary alteration. Three, though they are
not explicit, can be made so by slight and involuntary
alteration. What is the result? That they are made explicit,
that two out of the three become, in Mr Way's version,
applicable to 'Hades' and to nothing else.

> And to requite the service done of him
> Who *out of Hades* saved me, came I, ancient,
> If aught ye need mine hand or mine allies[2].

> Nought reck I of misfortune, shared with thee.
> Fair lot hath found me—I date it from that hour
> When safe to-day thou brought'st me from the dead[3].

Theseus.   Who sees thee play the woman thus shall scorn.
Heracles.   Live I, thy scorn? Once was I not, I trow.
Theseus.   Alas, yes! Where is glorious Heracles?
Heracles.   What manner of man wast thou *'mid Hades' woes*?
Theseus.   My strength of soul was utter weakness then[4].

And similarly, in the supposed allusion to Cerberus[5], which
we shall consider hereafter, Mr Way writes 'Cerberus,' as any
man, who meant Cerberus, instinctively would. But Euripides
speaks of 'a dog,' and, unless we correct him, of 'an unhappy
dog,' as no man, who thought of Cerberus, possibly could.

Equally decisive is the test by Euripides himself, by the
play itself. Amphitryon is meant by Euripides to assert that
Heracles has passed through Taenarum 'into Hades[6],' and he

---

[1] At *v.* 1336 Mr Way gives
> Yea, this requital will I render thee
> For saving me.
This is exact and, like the Greek, does not suggest Hades even remotely.

[2] *v.* 1169.   [3] *v.* 1220.   [4] *v.* 1412.
[5] *v.* 1386.   [6] *v.* 24.

says this, not that Heracles has gone among dead men. Lycus
thinks that Heracles, being dead, 'lies with Hades[1],' and says
it. Megara, who agrees with Lycus in thinking that her
husband, if he has gone to ' Hades,' has gone there as a dead
man and cannot return, expresses her meaning in the natural
language of mankind[2]. The Chorus speak of the hero's
voyage 'to Hades[3],' and of his return (when they are convinced of it) from 'the mere of Acheron,' and 'the house of
Pluto[4].' Heracles, when he means to describe himself as
having travelled in the underworld of popular religious belief,
uses, in almost every sentence, terms which cannot bear any
other sense[5].   All the personages of the play sometimes use
on this subject language which is applicable to this subject
only.   And so would Theseus, and so would Heracles in conversation with Theseus, if the thought in Euripides' mind had
been, that these persons were speaking of experiences which
they had shared in Hades.   But since, as a fact, the five
allusions (including the case of Cerberus) are all ambiguous,
since all speak in terms not of Hades, but only of 'dead men,'
'underground,' and the like, the inevitable inference is that
they are purposely ambiguous, and that, according to the
intention of the author, the speakers do not refer to Hades,
but to something totally different.

Nor should it be overlooked, that the incident which they
mention, the rescue of Theseus by Heracles, is apparently not
recent.   For Theseus describes his motive for repaying it as
dislike of a gratitude that 'grows old' or 'wanes with time[6].'
Now it is possible indeed, and the possibility is doubtless
provided intentionally by the composer, to interpret this as
meaning that Theseus loves to repay services promptly.
But this is not the only possible meaning, nor the most
natural.   A hearer who depended only on the words, who
had no preconception about the matter, would suppose
Theseus to reprobate the *forgetting* of benefits, and therefore
to have in view a service, which might conceivably have been

---

[1] *v*. 145.   [2] *vv*. 297, 491.   [3] *v*. 427.
[4] *vv*. 770–808.   [5] *vv*. 607–621, 1101–1104, 1276–1278.
[6] *v*. 1223 χάριν δὲ γηράσκουσαν ἐχθαίρω φίλων.

forgotten[1]. Here then is a sixth ambiguity, multiplying enormously the improbability that all six should be accidental. And if they are calculated, the inference is inevitable, that the popular interpretation, the interpretation which would commend itself to the prepossessions of a Greek populace, is not that which was intended by Euripides.

It remains then to ask—it is the only question which Euripides leaves open—what was the incident, *not connected with Hades*, to which the reminiscences of Theseus allude. Since Euripides leaves the question open, it follows practically, that we, at this time of day and with such illustration of the subject as we command, are unable to answer it. But not so his educated contemporaries. The rescue of Theseus from Hades, as an article of popular belief, an incident in the legend of Heracles, was, like the belief that he strangled the Nemean lion with his arms, a thing for which the rationalizers had to account. Herodorus and other such writers, who preferred to think that the lion was strangled by a noose or trap, were bound to transform on the same principles the rescue of Theseus, by showing a natural and mundane incident, out of which, by superstitious exaggeration and with the aid of ambiguous language, the legendary version might be evolved. They would have no difficulty. Euripides, without committing himself to details, shows us what was the general line of the explanation, and what were the ambiguities utilized. What Euripides implies, and all that he implies, is that Theseus was rescued by Heracles from 'underground' (νέρθεν), from a place where there were 'corpses' or 'dead' (παρὰ νεκρῶν). Various incidents may be imagined, possible and not improbable in themselves, which would satisfy this language. For example, the two friends might visit a mine or cave together, and be imprisoned with the victims of a fatal accident. Theseus, as he tells us, was utterly unmanned[2]; Heracles retained his courage and strength, and found an escape for both. Euripides gives neither these details nor

---

[1] See also *vv.* 1413–1415. Would any one naturally suppose here, that Heracles' πρόσθεν, *once, formerly*, refers to the day before yesterday? It is possible; but should we naturally suppose so?

[2] *v.* 1416.

any, but indicates plainly, to educated spectators or readers of his day, that it is some incident of this kind, some natural incident, something like what was figured in this connexion by rationalistic writers, that his Theseus and his Heracles jointly remember.

When therefore Heracles in his madness declares that he has delivered Theseus from Hades[1], he is not merely inventing, any more than when he says, in the same condition, that he has captured Cerberus. The latter delusion is founded, as we shall see, upon a real circumstance of his recent expedition to Taenarum, the former upon a more ancient reminiscence, of which his confused imagination disguises not only the nature but the date. If the civic theatre of Athens had permitted, in such a matter as this, the perfectly open exhibition of infidel views, this particular trait in the divagations of Heracles would have been somehow brought to the knowledge of Theseus himself: it might have been introduced, for example, into the speech hovering between sanity and insanity, which the hero addresses to his friend in the drama[2], and which we shall consider presently. And the refutation of it must then have been explicit. To save appearances, so plain a confrontation is avoided ; and the facts, that Theseus is ignorant of the expedition to Taenarum, and that the rescue, as supposed in this drama, took place at another time and in other circumstances, though conspicuous to instructed eyes, are conveyed in such a way that the ignorant and the superstitious would overlook them, and that, if the author should be molested (as once at least he was) by a prosecution for impiety, there would be room for a formal defence.

Beyond the incident of the rescue, we learn nothing about the relations between Theseus and Heracles, except in general this significant fact, that the admiration of the lesser man (for Theseus, though he has exploits to boast[3], is frankly the inferior) is totally free from superstitious imagination, and that his great friend, however glorious and beneficent his career, is to him just a mortal man and nothing more

---

[1] *v.* 619.   [2] *vv.* 1255 foll.
[3] *v.* 1327. Note that the Minotaur is merely 'a bull.'

Amphitryon continues, as before, to cite battles of gods and giants[1], Theseus never; and his reticence admits but one interpretation. That the gods are no better than others, he thinks very possible as a general proposition; and he characteristically finds it a reflexion rather consoling than otherwise. Their malice, and in particular the malice of Hera, is an idea quite acceptable to his intelligence[2]: she is doubtless an enemy of Heracles. But as to the part of Zeus in the parentage of his friend—he happens not to express an opinion[3]. And this example is typical. What Theseus is concerned for is solely the reputation of Heracles as a man, and his honour in the eyes of the world, which will suffer, he says, by so weak and ill-considered an act as suicide[4]. Most earnestly therefore does he labour to dissuade him from it, and to prove by word and deed that the friend of Theseus may still look forward to a tolerable future.

Such are the materials provided for the last and noblest scene of the play, one of the noblest in Greek drama or any drama. With reverent curiosity, profound yet self-restrained, Euripides, for the foundation of his tragedy, goes boldly down into those dim regions where soul and body meet, yet so as never to lose in vagueness and mysticism the difference between that which is obscure and that which is simply unknown. To the excited importunity of Amphitryon, Heracles, prostrate and shrouded, offers a resistance silent but furious[5]. Theseus with a more calm, though tender, authority forces him at last to look up and to speak[6]; but for some time it appears that even Theseus can effect no more. Hard and untouched, Heracles parries his affectionate insistence with curt replies, which cover rather than disclose the state of his mind. Only it is evident that between the two friends there is some spiritual barrier, some gulf of thought, unveiled and veiled again in a glimpse:

> *Her.* Ay, saw you ever misery that was more[7]?
> *Thes.* Nay, nay, from earth your sorrows reach to heaven.

---

[1] *vv.* 1192–1194. [2] *vv.* 1191, 1314 foll., etc.
[3] And note, in *v.* 1316, the word ἀλλήλοισιν.
[4] *vv.* 1246–1254 and *passim.* [5] *vv.* 1203–1213.
[6] *vv.* 1214–1228. [7] *vv.* 1239 foll. (A. W. V.).

A SOUL'S TRAGEDY

> *Her.* And therefore is my mind resolved to die.
> *Thes.* Think you your threatening touches Them above?
> *Her.* God hath his way; I with the gods have mine[1].
> *Thes.* Refrain your lips, lest the big word invite
>   The heavier blow!
> *Her.*   I am full, there is no place
> For misery more.

But when this aimless fencing has beaten itself out in strokes that do not meet—

> *Her.* Men help not: Hera wins!
> *Thes.*   And you accept
> A foolish death, by Hellas disallowed!—

Heracles, if not moved, is at last provoked to explain himself[2]. If Theseus will listen, he may have an answer, may know that for Heracles to live is, *as in the past it has been*, a thing unfit. His calamities began, not, as Theseus imagines, to-day, but before he was born, when his mother Alcmena was wedded to a homicide, the slayer of his own grandfather, one who by breaking the sacred chain of life had proved himself unworthy to continue it. How from such parentage should aught proceed but a thing born to be miserable? Thus, with ghastly composure, he begins, and thus he would have proceeded, tracing his whole career, his false glories no less than his latest exploit in the murder of his family[3], to the same source, the evil in the blood, revealed at last to all, but by himself long known and abhorred. That is why he must die. Thus he would have proceeded; but here the complicated horror of the situation becomes too much for his self-mastery. The father whom he denounces, the author of his being and his misery, whom yet (this is the worst and also the best of all) he tenderly loves, that father is present, though Heracles, absorbed in his revelation, had for a moment forgotten him. He sees Amphitryon's agony, and desires to console him, to console him (how else?) by wounding him again in the very heart of his fond and foolish pride, by acknowledging him as

---

[1] *v.* 1243 αὐθαδὲς ὁ θεός· πρὸς δὲ τοὺς θεοὺς ἐγώ. Note the change of number and compare *vv.* 1341, 1345.

[2] *vv.* 1255 foll.

[3] *v.* 1279.

his father indeed, him, and not Zeus.   And in this effort the
thread of his thought quivers and is snapped.   The delusions,
which he set out to confess and expose, rush back and possess
him.   He struggles, but is carried on; and the whole splendid
abomination of his legend rolls from his lips in a flood, blended
and inseparable, of sane irony and mad belief.   ' As for Zeus,
why what is Zeus?   The father whose blood devolved upon
me the enmity of Hera!...*and you, Sir, be you not wounded;
you, and not He, are my father, the father in whom I believe...
......and, She, ere I was weaned, laid open my infant cradle to
snakes, with shining eyes, ay She, the wife of Zeus, that I might
be slain!*...Then I came to the full muscles of a man, and
ever since I have had things to fight through...that I need
not tell.   What is the shape of foe that I have not met?
Lions?   Ay!   Three-bodied Typhons...Giants, Centaurs, an
army of them!   and a hydra, many-headed, that grew and grew,
which I did to death,...and others, hordes of them,...through
which I fought my way, till I came...to the place of the dead [1]
...to bring from Hades into day, as Eurystheus bade, the three-
headed Hound of the gate; and I crowned it all, ah me! with
this final feat, that I slew...my progeny...fair pinnacle to the
building of my toil!'   What is before him?   Where shall he turn?
Thebes is closed, and Argos, and every place which witnessed
his triumph and now will cry scorn upon ' the son of Zeus, the
murderer of his wife and children.'   Ay, the very elements, earth
and sea, will cry out against this second Ixion[2].   ' Let then,' he
concludes, still fighting, strangled and desperate, between the
two opposing thoughts which yet are in a manner united, the
hydra, veritably double-headed, of his sane and insane belief,
'let then Zeus' glorious Lady dance, and her sandalled footfall
ring upon Olympus' floor!   She hath wrought her will!   Him
who was first in Hellas, wholly and utterly hath she wrecked
and overthrown...'   But no, not wholly nor utterly!   For here,
with a last convulsive effort, he suddenly lays hold of reason,
and turns defiantly upon the capering puppet of his phantasy.
' A goddess!   That!   How should a man pray to that?

[1] See *vv.* 1097, 1101, and also *v.* 1222 compared with *v.* 619.
[2] The Greek *Cain*, the typical murderer.

Jealous!...jealous of her Zeus!...because of a woman...and therefore pursuing to destruction...one that did good to all his nation,...and was innocent'—and with this outcry, broken yet triumphant, neither deity nor devil, but once again a miserable, rational man, he bursts into saving tears[1].

To us, who have followed the scenes of the morning, this speech reveals not only the present storm, but all the life-long labour of the mighty, misbegotten intellect. But Theseus has neither witnessed the facts, nor received an account of them, and is moreover not fitted to comprehend them fully if he had. What Heracles means he does not understand, but he sees and is deeply moved by his tears[2]. He perceives also what is obvious, that the source of them is connected in some way with his friend's theology, and he offers accordingly such comfort as he can. Why be miserable because the gods are wicked? Theseus will show him a better way. Like men, the gods are not above evil, not by any means, if those say true who pretend to know. The disorders of Olympus, from love, ambition, and what not, equal anything to be seen below. Yet the inhabitants make the best of it, and are tolerant of their imperfect condition. Surely then, surely men should be not less patient, but should take things, and themselves, as they are. Heracles, being a homicide, must doubtless depart from Thebes, as custom prescribes; but Athens is open. Theseus is ready, and happily able, to endow him with all that

[1] See *vv.* 1353–1357. That this weeping of one who never wept before occurs first between the two great speeches of Heracles (*vv.* 1310–1340), and accompanies the sudden change of his mind there exhibited, may be fairly inferred, though it is not stated. What appears upon the text is that in the first speech Heracles is beside himself, staggering on, or rather over, the brink of insanity, but that in the second he has recovered, and is himself, completely and finally. Also that this recovery is effected by his own body and mind, since it will hardly be attributed to the observations of Theseus. The scene wants only proper action to be perfectly intelligible and even simple.

[2] *vv.* 1311–1312 should probably be assigned to the Chorus (Camper, Murray, and others). The following speech of Theseus begins in the middle of a sentence, and the first words seem to be lost. But of this I am not quite sure. At *v.* 1310 Heracles, who must stand up for the preceding speech, flings himself again in a passion of tears upon the ground (see *v.* 1394). Theseus kneels beside him, consoling. In these circumstances we may be meant not to hear Theseus, till he has been speaking, to the ear of Heracles, for some time.

a man can desire for this world and the next—wealth now,
chapels and memorial rites hereafter; gladly will he thus
recompense his rescuer, now friendless. 'While the gods
favour, friends are superfluous, and the aid of the god[1], so
long as he pleases, is enough.'
'Here is the man for a friend!' as Heracles presently
exclaims[2], with profound and merited gratitude. But as a
spiritual adviser in the case, Theseus imports only that touch
of the inadequate, the inappropriate, in short the absurd,
which is as seldom absent from the tragedies of life as from
those of Euripides, and is not the least poignant part of them.
The frailties of the Olympians are a strange comfort for
one to whom the Olympians are but a small and, as he says[3],
a 'secondary' part of that miserable misconception, that huge
error, by which he himself, his life and work and very mind,
have been inextricably entangled and distorted; one who
might perhaps have been happy as well as great, if men had
not believed in Zeus and Hera, and would have let him
deny such deities, as in his true mind he ever did and now
with all solemnity does. Now, for the first time since we
have seen him, he is truly Heracles, and his often quoted
profession of faith springs out, as the word for which we have
waited :

οἴμοι· πάρεργα μὲν τάδ' ἔστ' ἐμῶν κακῶν,
ἐγὼ δὲ τοὺς θεοὺς οὔτε λέκτρ' ἃ μὴ θέμις
στέργειν νομίζω, δεσμά τ' ἐξάπτειν χεροῖν
οὔτ' ἠξίωσα πώποτ' οὔτε πείσομαι,
οὐδ' ἄλλον ἄλλου δεσπότην πεφυκέναι.
δεῖται γὰρ ὁ θεός, εἴπερ ἔστ' ὀρθῶς θεός,
οὐδενός· ἀοιδῶν οἵδε δύστηνοι λόγοι.

But this is no time for argument; and upon the question
of the moment, the question of suicide, he has come, upon
better thought, to agree practically with Theseus. In refusing
his burden there might be cowardice; he will await death
patiently, and meanwhile will thankfully accept the offered
refuge[4]. The new strange tears, sign of a great and perhaps

---

[1] The change of number means nothing to Theseus, to Heracles (v. 1345) it does.
[2] v. 1404.   [3] v. 1340.   [4] vv. 1347 foll.

a lasting change, continue to flow, while he bids farewell to his father and the dead, and decides, after pathetic hesitation, that his deadly weapons, his glorious weapons, shall go with him still, and finally takes leave of Thebes, of her soil upon which he still lies prostrate, and of her people, to whom he commends the memory of his fate[1]. Here only, in his references to Thebes, do we perceive a trace of the crisis through which he has passed, a blank of thought persisting, and persistent to the end. When he trustfully bids all the folk of Thebes, as friends, to the funeral of his children, he shows that in his memory there is an unrepaired and perhaps irreparable gap. The story of Lycus, the fact that Heracles' enemies actually hold the town, all this is gone from him. Since he came to his senses, nothing has been said of it, and what was said and done before, even the slaying of Lycus by his own hands, he has forgotten. This natural touch, given without the least emphasis, and left, as in real life, to be marked or neglected as the observer shall please, is vividly characteristic of Euripides. Not less so is the single and final touch of irony, which warns us that the fierce feelings, and even the insane beliefs, which fill the preceding speech[2], may possibly still be revived:

> All ye of Thebes, together mourn us all,
> My dead and me, together all destroyed...
> *By Hera*,...all and with a single stroke.

From the hero's profession of faith, as we have called it, down to these closing words, all is valedictory, except a brief parenthesis[3], which refers to his recent expedition, the expedition to Taenarum, and is designed to satisfy, so far as is necessary and suitable, the reader's possible curiosity upon a point hitherto untouched. In the rumours at Thebes, which are exhibited in the prologue by Amphitryon[4], the purpose

---

[1] *vv.* 1353–1385, 1389–1393.   [2] *vv.* 1255 foll.
[3] *vv.* 1386–1388

> ἔν μοί τι, Θησεῦ, σύγκαμ'· ἀθλίου κυνὸς
> κόμιστρ' ἐς ˝Αργος συγκατάστησον μολών,
> λύπῃ τι παίδων μὴ πάθω μονούμενος.

So MSS. and Prof. Murray, adding however 'ἀθλίου ex v. praecedente traiectum videtur.' σύγκαμ' ἀθλίῳ· κυνὸς Pierson and others. Ἅιδου μοι κυνὸς F. G. Schmidt.
[4] *v.* 23.

of that expedition was said to be the capture of Cerberus for King Eurystheus; and in the report of Heracles, made in the first access of his madness[1], the capture is related with the addition of a remarkable detail. The captor, anxious to be at home, avoided the journey to Argos and the immediate delivery of the monster, which was left, as it were till called for, at the sanctuary of Demeter Chthonia in the town of Hermione. A glance at the map will explain this. Heracles went to Taenarum, and doubtless returned, by sea[2]—the best route for speed between Taenarum and Boeotia in an age when there were Centaurs in Arcadia and lions about the Isthmus. For a traveller proceeding by sea, Hermione, at the eastern promontory of Argolis, was the obvious place to leave anything destined for Argos. At Hermione therefore Heracles put in—with Cerberus tied to the mast, we should have to suppose, if the creature had ever existed. But since he is a myth, the product of superstitious or insane imagination, the only question which can arise is whether his appearance in the Theban rumours and in the report of Heracles had any foundation in fact, whether in short the expedition to Taenarum was connected at all with a dog. We are now informed, if we care to know, that it was. 'There is one task,' says Heracles to Theseus, 'which I must have your help to perform. There is a miserable dog[3], which by bargain I should convey to Argos. Come with me to close the matter, lest in the pain of my bereavement I...take some harm, if I be left alone.'

Words would be wasted in showing that the miserable dog of this allusion is not the Hound of Hell; and the attempts to correct the text, so as to make the reference possible, have had such success as should have been expected[4]. Palpably the facts were natural, which for the intention of the drama is necessary and also sufficient. That a dog which Heracles was bringing from Laconia to Eurystheus (under what precise

---

[1] *vv.* 607 foll.   [2] *v.* 427 ἔπλευσ' ἐς"Αιδαν.
[3] Or 'the miserable dog.'
[4] Nothing is efficient short of a violent change in *v.* 1386, like "Αιδου μοι κυνὸς, which makes the description of Cerberus explicit; and when we have done that, we have only made it, in its trivial curtness, offensive. Contrast *v.* 1277.

circumstances we are not told and have not the least interest
in knowing) would, if left on the road, be exceedingly unhappy, is more than probable. But it is worth notice, as a
trait peculiarly Euripidean, that Heracles, restored to himself,
though he is still in such distress of mind that he asks for a
companion to protect him against suicide, has sympathy to
spare for a neglected animal. We are reminded of Hippolytus'
appeal to the gratitude of his horses[1], and the tenderness of
Ion for the wild birds[2]. For all that is defenceless and liable
to suffer, women, children, slaves, Euripides has ever a word ;
and when, as in these cases, he will describe hearts more than
commonly noble and tender, he has a word for the dumb
creatures too. The honourable desire of Heracles to fulfil
an engagement, however justifiably suspended, is also an
appropriate, though more commonplace, trait.

About this dog, as about the rescue of Theseus, the Miss
Martha Buskbodies of the day, the consumers of fiction who
were not content without the sugar at the bottom of the cup[3],
could probably learn more, however little to the purpose, by consulting, as a Pattieson or Cleishbotham, one of those rational-
izing mythographers to whom we have before alluded. The
capture of Cerberus was the very subject for such handling as
that of Herodorus[4]. One circumstance, tempting to such an
interpreter, is indicated by the allusions of Euripides. The
legends were irreconcilable, or, as some would prefer to say,
demanded reconciliation. Not only Taenarum, but also the
cave of the Subterranean Demeter at Hermione, claimed to be
the place where the Hell-Hound was dragged into light[5]. To
bring him through Taenarum first, and leave him afterwards
at Hermione for a time, was an expedient as natural to the
reconciler as it was alien to the genuine spirit of legend ; and
it may well have been adopted by pious narrators, who had
no desire to eliminate the monster altogether. The effect
was none the less absurd, and the next step, that of the
rationalist, inevitable. Some such process may have preceded Euripides ; and the resulting version of the story might

---

[1] *Hipp.* 1240, with *ib.* 110–112, 1219.   [2] *Ion* 179.
[3] See the epilogue to *Old Mortality*.   [4] See Appendix, *Heracles* 1386.
[5] Pausanias 2. 35. 7.

be read into his allusion, by those who chose, without much profit indeed, but without offence. But what Euripides actually gives us is sufficient (let us repeat) for his purpose, and requires no further explanation but what any reader can provide for himself.

And now, to return to the drama, all is said; and nothing remains but to withdraw the actors. The brief dialogue in which this is accomplished offers nothing for remark, except the parting—for so Heracles conceives it—between the son and the father. In the preceding speech, Heracles has assumed that, when he and Theseus have departed from Thebes, Amphitryon will remain and reside there[1]. In fact, in the actual state of Thebes[2], this is impossible; and that Heracles can think of it shows only, what was noticed before, that about Thebes, and the present attitude of the Thebans towards himself and his family, his memory is not yet restored. So long as the Athenian army remains in its camp, Amphitryon under their protection can remain, and can perform, as requested by Heracles, the burial of the dead. But whenever Theseus and his force withdraw, the whole household, unless the king of Athens proposes to take the town and expel the occupants, must depart also; and we may presume that the aged Theban friends of Amphitryon, with their families if they have any, would not be forgotten; for they would certainly have a painful passage to Hades, if left to the dominant faction. In short, the departure must be an affair of negotiation; and the notion of Heracles, that his friend and he are to set off at once and at ease for Argos[3], is altogether illusory. Accordingly, when it comes to the point and the group divides, we find that every one, except Heracles, regards the separation as momentary; for between Theseus, Amphitryon, and the Theban elders, there passes not so much as a good-bye. Heracles, pursuing his idea, takes leave of his father passionately, and his father of course responds, for an explanation is not to be risked[4]. The one

[1] *vv.* 1358–1366.
[2] *vv.* 26–43, 272–274, 541–543, 588–592, 811–814, 1163–1165, and elsewhere.
[3] *v.* 1387.   [4] *vv.* 1408–1409, 1418–1421.

thing pressing is to persuade the sufferer upon any terms to quit the ghastly and beloved relics of his calamity[1]. Even Heracles at the last is dimly conscious of his error, and knows, in a confused way, that his father is not now to remain in Thebes, that they are to meet again, and shortly, in fact immediately:

> *Her.* O sire, farewell!
> *Amph.* And fare thou well, my son![2]
> *Her.* Perform, as I bade thee, the burial of my little ones[3].
> *Amph.* And who, my son, will perform mine?
> *Her. That will I!...*
> *Amph.* Thou wilt return...how soon?
> *Her. As soon as these are buried...*
> *Amph.* What then?
> *Her. I shall fetch thee from Thebes away to Athens.*

The confusion of his thought is still manifest, and we may conceive the sympathetic signs and motions of the others; but the last little cloud seems to be dissolving; and thus, broken but resigned, and murmuring his gratitude, he suffers Theseus to draw him slowly away towards the Athenian camp. The aged Thebans, bewailing themselves for the fall of their mightiest friend, follow after, while, Amphitryon having entered the house, the door closes upon the mourner and the dead.

Whether this play deserves to be called an abortion, whether it falls into parts which have little or no connexion, whether, in fine, the usual treatment of it is founded upon a

----

[1] *vv.* 1406–1418.

[2] We should remember that χαῖρε, as originally our 'good-bye,' is not in itself a formula of leave-taking, but of blessing. The ambiguity is frequently utilized in tragedy and is not without significance here.

[3] Throughout this scene παῖδες and τέκνα, used by Heracles as terms of affection and pity, not merely of age or relationship, include the mother, who, if we consider the career of Heracles and the fact that his three children are infants, may or even must be supposed much younger than her husband. See especially *vv.* 1380–1381 ἡμῖν τέκν᾽ εἷλες καὶ δάμαρθ᾽, ἡμᾶς ἔχεις παιδοκτόνους σούς, where in the word παιδοκτόνους the inclusion is formally signified. After this, the wife is not separately mentioned.

true understanding, the reader will judge. To me it appears, like most of the Euripidean plays, to have neither life, nor unity, nor sense, if we suppose that, as in Aeschylus and Sophocles, the story is a legend or legendary in character, and that the theology and miracles of popular religion are part of the assumptions, but to become luminous, profound, and intensely interesting, so soon as we comprehend, and follow to the consequences, the saying attributed with justice and probably with truth to Euripides himself[1], that the facts of his drama are 'the familiar things we use and live among.'

Doubtless upon this understanding criticism may still find something to say. The *Heracles*, being the work of a man, is presumably not perfect. It may for example be fairly asked, whether the theology of Heracles would be found, even in a solitary and superior mind, among people materially so rude and mentally so backward as the play depicts. It is a fair and relevant question, because Euripides, like Shakespeare in a historical play and not like Shakespeare in *The Tempest* or *A Midsummer Night's Dream*, pretends to show us possibilities, to show what the life of Heracles, who for Euripides as for all his contemporaries had been a historical person, may really have been like, and also to show incidentally how we may account for the distorted reflexion of it in legend. If he assumes anything which is not possible, that is in him a fault, as it would not be necessarily, if chargeable (let us say) on the *Agamemnon* or the *Oedipus Tyrannus*. I do not presume to answer the question of possibility ; though this I will say, that an answer unfavourable to the view of Euripides should not be given in haste. The more we learn about primitive or uncultured men, the less we shall be disposed to lay down, that they are universally incapable of lofty and penetrating speculation in the region of theology. Long before there was a clearing in the forests of Thessaly and Arcadia, Thebes, or any other township, may well have contained a man or two, who,

---

[1] Aristophanes, *Frogs* 959, οἰκεῖα πράγματ' εἰσάγων, οἷς χρώμεθ', οἷς ξύνεσμεν.

like the man in Voltaire, knew of these matters what has been known in all times, that is to say, very little.

Given the possibility of such a Heracles, we may, I hope, agree that Euripides has made him tragic, consistently tragic, and tragic beyond description. Or if not, if, when all is said, the play should be still a thing about which we differ, the more truly then does it resemble the world. For the world is another such thing.

A FIRE FROM HELL.

(ORESTES.)

The most tremendous of all things is the magnanimity of a dunce.
SYDNEY SMITH.

IT would not be easy to imagine a greater contrast between
two plays, designed by the same hand for the same theatre,
and nominally included, as tragedies, in the same species of
drama, than is presented by the *Heracles,* from which we
pass, and the *Orestes,* upon which we are to enter. In particular, they exemplify a distinction which, though it is for
Euripides of much importance, is liable to be overlooked,
partly because obscured by the conventional necessities of
Athenian practice, partly because for Aeschylus and Sophocles
it can hardly be said to exist. This distinction is that of
time, of the epoch in the world's history and in its social,
political, religious development, at which the stories respectively are placed. For the purpose of Aeschylus or Sophocles,
if we ask *when* the events are supposed to pass, it would
generally be sufficient to reply, 'In antiquity.' The time is
remote, so remote that without shock to the imagination
much may be accepted as possible, if the legend or the treatment so requires, which could not have been attributed to the
fifth century. In the *Persae* of Aeschylus, though the events
are contemporary with the audience, remoteness of place, it
has been truly said, does the work of remoteness in time: at
Susa, in the unknown scene of a Persian palace, the apparition
of a dead king, visible and audible to his councillors, might
pass with the other strangeness of the situation. It would

have been another thing to show on the stage how the contemporary Pheidippides encountered Pan in the pass of Parthenium, or Demaratus beheld the supernatural procession of the initiated moving across the plain of Eleusis. But in general, remoteness of time is the condition, and in this remoteness there is little discrimination. Slight differences of colour there are: the world of the *Trachiniae* is somewhat more fancifully depicted than that of the *Philoctetes*; the Argos of the *Suppliants* and the Argos of the *Agamemnon* are societies not exactly alike. But there is no system in these differences, and generally speaking all marks of date are sunk in a haze of poetry. For the intended purpose, this method, commonly distinguished by the name of *the ideal*, was not only commendable but necessary: in no other way could the hypotheses of legend have been made acceptable, under the trying conditions of drama, to the given audience. And it is perfectly legitimate, as a matter of taste, to prefer such ideal drama to other species. Only let us not confuse the species, or attribute to Euripides an obscurity and negligence in the distinction of time and circumstance, which would have been as inconsistent with his purpose, as it was necessary to that of Aeschylus.

To borrow from antique legend the names and relationships of the principal characters was, for the Attic tragedian, generally necessary; but we see from Euripides that this requirement sometimes became, as was to be expected, purely conventional and fictitious. The names tell us nothing, in his case, about the conditions of the story, which can be learnt only from the play itself. They may be antique, as the legendary names suggest, or they may not. Heracles and Orestes, according to legendary chronology, were persons nearly contemporary; but the Euripidean stories bearing their names are as wide apart as *Ivanhoe* and *Guy Mannering*. The social, political, and religious conditions of the two are mutually exclusive, and the events of each story inconceivable in the conditions of the other. The world of the *Heracles*, though not, like that of Sophocles' *Trachiniae*, miraculous, is nevertheless far remote from the age of the dramatist, and

utterly unlike it.   The world of the *Orestes* is in all essentials
that of the fifth century, the state of society such as existed
then, and, in some most important particulars, such as
notoriously had not existed long.   Nothing is antique, not
even possibly antique, except the names of the *dramatis
personae*, whose minds, conduct, and status are, like the
surrounding society, absolutely modern.   They may call
themselves children of Agamemnon or Menelaus, and speak
of the Trojan war as a recent event.   But the ' Argos,' in
which they reside, is a fully developed democracy, with a
popular assembly as completely sovereign as that of Athens
in the age of Pericles or of Cleon, and is assumed to have
been such in the past for so long a period as the story
takes into account.   Agamemnon was 'not a king[1],' and his
' almost superhuman power' was exercised by appointment
and public choice, like the command of Cimon.   The
house of Pelops, being ancient, illustrious, and formerly royal,
has the sort of dignity which in fact remained to many such
houses in Athens and other democratic communities, a dignity
which under favourable circumstances conferred influence.
But in a legal view the family has no advantage whatever,
no more than the Athenian Erechtheidae, Alcmaeonidae, or
Butadae of the fifth century ; and if for the time being the
family is for any reason unpopular (and at the time of the
drama it happens to be so to the highest degree), its chiefs
are so far from wielding authority, that their position is both
humiliating and perilous.   The conception of equality before
the law is not merely prevalent in theory, but established
and applied in fact without possibility of protest.   The state,
like many Greek states in the fifth century, including Athens
itself, and like modern France, retains from its past history
a nobility or the remains of one, but of political royalty or
political aristocracy nothing whatever.

Such, and so profoundly different from the heroic age, is
the political atmosphere of the play ; and in religion the stamp
of modern feeling is, if possible, sharper still.   In the *Heracles*,
the conditions of belief, like those of the world and of society,

[1] *Or.* 1168.

are primitive. Not only is the past conceived as miraculous, but miraculous stories, related of a living and familiar person, though they excite much jealousy and scepticism, as assuredly they would have done in most Greek societies for many generations before the time of Euripides, nevertheless obtain a measure and kind of assent, which in most societies of the fifth century would have been inconceivable. To find such a class of persons as is represented by the Chorus of the *Heracles*, to find even an individual Amphitryon, would then have been scarcely possible in Athens, Corinth, or Syracuse, probably not easy in Sparta, Thebes, or Tegea. At the date of *Heracles*, the popular theology, whatever may have been dared in speculation by a solitary thinker, is generally accepted without question and has a universal influence over private and public affairs. But in the 'Argos' of *Orestes*, as at Athens in the age of Euripides, that theology has not only lost much of its hold upon individuals, but, what is of far more importance, in matters of legal and political action it receives not even the semblance of respect. When a deed, done with the previous sanction of the oracle at Delphi, is arraigned before the Argive assembly sitting as a criminal court, the religious justification is not even pleaded. It is on all sides simply ignored, and condemnation passes after a debate in which, so far as appears, the name of Apollo has never been mentioned[1]. And in the age of Euripides, such a course, on the part of a defendant before an Athenian tribunal, would have been both probable and prudent. Few dicasts would have been propitiated, and not a few possibly exasperated, by an attempt to bolster up a case otherwise indefensible with an alleged effusion of the Pythian prophetess. The procedure is in perfect accord with the rest of the play, and would have agreed with the *Andromache* or *Ion*. But it would have been monstrous in the *Oedipus Tyrannus*, and not less so in the *Heracles*, the *Hippolytus*, or even the *Iphigenia in Taurica*.

Into the midst of such conditions, political, social, and religious, Euripides in this play, which differs widely even

---

[1] *vv.* 866 foll.

from others of his own upon the same theme, has transported
the ancient story, which told how a son, under the special
command of the Delphian god, avenged his murdered father
by slaying the murderess and adulteress, his mother. It was
a daring experiment. The conditions changed are precisely
those upon which the legend depends for its interest; and to
find a new interest, compatible with the transference, might
well be thought impossible. Sympathy, general or at least
predominant, with the avenger, the final justification of the
avenger, these are the pillars of the legendary structure, and
must, we should suppose, be the support of any practicable
drama founded upon it. But by the change of conditions
this support is destroyed. The matricide is no longer defensible, and scarcely pitiable. His act is a different thing;
his guilt is multiplied tenfold, his pleas disappear; and nothing
is left, out of the material presented by the original version,
which can suspend our judgment or divide our emotions.
The names of Agamemnon and Clytaemnestra, of Orestes and
Pylades, may remain; but the moral interest, which they
represented, is destroyed. If it were now conventionally
necessary that the persons of all plays should be taken (let us
say) from the history of the seventeenth century, a playwright,
who chose nevertheless to exhibit the laws, beliefs, and
manners of the present day, could not, without inventing
some entirely new line of interest, take for his subject the
murder of the Archbishop of St Andrews. He might, without
exceeding the bounds of possibility, show a prelate put to
death by fanatics; he might call the victim Sharpe, the
assassins Burley or Rathillet, and the place Magus Muir. But
if his Scotland was, in religion, morals, and politics, the Scotland of the twentieth century, then the balance of principles,
the conflict of rights, the division of sympathies, all which
makes the historical incident suitable for artistic treatment,
would in the transference vanish. So with Orestes. His
legend, as originally conceived and as handled by Aeschylus,
rests upon presumptions which, in the circumstances given
by Euripides, cease to be possible. It presumes, in the first
place, the general justice and normal toleration of private

revenge. As the slayer of his mother, Orestes may be open
to condemnation, but he is praiseworthy as the avenger of his
father. For slaying Aegisthus, the accomplice of Clytaemnestra,
the Aeschylean Orestes will not even condescend to excuse
himself[1], though Aegisthus too was a near kinsman ; nor has
that incident any effect upon his subsequent fate or the final
review of his conduct. So long as the story was left in the
original atmosphere of antiquity, this presumption was natural.
Such had in fact been the ethics of the past. It was easy
too, and Aeschylus does it, to strengthen the plea of private
wrong, in case any doubt should be entertained of its sufficiency, by public motives of the most respectable kind—to
insist on the fact that Agamemnon was a king, a lawful
governor, that Clytaemnestra was guilty of treason in killing
her husband, and of usurpation in taking his throne, and that
the man who pulled down her and her paramour, whatever
might be his position as a son, was a citizen of the highest
merit, the deliverer of his country from a detestable despotism[2].
For the Argos of Euripides, a democratic state resting on fixed
laws, tribunals, and criminal procedure, none of these defences
or palliations are conceivable. Such a state could not exist,
unless private revenge were itself a crime, disallowed by
opinion, and normally visited with punishment as an insult
to public authority. The necessity of this doctrine, as an
elementary principle of common sense, a rudiment of traditional morality, familiar to every one who has any notion of
right and wrong, is explained, under contemptuous protest
against the explanation of a thing so obvious, by one of the
personages in the play[3]; and the behaviour of the Argive
public is, as of course it must be, in accordance with that
exposition. Doubtless it was the duty of a son to prosecute
the enemies of his father, to prosecute them to the death, but
not to assassinate them. The law was ready to his hand, and
no other weapon permissible. So thought, so must think,
the Argives of such an Argos as is presented by Euripides.
Away then goes the foundation of Orestes' case, as con-

[1] *Choephori* 989 (Dindorf).   [2] *Cho.* 973, 1046, *Eum.* 631 etc.
[3] *vv.* 491 foll.

ceived by the legend, and away go also the palliations adopted by Aeschylus. There can be no tyrannicide, for there is no tyrant. Clytaemnestra and Aegisthus are private persons; and the murder of them, though highly sensational, has no political importance whatever. Nor had the murder of Agamemnon. The legendary version conceived Agamemnon as the lord of a strong castle and subject territory; the Aeschylean version invested him with political royalty and a sort of empire. Either way, those who slew him could maintain their usurpation by the very strength which it brought, or with the aid which it enabled them to purchase. Not so in our modern Argos. Here Aegisthus and Clytaemnestra could not, by suppressing their enemy, acquire the means of protecting themselves against punishment for their act. Their impunity of seven years or thereabouts, an element in the story not open to modification, becomes now intelligible only on the supposition, that the disappearance of Agamemnon did not, for some reason, arouse any effective resentment, or even excite remark. A reason is provided. Agamemnon, as seen in the retrospective glimpses of this play, is a personage of great but equivocal celebrity (κλεινός, εἰ δὴ κλεινός[1]), who by drawing his compatriots into a long and distant enterprise, fatal to many families[2] though profitable and interesting to his own, had made himself famous indeed, but to the last degree unpopular, so that if many knew or suspected how he died, few or none very much cared. His wife had wrongs; her own infidelities were obscure and not scandalous[3]. His own brother Menelaus, absent at the time of his death and for years after, was, when he heard of that event, moved indeed, as he tells us, to tears, 'many tears,' but was not the less anxious to remain on good terms with the wife and family; and he regards the conduct of the son, his nephew, in disturbing a situation not (all things considered) infelicitous, with horror and disgust![4] The very daughter of Agamemnon, though a principal in the scheme for avenging him, never speaks of the father, whom she must have known, with any personal affection[5].

---

[1] v. 17.   [2] vv. 58, 102, 432, etc.
[3] vv. 27, 561, etc.   [4] vv. 360–374.   [5] Electra *passim*.

The father of Clytaemnestra, though detesting the crime of his daughter, and more than willing to see her punished in a legal way, has not a word of personal regret for Agamemnon[1]—who, in short, was not regretted, as it seems, by any who knew him, except indeed in a military fashion by some of his noble companions in arms[2]. All this is very well, very natural, very consistent with the political and social frame of the picture; but it is a most unhappy and disastrous preparation for the entrance upon the scene of a person claiming, for the sake of Agamemnon, to defy law, morality, and nature, and pleading a divine command.

And the command itself, the sanction of Delphi, what has become of that? Here, in the traditional story, lay the pith of the matter. Orestes is a man divinely commanded, for special reasons, to do an act naturally abominable. The oracular command, its reality and authority, make the cornerstone of his case. Sophocles in his *Electra* supposes this justification to be so clear as to lift Orestes himself above doubt or scruple, and commend him to unqualified sympathy. Aeschylus, more faithful apparently to tradition and history, represents it as raising a painful question, a question, humanly speaking, insoluble. The Areopagus of Athens is divided upon it equally. For both Aeschylus and Sophocles, the supernatural origin of the message is a certainty, and its weight indisputable. In the *Eumenides*, Apollo himself proves it as a witness in court; in the *Choephori* we learn that it was given to Orestes repeatedly, by the mouth (so the language suggests) of the God, and under appalling penalties in case of disobedience. But in our play, in the modernized *Orestes*, what becomes of all this? How could it possibly stand? In such an Argos as Euripides depicts, what would it matter that an act condemned by law and public opinion had been sanctioned, or supposed to be sanctioned, by a response from the woman of the tripod? So much the worse for Apollo. Some are scandalized[3], the majority simply indifferent[4]. It is as if now, in some state where

---

[1] *vv.* 496 foll., and Tyndareus *passim.*   [2] *vv.* 890–900.
[3] *vv.* 194, 807–843, etc.   [4] See the trial (*vv.* 866 foll.) and *passim.*

marriage with a deceased wife's sister is recognized by law, a man so married were to commit bigamy, and were to plead the opinion of his spiritual director, that his previous contract was invalid. Even the sincerity of such a plea would be questionable, and its weight nothing. So with Orestes and his oracle. He, and he alone, is affected by it. Pylades, his counsellor and in truth the author of his acts[1], never mentions the oracular command, and is, as we shall see, a character not conceivably open to such influence. Electra, his other instigator, mentions it only to complain that it has not been followed by support[2]. No one, whose opinion carries weight, none but women[3] and rustics[4], even allows it for supernatural, and no one allows it for authoritative. Orestes himself, though it seems to have quieted his scruples for a time, finds it impotent against his remorse and useless for his defence. He pleads it to his uncle, and his uncle sneers[5]; he pleads it to his grandfather, and his grandfather ignores it[6]. At his trial he does not plead it at all[7]. The high language, in which he extols the wisdom of Delphi as universally acknowledged and obeyed[8], is such as in the fifth century might doubtless have been frequently heard, and still represented something real. Delphi was much consulted, had much influence on private affairs and some on public. But it did not then command in Athens, and it does not command in 'Argos,' that sort of authority which could serve an Orestes. The compromise is familiar, and analogies abundant both in other times and in our own. It follows as a necessity from the time and circumstances adopted for this play. But it destroys the interest of the story, as that interest was conceived by tradition.

We may indeed doubt whether the part of Delphi is, strictly speaking, possible in the altered circumstances, whether in the sixth or fifth century an encouragement to matricide could have been procured from the tripod at all.

---

[1] *vv.* 1090, 1158.

[2] *vv.* 162, 191, etc.

[3] *vv.* 191 foll., etc.

[4] *v.* 955, see *vv.* 866–870.

[5] *vv.* 416–417.

[6] *vv.* 591 foll., and Tyndareus *passim*.

[7] *vv.* 932 foll.

[8] *vv.* 591 foll.

But we do not know the contrary, and may be content to suppose with the dramatist. Nor in any case is the doubt important. Suppose a youth so wrong-headed and weak as the Orestes of this play, and suppose him to be guided by such a fool as Pylades and such a fiend as Electra, and then the murder of Clytaemnestra is the natural consequence of their characters and situation. The 'supernatural command' is an extra, and almost a superfluity. Apollo is a fly on the wheel.

Other changes follow, minor but not insignificant. As presented by tradition, the enterprise of Orestes excites a certain sympathy by the mere peril of the execution. In Aeschylus he must make his way into a guarded fortress; both in Aeschylus and in Sophocles he must sustain, by presence of mind, the dangers of an impersonation. Something of this remains even in the *Electra* of Euripides. But in our play there is nothing to show, nor is it probable, that the assassins had any difficulty at all. For anything that appears, Pylades and Orestes may have given their names at Clytaemnestra's door. In such an Argos as is here represented, not even murderers would expect to be murdered, or at any rate not by their sons. When Menelaus can suppose that Orestes and his mother are living peacefully together[1], we cannot suppose that she would refuse to see him ; nor would she dare to refuse, considering the legal danger in which she stood, and his power to use it[2]. Again, her relations with Aegisthus have not here, and could not have, that cynical stamp, which in Aeschylus so powerfully directs sympathy to the hand which punishes. The play assumes that these relations were known[3], but it also assumes, as a necessary condition, that they had been so conducted as to cause no open scandal.

Where then—we come back to the question—could lie the interest of an Orestes so circumstanced? Not in the moral quality of his act. It is plainly indefensible and inexcusable. Not in his fate. That is a foregone conclusion. His life indeed, by Greek law as it mostly stood in the age

---

[1] *vv.* 371–373.   [2] *vv.* 500 foll.   [3] *vv.* 619–620, etc.

of Euripides, and is supposed in Argos, is not absolutely and certainly forfeited. Exile, still a very formidable penalty, might be awarded by sentence[1]. In an ordinary case the homicide might even be permitted to accept exile by leaving the country before trial; but in a grave case, this freedom of choice might not be conceded, and it is not conceded to the matricides, who up to the day of trial are prisoners in their own house. There remains the possibility that they may escape with their lives; but this is no issue suitable for the purpose of a dramatist, since neither decision could please. The whole affair, so framed and circumstanced, becomes simply revolting, and not susceptible, as it might seem, of artistic treatment.

A line theoretically open, if the author were a religious enthusiast and could expect sufficient support from his audience, would be to make Orestes a martyr, sealing by endurance to the death his faith in Delphi and his testimony against the errors of an infidel world. Needless to say, Euripides has not taken this line; nor was it practically open to an Athenian dramatist in the year 408 B.C. But if not this, nothing seems to be left.

And yet the *Orestes* was one of the triumphs of the stage[2], and may still be described as supreme in its kind. A tragedy in the strict sense it hardly is or could be. But for excitement, for play of emotion, for progression and climax of horror, achieved by natural means and without strain upon the realities of life, it has few rivals in the repertory of the world.

The chief instrument of effect is the fury, the insanity, of despair. Villains of some sort, and fools of the worst sort, the assassins of Clytaemnestra must be. But for this very reason they are hideously dangerous to themselves and to others, moral explosives of enormous force and instability. What hope they have they will throw away, pursuing their

---

[1] See *vv.* 898–900 and 441. The anticipations of Electra (*vv.* 49–51) and of Orestes (*v.* 442) that the only alternative considered by the assembly will be between execution (by stoning) and permitted suicide, are an illusion of their terror, and are refuted, like their anticipations generally, by the actual proceedings.

[2] τὸ δρᾶμα τῶν ἐπὶ σκηνῆς εὐδοκιμούντων, *Orestes* Hypothesis II.

fate as blindly as they have pursued their crime. And when
they are condemned, when nothing is before them but death,
if then they have the chance to die killing, to strike, wound,
slay some one, any one, to avenge themselves at the cost
of human creatures, however helpless, however innocent, is
there anything which they may not conceivably do, any
extremity to which, in the name of justice, they may not
go, any demoniac sacrifice which they may not rapturously
solemnize[1]? Here is material not exactly for tragedy (it is
not deep enough), but for a highly spiritual sort of melodrama.

In one thing the traditional story was favourable to such
handling: the three conspirators can all be conceived as
grossly, totally inexperienced and ignorant of affairs. Orestes
is but a boy, about eighteen or nineteen years old[2], Pylades,
his cousin and comrade, not older. Pylades has wild spirits,
no fear, no scruples, and no sense. Orestes, when the action
begins, is half insane with fever, and before it ends, a maniac.
Moreover he is governed by Pylades. They are united by
that boyish sort of romantic devotion, which for sheer
unreason surpasses perhaps even love itself, and attracts the
like unreasonable sympathy. Amid all the atrocities which
the pair perform, a certain pathos cleaves to the heroic
obstinacy of their folly. In Electra, a woman of middle
age[3], perhaps thirty or something more, is concentrated what
little wisdom the party can boast. The most fatal blunder
of the two young men would have been prevented by her,
if she had had the chance[4]. But as a woman she is unable,
according to the notions of those times and of most times,
to measure public forces or estimate fairly the possibilities
of a political situation. Family pride too[5], in her as in her
brother and cousin, forbids respect for a democratic govern-

---

[1] See *vv.* 1–3, which are more true, as a compendium of the sequel, than the
speaker intends. Her characteristic assumption that guilt is a συμφορὰ θεήλατος
is also noticeable, and a key to the situation.

[2] *v.* 377. The time of the play, according to the received chronology of
Menelaus' return, is about seven or eight years after the fall of Troy.

[3] *vv.* 201 foll.   [4] *vv.* 846–850. See hereafter.   [5] *vv.* 960–1012.

ment and equal law; she regards the Argive assembly as
the natural enemies of her house¹. Lastly, she is a fiend,
by her misfortune perhaps rather than by her fault, but a
fiend she is. The crowning horror of horrors is her particular
work².

Such is the machinery of destruction, the spring of the
catapult. It remains to provide victims within range of the
bolt, and a turn of fate to produce the discharge. The
solution of this problem, by means of Menelaus and his
family, is the making of the play and a masterpiece of
dramatic ingenuity. Since the fall of Troy, some seven
years, Menelaus with his recovered Helen has been wandering,
not unprofitably, about the world. Loaded with wealth and
Oriental treasures, including a train of eunuchs for the service
of Helen, they reach the port of Nauplia on the day before
that which is to determine, as between death and banishment,
the fate of Orestes and Electra. Their entrance into Argos,
as here described, suggests that in truth they dared not return
sooner. The popular hatred of the Trojan war, its causes and
authors, as imagined and used by Aeschylus in the *Agamemnon*, has in the *Orestes* a still wider and deeper effect. Even
so long after the war, Helen and her servants must be conveyed by night into the mansion of the family, now become
the prison of its inheritors; and there she lies concealed³.
She shows some alarm, but not a trace of real remorse, laying
the responsibility of her conduct upon compelling Powers with
the same facility which we observe, modified by temperament,
in Electra⁴. She is indeed for the present perfectly comfortable,
agitated rather agreeably than otherwise by the emotions
of the hour, shedding easy tears for poor sister Clytaemnestra so terribly taken away, poor Electra 'still unmarried,'
poor Orestes, so ill, and both of them in such dreadful danger.
None of this distracts her from the usual cultivation of her
person, or from the important business of stitching a piece of
embroidery, to be offered in token of sisterly sorrow at poor

¹ *v.* 974.
² *vv.* 1191 foll. See hereafter.
³ *vv.* 57 foll., etc.
⁴ *v.* 79, compare *v.* 2.

14—2

Clytaemnestra's grave[1]. She has moreover 'a certain consolation,' as her niece observes, in recovering her daughter
Hermione, abandoned in infancy, for the sake of Paris,
seventeen years ago, and tenderly reared by Clytaemnestra[2].
This girl, a simple and beautiful figure, mourning with innocent affection for her murdered foster-mother, yet unable to
wish the death of her cousins, the murderers[3], shows in such
darkness like a diamond. She becomes at last the pivot
of the diabolic engineering. Electra hates her.

Menelaus, though in character vulgar and below vulgarity,
emphatically πονηρός as Aristotle calls him[4], is the chief lever
in the mechanism of the plot ; and it is important to estimate
rightly not so much his acts and motives, which are simple,
as the disturbed reflexion of them in the minds of his nephews
and niece. This is a monstrosity, and yet a natural monstrosity. The contrast between the commonplace of his
behaviour, selfishly prudent, rationally mean, and the appalling
train of passion to which, without suspicion, he applies the
spark, is in the best vein of that natural supernatural which
Euripides loved to study. He is like a soldier who, watching
the couch of a wounded comrade, and choosing to let him die
in darkness rather than to burn his own fingers, should drop
a match, which, falling upon powder, hurls the whole place
into the air. A low-minded, sensual, prosperous man, he is
suddenly compelled to be either a little brave or a little
dishonourable. Bravery will be quixotic, for it can do no one
any good, and is certain to hurt him a little. The dishonour
is purely sentimental, and will have no consequences. Naturally he accepts the dishonour,—and Hell opens under
his feet.

The children of Agamemnon see, and every one sees, that
Agamemnon's brother, the husband of Helen, is bound to
them by no common tie. Menelaus has drawn upon the
fraternal interest so largely, that scarcely any counter-claim
can be excessive[5]. He at least cannot with decency abandon

---

[1] *vv.* 122, 1431 foll.
[2] *vv.* 62–66, 1340.
[3] *v.* 1323, *v.* 1345.
[4] See note in Appendix on *Or.* 1554.
[5] *vv.* 244, 448 foll., and *passim.*

the children and the avengers, however misguided, of his benefactor. Insensitive as he is, he cannot without embarrassment withdraw from the house where his nephew and niece are agonizing. But he does withdraw; and nothing is seen or heard of him again until all is over. In particular, after the trial and condemnation, he does not return to the house with Orestes, unwilling, as he has every reason to be, to embarrass his own very dubious relations to his countrymen with a fresh load of popular hatred. He allows Orestes to be reconducted by others, an act or omission which is the necessary condition and cause of the horrors which ensue.

All this, he thinks, is the reasonable course; and so, in a certain sense, it is. For any practical purpose he is powerless. The danger of the criminals lies in the legitimate animosity of the public. To turn this sentiment into the least fatal channel is the only substantial service which can be rendered to them; and this should be the work of persons acceptable to the people and influential in the assembly, such persons as do in fact undertake it. Menelaus, himself threatened with no small peril from the same quarter, Menelaus, the obsequious husband who under cover of night has smuggled into Argos a woman so odious that she dares not be seen, is an orator who cannot even appear, and would extinguish the last hope if he did. He cannot improve the prospects of the culprits; but he may very easily injure his own, as is made superfluously clear to him by an incident which shortly follows his arrival[1]. He decides to keep out of the way; and his action, though grossly indelicate, is innocuous to the criminals and apparently prudent. He protests, quite honestly, against the unreasonable clamour of Orestes[2].

Unhappily for his calculations, Orestes is something more than unreasonable. A week of fever[3] has brought him to the verge of insanity; and the other two criminals, whom Menelaus does not meet, are in a condition more dangerous than madness itself. All of them imagine that their wealthy relative, arriving at this crisis, must be able in some way to save them. They have no ground for so imagining; they

[1] *vv.* 470 foll.   [2] *vv.* 682 foll.   [3] *vv.* 401 foll., 422–423.

suggest no possible way, because there is none ; but with their proper contempt for his disregard of dignity and sentiment is mingled the conviction, that he could have done *something*, and that by omitting this something he has done them a cruel wrong. In a vague way they seem to expect the use of force[1], a notion as impracticable as outrageous. And they are especially indignant that Menelaus did not address the Argive assembly[2], a view which does not surprise us, when we see what is their knowledge of such an assembly, and with what wisdom Pylades and Orestes essay to manage it. Their expectation is a chimera, bred, like all their ideas, of ignorance and truculence.

But it proves a Chimaera indeed, a monster breathing fire, when, after the condemnation of Orestes and Electra, barely graced so far that they may escape stoning by suicide, the trio meets again at the house. The furious Pylades, whose position, though different, is equally desperate[3], suggests that they may not only punish the treachery of Menelaus, but also obliterate the reproach of murder (*sic*), by gloriously executing the abominable Helen. Electra dexterously engrafts upon this admirable plan the assassination, disguised as the capture, of her innocent supplanter, Hermione. The scheme is to be consummated, if necessary, by burning the house over their heads. The objections of Orestes, last efforts of a conscience vanishing in frenzy, are stifled or thrust aside. The frightful programme, frightfully diversified by mismanagement and misadventure, proceeds *crescendo* to its finale. And when that is achieved, when nothing and nobody is left to be saved or to be blessed, the real though unseen Furies of Arson, Murder, and Madness resign stage, actors, and audience to the not inappropriate benediction of Apollo.

As we have mentioned the house, which shares and partly determines the fate of its inhabitants, we may call attention here to the uncommon importance, for this play, of conceiving rightly the place of action. It is the house-in-town of a noble family, such as might perhaps oftener have been found in

---

[1] *vv.* 52, 243, 711, and the rest of that speech.
[2] *v.* 1056.   [3] *vv.* 763 foll.

Thebes, Argos, Sicyon, or other antique centre of city-life,
than in Athens, whose people remained principally rural in
habit until forced to congregate by the Peloponnesian war.
It is utterly unlike anything to be seen among ourselves,
though the cities of Italy and of some Roman provinces
present specimens distantly similar. Built for defence against
rivals or rebellions, its walls of stone, two stories high and
perhaps more, are unbroken except for one great gate, by
closing which it is instantly converted into a fortress. Unless
this arrangement is clearly grasped, the latter part of the play
will be unintelligible[1]. The interior structures, probably of
wood and, in the more sumptuous portions, of precious wood[2],
surround and are lighted from a labyrinth of little courts. In
front, and probably elsewhere, the parapet of the outer wall is
accessible, for defence, from within. Being old and somewhat
out of date, the house shows touches of ruin. The parapet
is loose[3], and half-way up the sheer front, where the stories
join, the line of *metopa*, or interspaces between the beam-ends,
shows at least one gap, from the loss of the closing stone.
This orifice, some twenty feet or more from the ground, is
accessible from the inside to a climber sufficiently desperate[4].
Before the gate is a yard or forecourt, represented in the
theatre by the orchestra[5]. That Orestes in his fever should
lie and be nursed here, rather than within, may perhaps be a
theatrical fiction, but may also be copied from life. The
Athenians of that day knew nothing of domestic state and
little of domestic comfort; and living themselves chiefly in the
open air, would probably find it natural that such a patient
should prefer the *aulé*. This yard is not defensible, but is of
course enclosed, though the boundaries are mostly outside the
scene; one passage, which seems to speak of looking 'through'
them, suggests that they may partly consist of a railing, *grille*,

---

[1] The scheme of Electra, for securing a hostage and then making conditions
with Menelaus (and the government), assumes this as an essential condition.

[2] *v.* 1371.   [3] *v.* 1570.   [4] *vv.* 1369 foll.

[5] The action shows no trace of a stage, and any such erection would have been
on this occasion highly inconvenient. There may, however, be steps to the house
and a space at the top of them.

cheval-de-frise, or the like[1], but the detail is of no moment. The approaches to the orchestra (πάροδοι), one or both[2], figure entrances to the yard. The scenic apparatus, then, is nothing but a back-wall, practicable from within, with a door in it and also a hole; but not all the machinery of Bayreuth could achieve a more heart-shaking series of effects than Euripides has got out of this.

Of the Chorus we need say little, and would gladly say nothing. The plot, like many or perhaps most of the plots best suited for a drama, excludes, as matter of credible reality, the presence throughout of a numerous body, the Chorus of the Greek theatre. Like the counsels of Medea, the counsels of Pylades and Electra could not conceivably be executed, if known; and the fifteen accessories, in these plays and to some extent elsewhere, must be accepted as a convention beyond criticism, an exhibit not offered for competition[3]. Greek women of aristocratic caste, living under a democratic government, would be as nearly capable of acting insanely, in a matter touching their prejudices, as any human beings, not insane, could be; this much and no more can be said for the Chorus of the *Orestes.* A touch of bitter humour is given to their first appearance, in the fact that, by an exception perhaps unique, they are as unwelcome to the *dramatis personae*[4] as assuredly they were to the constructor of the piece. In a single scene[5] their importunity is utilized with some effect; elsewhere, their presence being once for all condoned, they serve to prompt and sustain the excitement of the spectators[6]. But their real function is simply to fill with their odes the necessary pauses in the action; and this is judiciously cut down to a minimum.

There are hardly any 'supers[7].' The slaves of the house

---

[1] *v.* 1267; see note in the Appendix.
[2] More probably only one is used.
[3] See p. 125, and the end of this essay.   [4] *vv.* 131 foll.
[5] *vv.* 131–210.   [6] Especially in *vv.* 1246–1553.
[7] The servants who lead Tyndareus (*v.* 474), and those of Helen, seem to be all. Some of the latter, remaining for a moment behind their mistress, are apparently addressed in *v.* 128 εἴδετε; but see the end of this essay.

have fled or been withdrawn[1], a grim circumstance which
Euripides after his fashion exhibits without comment ; and for
several days, from the funeral of Clytaemnestra to the arrival of
Helen and her suite, the brother and sister, with the waif
Hermione, have been alone in the desolate place. The public
order forbidding intercourse with the criminals to citizens
of Argos[2] does not apparently exclude the family (Menelaus),
and is relaxed in effect, but merely by way of theatrical
convention, in favour of the Chorus. All the approaches are
guarded, and escape is impossible[3].

We will now survey the scenes in order, noting specially
such points as have not been anticipated.

A prologue, spoken by Electra, exposes the story down to
the arrival of Helen, and fixes the tone of the play. Disbelief in the miraculous[4], reproach of the oracle[5], which has
commanded but not helped, contribute with many other signs
to show how far we are from Aeschylus and the *Orestea*. In
view of this essential purpose, we may condone one allusion
dubious in literary taste, but characteristic and effective.
Orestes is described as the victim ' of *frenzies* ; for,' says
Electra, ' I scruple to give the name *Eumenides* to the powers
which terrorise him[6].' The true and ancient name of these
mythical avengers was Erinyes. Superstition discouraged
the mention of them by name ; but Electra has no such qualms
(*v.* 238), nor will her scruple bear such an interpretation.
She avoids the name Eumenides because its signification,
Gracious Ones, is, to her thinking, so horribly inappropriate.
The sneer is in truth directed against Aeschylus, who, for a
special purpose, had cautiously promoted the identification of
the Erinyes with the Eumenides by the title of the last play
in the *Orestea*[7]. 'Eumenides' became at last a literary
synonym of 'Erinyes'; but the transition was slow, and our

---

[1] See especially *v.* 303, where Electra is told to get herself food, and
passim.

[2] *vv.* 46, 428 etc.   [3] *vv.* 444, 760 etc.   [4] *vv.* 5, 8.

[5] *v.* 28.   [6] *v.* 37.

[7] The name *Eumenides* is not found in the play as we have it, and according to
the better opinion never was.

play, the *Orestes*, exhibits such uses of the newer title (*vv.* 321, 836), as were apparently still not common. The sarcasm of Electra accents this modernism, explaining in what spirit the language of Aeschylus is adopted ; and though it is scarcely within the rules of art, nothing could better signify the atmosphere of the play. For Euripides, the sick delusions of Orestes are of course merely natural (whatever that may mean), and the powers inflicting them need no name but *maniai,* 'frenzies.'

The political notes in the prologue are simple, except at one place, where a hint may be differently interpreted. The adultery of Clytaemnestra, as motive for the murder of her husband, is unfit, says Electra, for an unmarried woman to relate, and is therefore ' left obscure, *a point for common consideration*[1].' Her doubt is ironical, but not at all so the suggestion that the matter is proper for enquiry. The death of Agamemnon, and everything connected with it, ought long ago to have been the subject of a public enquiry. The inefficient provision for justice, where private initiative failed, was a common defect of Greek states, and of modern states also until recent times. It is the one excuse for Orestes, which the circumstances of this play admit ; imperfect as it is, it would, as we shall see, in all probability have induced the assembly to spare his life, if he had not himself been his own worst enemy. For this reason, it is properly touched upon in the exposition.

It need hardly be added, that Electra is also ironical in affecting, at her age and in her position, the delicacy of a girl. The accusation, from which she thinks fit to avert her maiden thoughts, she has in fact agitated with deadly persistency[2]. She

---

[1] *v.* 27 ἐῶ τοῦτ' ἀσαφὲς ἐν κοινῷ σκοπεῖν. The rendering 'I will not consider this in public' is incorrect, and would moreover imply a reference to the spectators (since there are no other hearers of Electra's soliloquy) which Tragedy does not permit. Nor does 'I leave...for whoso will to guess' (Way) quite represent the words : ἐν κοινῷ, however meant by the speaker, directs our thoughts to the public assembly, τὸ κοινόν.

[2] *v.* 619. The impatient dismissal of this subject by Tyndareus, assuredly no friend to Clytaemnestra, is a noticeable touch. We are clearly meant to understand

is but emphasizing, as elsewhere[1], the injury of her enforced celibacy, a topic taken over into this play from previous versions of the story by Euripides and others, but receiving here, like most topics, a new colour. It is no longer merely a wrong, but a physical and moral lesion, the source of her peculiar wickedness, οἷα δὴ γυνή[2]. Her hideous malice against the young girl, her cousin, is at bottom nothing but the familiar vice of an old maid, wrought up to the pitch of devilry by circumstance and occasion. She is a tragic 'cat.'

To her enters Helen, on whose character we have touched before. A brief conversation of masterly skill reveals the whole woman. It is enough to mention the main purpose of her coming out. She proposes that, as she (by the ill-guiding of the gods) will be in danger of her life, if she quits the house, Electra shall be so kind as to leave her brother, sleeping for the moment the sleep of exhaustion, and go, through the city which has excommunicated her, to the grave of Clytaemnestra, carrying gifts, which, to discharge the tender feelings of Helen, some one, it is plain, must present at once! And this she proposes weeping, with absolute sincerity, over the distresses of the family! The indulgence of the world for a lovely woman has destroyed in her the power to perceive anything but what at the moment it suits her to perceive. Even Electra, watching her tricks, is almost as much amused as indignant[3]. The immediate question, who shall be Helen's *choephoros*, is decided by a whimsical stroke. Electra after some fencing suggests Hermione, to which Helen incautiously answers that 'the street is no place for maids.' Seeing that not only Electra is a 'maid,' but Helen, wishing to command her services, has been pleased to lay particular and repeated stress upon that point[4], the argument is double-edged ; and it is received with a smile which cannot be misunderstood. Helen, in some confusion, changes her tack, and withdraws without further

---

that there had been exaggeration, if not falsehood, about it; and the fact is that, in the present setting of the story, it ceases to be important.

[1] *v.* 205, and see *v.* 72.　　　　[2] *v.* 32.
[3] *vv.* 126 foll.　　　　[4] *vv.* 72, 92.

pressure her objection to sending her daughter, who is summoned and sent accordingly[1]:

El.   I cannot, will not see my mother's grave!
Hel.   But yet,...a servant?   Surely such were no...
         Fit bearer!
El.   Why not send Hermione,
         Your daughter?
Hel.   Crowded streets are not for maids!
         (*Electra is silent; they regard one another; then Helen*
                        continues hastily)
         Yet after all...my sister fostered her,
         And has a claim...yes, your suggestion, girl,
         Converts me quite,...my daughter...she shall go;
         A good suggestion...(*calls*) Child, Hermione!

The part of Hermione, although small, is theatrically important, and even principal. Here, though silent, she is kept before us long; for Helen has not only to give directions, but to cut, as an offering to the grave, a piece (it should be a lock) of her own hair, a matter for care and economy[2]. We have thus time to take an impress of the pathetic figure in her solitary black, stone-cold, rigid with the horror of her bereavement, obeying without a word the unkind, though welcome, commission of this idol-mother, all jewels and tears, who has come out of night with the voice and the features of the foster-mother lost[3]. The rite which she goes to perform, the *choephoria* or communion of the dead, was perhaps the most tender of Greek offices, and moreover—a point not less relevant to the use eventually made of it in this play— had been staged by Aeschylus as the central solemnity of the

---

107 ΗΛ.   τί δ' οὐχὶ θυγατρὸς Ἑρμιόνης πέμπεις δέμας;
     ΕΛ.   εἰς ὄχλον ἕρπειν παρθένοισιν οὐ καλόν.—
            καὶ μὴν τίνοι γ' ἂν τῇ τεθνηκυίᾳ τροφάς·
            καλῶς ἔλεξας, πείθομαί τέ σοι, κόρη·
            καὶ πέμψομέν γε θυγατέρ'· εὖ γάρ τοι λέγεις.

The passage, for want of perceiving the double edge of *v.* 108, has been wrongly distributed, and otherwise mistaken. It is possible that Electra was made actually to repeat Helen's words (*v.* 108) with emphasis, but this would be no improvement. That Helen sees the point and acknowledges defeat is shown by the κόρη (*maiden*) of *v.* 110.

[2] *vv.* 126 foll.   [3] See *vv.* 245 foll., as explained hereafter.

Orestea. The purpose of it was, by prescribed offerings and persistent prayer, to make temporary connexion with the departed. It could not therefore be performed with haste; and though Helen comfortably tells her daughter to return 'the very moment it is done,' she is absent, as was to be expected[1], for some hours. Electra, whose part of daughter to Clytaemnestra she has filled from infancy with unconscious usurpation[2], watches her departure with feelings which can be imagined.

Scarcely are the prisoners alone again when the Chorus, the inevitable visitors, arrive, full of curiosity, and throwing Electra into an agony lest her patient should lose his sleep. With fifteen persons engaged in being quiet, there is no little noise; and at the first moment when Electra is not on guard, one of the ladies gets to the bed of Orestes, and is remarking that there is a slackness in his attitude which she does not like, when the strange voice wakes him[3]. His sister, after tenderly composing him, hastens to communicate, 'while he can understand[4],' the arrival of Menelaus; and the very shock of hope exposes him to an access of delirium. Here occurs a dramatic effect of great power and simplicity. The voice of Orestes has aroused the curiosity of Helen, who, not choosing to present herself to the visitors, goes up with some of her attendants to survey the scene at ease from the parapet. There she is espied by Electra, at the moment when Orestes is asking excitedly, whether really, really his uncle has come. 'He is here' Electra answers, pointing up,

> Arrived—and there thou hast the proof of it—
> With Helen, whom he brings from taken Troy.

The effect is prompt, and astonishing. Orestes gazes fixedly at the place where the figure of Helen is visible, replying to Electra with increasing distraction, till he reveals with a shriek that what his eyes see there is *his mother*, and that his imagination has converted Electra and her companions into fiends, whom the ghost is urging on. The natural resemblance of two sisters, and the fact that Helen's presence really is

---

[1] *vv.* 1211–1215. [2] *v.* 1340. [3] *vv.* 195–210. [4] *v.* 238.

almost incredible, make the delusion as likely as it is startling, while it serves the purpose of showing that the supernatural perceptions of Orestes are but fancies, that we are not in the world of the *Eumenides*, where ghosts and furies actually walk. Here, as in the *Iphigenia in Taurica*[1], that there may be no doubt of this, we are shown of what they are made. 'Happier were Menelaus,' says Orestes, gazing darkly at Helen,

> More blest he were had he escaped alone :
> Sore bane he bringeth, if he bring his wife.

El. As beacons of reproach and infamy
    Through Hellas were the daughters Tyndareus gat.

Or. Be thou not like the vile ones !—this thou may'st—
    Not in word only, but in inmost thought!

El. Woe's me, my brother ! Wildly rolls thine eye :
    Swift changest thou to madness, sane but now !

Or. Mother !—beseech thee, hark not thou on me
    Yon maidens gory-eyed and snaky-haired !
    Lo there !—lo there ! they are nigh—they leap on me[2]!

We see that Electra, not perceiving the rush of her brother's thoughts from Helen to Clytaemnestra, innocently spurs it by her allusion to the daughters of Tyndareus. After a terrible struggle, he breaks from the women, and raves about, repelling the fiends with an imaginary bow and arrows (in the ancient legend real), which were 'given me by Apollo for such defence.' The acme is reached when some of those within, fascinated by excitement, are again seen on the parapet. The maniac fancies that he is driving his Furies into the air :

> Do ye not hear?—not see the feathered shafts
> At point to leap from my far-smiting bow?
> Ha ! ha !
> Why tarry ye ? Soar to the welkin's height
> On wings !

They vanish, and he swoons[3].

---

[1] *vv.* 281–294.   [2] *vv.* 247 foll. (Way).

[3] *vv.* 273 foll. (Way). By want of stage-directions, this scene is made incomprehensible. Electra (*v.* 245) proves the arrival of Menelaus by that of Helen, a convincing proof—if itself proved. But the only conceivable proof is that Helen *is seen*. Moreover, without this outward occasion and the other connected circumstances, the abrupt access and ending of Orestes' fit are inexplicable to the imagination. For the use of the roof and parapet compare *v.* 1567.

Recovering, he is helped to his couch, and there bemoans himself and his errors[1]. His saner thoughts are scarcely the less distressing. Apollo has betrayed him; Agamemnon himself would not have counselled a deed which has proved so fruitless; Electra, so faithful, must perish too. Viewing these reflexions in the light of the whole play, we notice here, as in all that he and his accomplices say, that of crime as crime, as an offence against law, they seem not to have the conception. Beyond himself and his family, Orestes sees nothing. Argos is nothing but a menace. That murder is an outrage against society, and matricide against humanity, are thoughts which his mind does not form, and, as we are to see, cannot grasp. So perfect an insensibility of the civic nerves would scarcely now be possible, at least we may hope so, in a youth neither dull nor unfeeling; and it must have been abnormal in the republic of Athens. But among the young members of the aristocratic treason-clubs, something like it may have been not uncommon: the Orestes and Pylades of this play may help us to conceive such a *hetaireia*[2], its effect upon life and affairs. The mutual tenderness of Orestes and his sister, the vividness of their feelings so far as they can feel, while making more conspicuous the narrowness of the range, sustain our interest. For the moment indeed we are conscious mainly of their misery.

Electra having been with difficulty persuaded to go in and take a rest, Menelaus, arriving shortly after from the port, is received by Orestes (and the Chorus) alone. Not suspecting the ghastly figure on the couch to be his nephew, with whose features he is of course unacquainted, he explains his disappointment and perplexities to the sympathetic ladies. Of his character we have spoken already. He is vulgarity itself; and his actions, apart from the incalculable effects which they happen to produce, would call for no remark. A trait in him, suiting the rest, is that, though without real religion, his fancy is grossly superstitious,—like a sailor's, as Euripides

---

[1] *vv.* 277 foll.

[2] The point is actually indicated; see *v.* 804, as respective to the rest of that scene.

seems to suggest[1]. It is everywhere evident that in the situation he is not likely, and indeed not able, to be of use. He is however genuinely shocked at the condition of Orestes, and the dangers which Orestes describes. The political part of this description[2] should be read with scepticism. It is, as we might suspect from the ignorance and isolation of Orestes, and as we afterwards discover, a complete misrepresentation. Placed as he is, Orestes plainly cannot have accurate information on the state of affairs, nor is he qualified to estimate rightly such information as he may have. The slayers of Clytaemnestra are not the objects of any such general and implacable persecution as he suggests; nor (which is still more important) is it in the least true, either that the friends of Agamemnon are passive, or that their enemies, the friends of Aegisthus, 'command the obedience of the city[3].' All this, as the proceedings of the assembly prove, is a wild exaggeration of half-known and unfamiliar terrors, a travesty of the real situation, which, though grave enough, is different, and not at all desperate. For the present we will merely remark, that the formidable Oiax, who, according to Orestes, is bent on 'hunting him off the face of the earth,' is never heard of again, and that neither Oiax, nor any 'friend of Aegisthus,' so much as takes part in the debate. Oiax has nothing to do with the present case; and his enmity, if it exists, could not have any influence on the assembly. In the statement about him we have incidentally the device, beloved of all dramatists, by which a speaker is made to criticize unconsciously his own position. The motive for the supposed zeal of Oiax is revenge for Palamedes, put to death by Agamemnon at Troy. The brother of the slain, says Orestes indignantly, visits upon him, the son of the slayer, the deed of his father,

> a deed
> Not mine at all! And yet my life is sought
> At three removes[4]!

---

[1] vv. 360–369, 409, with which contrast v. 417. The story about Glaucus, a characteristic piece of Euripidean work, will be considered hereafter, in connexion with the appearance of Apollo.

[2] vv. 427 foll.   [3] v. 436 οὗτοί μ' ὑβρίζουσ' ὧν πόλις τανῦν κλύει.

[4] v. 433   ME. ξυνῆκα· Παλαμήδους σε τιμωρεῖ φόνος.

OP. οὗ γ' οὐ μετῆν μοι, διὰ τριῶν δ' ἀπόλλυμαι.

In διὰ τριῶν, three off, the preposition is used, as in δι' ὀλίγου, at a little distance, etc.,

The doctrine of the *vendetta*, or representative retaliation, by which, if A has offended B, the representative of B has against the representative of A as good a cause as principal against principal—this notion, when Orestes is to suffer by it, he can perceive to be pernicious and unreasonable. Yet upon what other ground is he standing himself? If, for the purpose of slaying Aegisthus and even his own mother, Orestes may claim the full immunity of Agamemnon, why is it unreasonable that he should be saddled, in another case, with the full responsibility of Agamemnon? 'At three removes' a *vendetta* is monstrous; but at two (Orestes—Agamemnon—Aegisthus) it is plain justice! The plain fact is that the *vendetta* is vicious in principle, the negation of all civilised morality; and Euripides makes occasion to expose this by the mouth of the avenger himself.

At length Orestes brings the dialogue to the point at which he aims, by flinging himself at his uncle's feet:

> In thee mine hope hath refuge yet from ills.
> Thou com'st to folk in misery, prosperous thou :...
> Requite, to whom thou ow'st, my father's boon[1].

And at this instant enters, led by his attendants, an aged man in deep mourning. It is Tyndareus, king of Sparta, the father of Clytaemnestra. This entrance is a turn of that sort which, depending on surprise, is impaired by knowledge of the whole work. We have been compelled to spoil it, by noticing the grandfather, in the course of our observations, as one of the *dramatis personae*. But in the drama nothing could be less expected, or more interesting. Here, and not too soon, we listen to a personage who claims pure compassion, one that has been wounded repeatedly in affection and honour, wounded by the act of his grandson more deeply than ever, and who is placed moreover in the cruellest of

to express interval. The point is that to connect Oiax with Orestes requires three steps, Oiax—Palamedes—Agamemnon—Orestes, and that Orestes is thus artificially fixed with a responsibility 'not his own.' Other versions, such as 'my life is sought by three,' do not fit the context.

[1] *vv.* 448 foll. (Way).

straits. And coming at this moment, he is more than this. He is the answer to the blind cry of Orestes for help. Here, if we pity Orestes, or if he pities himself, is where he should have sought the key to the lock, the finger to the knot ; and we wonder that we did not think of it sooner. For why has this tottering man made the journey from Sparta to Argos ? Why is he here this morning ? Why, of all places, in this house ? Because—it is obvious before he betrays it—he has been agitating, *and has not solved*, the dolorous problem presented to him by the coming trial. Even in modern life such a position might be not only painful but difficult. When the machinery of justice depended so much as it did in Greece upon individual impulse, the perplexity was intense. Clytaemnestra was a dishonour to her father, a bitter disgrace ; but after all she was his daughter, and she had such rights as belong to a criminal. The law, most venerable of names to the old Spartan[1], is concerned in her rights. Of these rights he, as society was then constituted, is a legal guardian and, in the circumstances, the sole. It is his duty to pursue her murderers, if it may be, to the death. And yet, who else is the natural director of his misguided grandson? He has loved the boy (it is Orestes who tells us so[2]) like a child of his own. And now, though abhorring, though furiously hating, he loves him still, or he would not be here. And the boy is alive, and, by grace of the law, may yet live. The king of Sparta could not decently, or perhaps legally, address the Argive assembly on such an occasion in person. But he could, and he does, appear by a representative—by counsel, as we should say, though the analogy is not exact. Must he not so appear ? And if he should, what are to be the instructions ?

The scene which follows is psychologically the best in the piece, as it is also the turning point, though remote, of the catastrophe. To appreciate it fully, we must know, that the representative of Tyndareus is *the only person*, who in the subsequent debate pleads against Orestes[3]. The grandfather, as he tells us, had already once decided on this course, but had revoked the decision. In consequence of what now

---

[1] *vv.* 487, 523, and Tyndareus *passim*.   [2] *vv.* 462 foll.   [3] *vv.* 902-916.

passes, he returns to it[1]. But the old man meant, so far as in the storm of his feelings he knew what he meant,—he hoped, as he proves by seeking this interview, that it would end otherwise. Affection in him so struggles with anger, that in the midst of expounding to Menelaus the enormity of Orestes' crime, he bursts into tears, when he attempts to address the boy himself[2]. He comes to make the offender suffer as he ought, to confound him, crush him, and break him to pieces. He is indignant—and this feeling, like all else in the miserable situation, is inevitable—that he should have been forced to seek, when his pardon and aid should have been sought. He will not admit that he has taken the first step. He is in Argos (so he says) for the purpose of 'causing offerings to be made[3]' at the grave of his daughter—a thing which plainly could not have been done without a journey! He has come to the house (so he says), because, after so long a separation, he could not keep away from his son-in-law[4]—with whom nevertheless he instantly quarrels, and whom he presently joins with Helen in a sentence of scathing contempt[5]. He is astonished and shocked (so he says) to find Menelaus conversing with the matricide[6]—than which indeed nothing, in that house, could be more surprising! Nevertheless he is there; and when all is said, he must have come there in order to be asked, and to grant, forgiveness. But that forgiveness is never asked. And yet Orestes knows that he needs it; he can admit to Menelaus, while the old man approaches, that here indeed is one whom he has foully injured, whose love he has cruelly repaid[7]. But his fate, that fate which consists in a man's being what he is, refuses him the chance to save himself by just saying *that* to his grandfather. Partly by ill luck, but chiefly because he is perverse, conceited, and half-crazy, he gets to argument with his grandfather, and fixes in

---

[1] *v.* 609. Tyndareus to Orestes, μᾶλλόν μ' ἀνάξεις ἐπὶ σὸν ἐξελθεῖν φόνον, 'Instead of winning me (μᾶλλον), thou wilt make me thy prosecutor again,' 'wilt *recall* me to the seeking of thy life.' The change of ἀνάξεις to ἀνάψεις, 'thou wilt kindle me more' (recentiores libri pauci), or ἀνάξεις (modern), is an error, and not insignificant.

[2] *vv.* 526 foll.   [3] χοὰς χεόμενος, *v.* 472, and see *v.* 611.   [4] *vv.* 470 foll.

[5] *vv.* 518–522.   [6] *v.* 481.   [7] *vv.* 459 foll.

the mind of the one man, who can protect him, the conviction
that he is no fit object for mercy.

It is his ill luck that his uncle is there. As Tyndareus
comes near, he cowers down, abashed and conscience-stricken[1].
If the grandfather could have found him so, and alone, pity
might have had the first word. As it is, the first movement
of Tyndareus is to defend his dignity by denouncing his
son-in-law (whom he despises, and suspects very justly of
regarding the young man's case in no proper spirit) for having
anything to do with such a villain. To Menelaus, the disgrace
of the criminal, from which the old king shrinks as from a fire,
is nothing; and the imperious tone of the rebuke nettles his
self-complacency. Why should he not stand by his own
brother's son, and him so unfortunate? Kin must have its
due. 'You have been too long abroad!' answers Tyndareus,
rigid with indignation; 'In Greece, the first claim is that of
the law.' 'Anger and age,' retorts Menelaus, 'mislead your
wisdom.' 'Wisdom!', thunders the king,

> Dispute of wisdom—what is that to *him*?
> If there's a common sense of right and wrong,
> Here is the dullest fool that ever was!

There is nothing to be argued. A man must not take the
law into his own hands. If the mother was a vile wretch,
as she was, the courts were open, and the old, the regular
way[2]. Any one can see, Menelaus must see, that otherwise
the series of murder must be perpetual. Wicked wives are as
hateful to Tyndareus as they—should be to the husband of
Helen! But one must support the law, or we go back to
savagery. So he runs fluently on. But when he turns to his
grandson, grief and sheer pain overwhelm him, and the oration
breaks down in sobs and wild lament:

---

[1] *v.* 467. On the movements see note in Appendix.

[2] In *v.* 515 φυγαῖσι δ' ὁσιοῦν ἀνταποκτείνειν δὲ μή the argument is not for
punishment always and only by *exile*. Tyndareus is at this very moment demanding
the penalty of 'a life for a life.' The point is that the murderer must be pursued
through φυγαί, that is, by making him a defendant (φεύγων) and putting him to the
bar of the law, not by another murder. The question of death or exile is
secondary, and will depend on the case.

What heart hadst thou, O miscreant, in that hour
When suppliant unto thee thy mother bared
Her breast? I, who saw not the horrors there,
Yet drown, ah me! mine aged eyes with tears...
    One thing, in any wise, attests my words—
Thou art loathed of Gods, punished for matricide
By terrors and mad ravings[1]. Where is need
For other witness of things plain to see?
Be warned then, Menelaus : strive not thou
Against the Gods, being fain to help this man.
Leave him to die by stoning of the folk,
Or never set thou foot on Spartan ground.
Dying, my daughter paid but justice' debt ;...
Yet...it beseemed not *him* to deal her death.
I...in all else have been a happy man...
Save in my daughters : herein...most ill-starred[2].

So he ends, and...*he does not go away.* He will cast off the
criminal ; everyone shall cast him off ; but he does not go[3].
Menelaus, who has had time to cool and to grasp the
situation, is silent ; and the way is open for Orestes.

It seems impossible that he should not take it, impossible
that, if he cannot understand, he should not now feel, what
is to be done. Whether the doctrine, which his grandfather
asserts to be the alphabet of morality, be true or false,
universal or peculiar—and modesty might at least suggest
misgivings,—the duty and interest of Orestes are the same.
His duty is to heal where he has hurt, his interest, to appease
the opponent. Whatever may be his rights, he is here and
now in the wrong, and it seems impossible that he should do
anything but confess and have done. But no! His case, as
he sees it, possesses his brain ; he has the weak man's love of
dissertation for its own sake[4]; and he insists on having his
turn.

---

[1] This he has learnt at the grave of Clytaemnestra (*v.* 472) from Hermione
(*v.* 114). It is in fact her report of Orestes' miserable state, which has sent the
grandfather to see for himself ; this is the real meaning of *vv.* 532–533.

[2] *vv.* 526 foll. (Way) with some changes of punctuation.

[3] The Chorus fill the pause with the usual distich. See Appendix, *Helen* 944.

[4] This comes out again in the sequel (*vv.* 640 foll.) ; where see the epigram of
Menelaus (*v.* 638) on the merits of speech—and of silence. Menelaus is of course
well aware that Orestes has done his best to ruin himself.

His speech is painfully interesting. With the natural eloquence of sincerity and passion, it has that pathos which, apart from judgment or in spite of it, must belong to an act of unconscious suicide, committed by one young, inexperienced, and distracted by physical and mental suffering. But, for all this, it reveals a perverse and unkindly nature, an intelligence defective and twisted, feelings blind and irresponsive to a plain appeal. The legal conception of crime, the civic conception, is so totally incomprehensible to him, that he fancies himself to be refuting his elder's 'high-sounding' vindication of law[1], when he claims to be himself a reformer of the law! After his patriotic deed, wicked wives will no longer imagine that maternity is to protect them against their sons; that is a 'law' which, thanks to him, will be law no longer[2]. He insists on the sacred duty of avenging his father, precisely as if this, and not the way of doing it, were the essence of his alleged offence[3]. But more unhappy and repulsive than these intellectual errors is the perversion of his feelings, the insolence and cruelty (no softer terms are adequate) with which he handles the wounds inflicted by himself upon his progenitor. He begins indeed not ill, requesting audience with respectful humility[4]. But this modesty is discharged by the mere profession. He instructs his ancestor in the important truth (learnt apparently at Delphi[5]) that the father, as 'sower of the plant,' is the true parent of a child, the mother only the ground in which it grows—an inferior obligation[6]. He reminds the parent and king, that his daughter was not only a murderess but an adulteress; and enlarging upon this opportune theme, he arrives at the conclusion that Tyndareus himself is author of all the mischief!

> Thou, ancient, in begetting a vile daughter
> Didst ruin me; for, through her recklessness
> Unfathered, I became a matricide.

---

[1] *v.* 571 ὡς σὺ κομπεῖς.

[2] *vv.* 564–578, especially *v.* 571 τόνδ' ἔπαυσα τὸν νόμον, and *v.* 576 compared with *v.* 500.   [3] *vv.* 546–563, 579–584.   [4] *vv.* 544–545.

[5] Apollo, in the *Eumenides* of Aeschylus (*v.* 657), has recourse to it in a moment of embarrassment. This would alone suffice to prove that Orestes, in the conception of Euripides, here speaks as a fool.   [6] *vv.* 552–556.

He might, he says[1], have been virtuous as Telemachus, if he
had been given a mother like Penelope! This strain of insult
runs through the whole, and reappears, with the improvement
of a sententious pity, in the conclusion:

> Nay, say not thou that this was not well done,
> Albeit untowardly for me the doer.
> *Happy the life of men whose marriages*
> *Are blest: but they for whom they ill betide,*
> *At home, abroad, are they unfortunate.*

But for the practical effect of the speech all these things
are indifferent. It is enough for Tyndareus that the murderer
justifies his act. No sooner does he catch a glimpse of
this intention than he turns away[2]. Every word serves to
bring him back to the resolution, which he now announces,
that he will prosecute to the death so hardened a villain,
him and his sister also, the worse of the pair. It should be
noted here that Electra has lived in Argos, at her home,
within reach of Tyndareus' observation, whereas Orestes has
been in Phocis for years. About the character and merits of
his granddaughter, it does not appear that the king ever
entertained any doubts[3]. With a threat flung at Menelaus
he goes; and Orestes, after defying him, turns to the really
important business, as he conceives it, of securing the aid of
his uncle[4].

That personage, now thoroughly and most reasonably
alarmed, is pacing to and fro,

> Treading the mazes of perplexity,

and begs not to be interrupted in studying the difficulties of
the situation. His chief desire, beyond doubt, is to get
decently out of the house. But to do him justice, the
intentions which he finally announces[5] are the best possible:

---

[1] *vv.* 585–590.

[2] At *v.* 547, I think. A movement is implied in ἀπελθέτω δή, 'Go away
then' (*v.* 548); Orestes' only feeling is relief, that the venerable appearance of
his grandfather no longer embarrasses his eloquence.

[3] *vv.* 615–621. The fine metaphor in *v.* 621, ἕως ὑφῆψε δῶμ' ἀνηφαίστῳ πυρί,
is a compendium of the play, both in the moral aspect and in the scenic. I take
from it the title of this essay.   [4] *v.* 630.   [5] *vv.* 682 foll.

he will try to recover Tyndareus (this of course he perceives to be vital), 'to persuade him and people generally to be moderate in extremity[1]'—that is, in plain words, to be satisfied with the penalty of exile. Whether this operation is to include an attempt by himself to address the civic assembly, he does not decide, and really seems not to know. A popular meeting, he shrewdly remarks, however hostile, will give surprising chances to the wary:

> When the storm is lulled,
> Lightly a man may win his will of them.

Except as to the assembly (where, if present, he does not speak, but on the other hand is not wanted and has no opportunity), the play gives not the least evidence either that his promises are performed or that they are not. Nor does it matter. It is plain, on the one hand, that he can do little or nothing, on the other, that if he could he would not, at any considerable risk to himself. Tyndareus, the one man whose character, dignity, and relation to the case, make even his neutrality invaluable to the accused, and his least aid almost decisive in their favour, Tyndareus, who loved Orestes, the perverse and miserable youth has rejected, and sent to the side of his enemies. Menelaus, who cannot save him, and who, though not indifferent to his nephew, cares more for his own little finger, Menelaus he very consistently pesters with entreaty.

In spite of his uncle's evident and quite justifiable impatience, he insists that, before decision, his uncle's deliberation shall have the benefit of his arguments. Menelaus, who has heard him argue, ironically consents:

> Speak; *thou hast spoken well.* Silence than speech
> Sometimes is better, and than silence speech[2].

Thus encouraged, and opening with the remark that, for clearness, it is best to be long, he delivers an address, which the

---

[1] *v.* 704 Τυνδάρεών τέ σοι πειράσομαι | πόλιν τε πεῖσαι τῷ λίαν χρῆσθαι καλῶς.

[2] *v.* 638   λέγ', εὖ γὰρ εἶπας. ἔστι δ' οὗ σιγὴ λόγου
κρείσσων γένοιτ' ἄν, ἔστι δ' οὗ σιγῆς λόγος.

modern reader could well spare. The substance indeed is
not out of character; for it exhibits the same blindness to
fact, the same lack of grasp upon the realities of the situation,
which belong to the speaker everywhere. What is here
wanted, if anything, is practical suggestion. It is not the
fault of Orestes, that in that line he can contribute only
this: impossibility is friendship's true opportunity[1]. But
since that is all, this is another of those occasions where,
as Menelaus observes, it is better to say nothing. The
obligations of Menelaus to Agamemnon, which he proves
with pedantic formality, need no proving; and adjurations
without counsel go wide of the mark. So far however, there
is nothing to surprise us; what does surprise, and seems now
simply impossible, is the style. This—utterly remote from
the natural force of the speech to Tyndareus, unlike any
other speaking in the play, and most unlike that common
element in it all, which comes from Euripides himself—is
a rhetoric frigid and artificial beyond anything now conceivable:

> Grant I do wrong: I ought, for a wrong's sake,
> To win of thee a wrong; for Agamemnon
> Wrongly to Ilium led the hosts of Greece:—
> Not that himself had sinned, but sought to heal
> The sin and the wrong-doing of thy wife...
> Aulis received my sister's blood[2]: I spare
> Thee this: I bid not slay Hermionê.
> Thou needst must, when I fare as now I fare,
> Have vantage, and the debt I must forgive[3].

This incomparable oratory, which (let it be repeated) is as unlike what Euripides offers for real eloquence as anything can
possibly be, and which caricatures the worst features of a
school that was no longer in fashion, is apparently supposed
to represent what might be produced, if a young man of no
sound judgment, fresh from a rhetorical education, should
suppose himself called upon to apply his lessons to practice.

---

[1] *vv.* 665 foll.   [2] See note in the Appendix, *v.* 658.
[3] *vv.* 646 foll., 658 foll. (Way). The translation does more than justice. Note
especially the artificial placing of ἀδικῶ...ἄδικον...ἀδίκως in the first passage.

Happily modern education, whatever its defects, does not err in this way or to this extent; and we cannot but suspect Euripides, perhaps unjustly, of over-painting. The orator's unwilling appeal to the name of Helen is more naturally turned, but becomes, for this reason, something very like an insult to Helen's husband[1]. The peroration, after promising better for a moment, is then marred by the conscious formality of composition:

> O brother of my father[2], deem that *he*
> Hears this, who lies 'neath earth, that over thee
> His spirit hovers: what I say he saith.
> This, urged with[3] tears, moans, pleas of misery,
> Have I said, and have claimed my life of thee,
> Seeking what all men seek, not I alone[4].

Menelaus, whom we may suspect of not listening, replies, as we have seen, by a profession of good will, which may or may not be sincere, and by an explanation of what is practicable, which could not be improved[5]. He then hurries off, pursued by the taunts, prayers, and curses of the unhappy Orestes, who now gives himself for lost. With rapture therefore he welcomes the sudden return of his comrade and confidant, Pylades.

And if pluck, audacity, and devotion could save him, he has found them indeed. Pylades is ready for anything,

---

[1] *vv.* 669–672.

[2] ὦ πατρὸς ὅμαιμε θεῖε. The flattering equivocation in θεῖε (adjective or substantive) must not be missed. No native ear could miss it, and such a speech as this would not be complete without one such *démodé* decoration.

[3] Rather 'in the way of,' 'in the pathetic *line*' (ἔs τε δάκρυα καὶ γόουs καὶ συμφοράs) as contrasted with the practical application. But modern English (fortunately) can scarcely give the effect.

[4] How pathetic in the murderer of his mother! We may take occasion to note that this Orestes, among other winning traits, is a coward, contrasting in this strikingly with Pylades, who is 'as brave as a weasel.'

[5] *vv.* 682 foll. The question, whether Menelaus has any armed force at his disposal, is unanswerable and immaterial. It is inconceivable that he should be in a position to control the state. He says that he has no force (*v.* 688), and, since he has been travelling, not fighting, he probably speaks the truth—the more probably that he does not pretend any moral objection to violence. Electra (*v.* 54) can know nothing exact about the matter, and what she says is on any interpretation vague; see Mr Wedd's note.

not less so because, as he presently relates[1], he has found
no countenance in his native Phocis, has been turned out
of doors by his own father, and is actually, as we say, 'on the
street.' Unhappily, what Orestes wants is an intercessor, which
Pylades cannot be, and an adviser, which he can.

The report of the approaching assembly, and the sight of
the preparations, have made him almost as excited as Orestes[2].
In a rapid dialogue (the rapidity is emphasized by a change
of metre) the two young men, having first inflamed each
other by recounting the behaviour of their unnatural kinsfolk,
deliberate (if the word is applicable) about the trial; Orestes,
who apparently misapplies the remarks of his uncle[3], proposes
that he should go to the assembly and speak for himself.
A modern reader may here be reminded that Orestes is
not in form a defendant, for the proceeding is not in form
judicial; as an Argive by birth, he can attend the assembly
if he pleases. Pylades, upon the ground that, since the case
is otherwise desperate, to do something is at worst 'a finer
way to die[4],' decides that Orestes shall go, and—which indeed
follows of itself, for the fevered prisoner is in no condition
to go alone—that he himself will conduct him and appear at
his side. The supreme courage of this act, since Pylades,
once known to be in Argos, cannot hope to escape with
life[5], and the sympathy for both lads, which their isolation
and attachment excite, makes pathetic their prodigious mistake. A spectator, who knew what an *ecclesia* was like—and
few Athenians were without this knowledge—must have been
almost intolerably agitated by the desire to stop them. What
Orestes is as an orator, we have seen; we know his opinion
of his case; we can anticipate the skill with which he will
adapt himself to his audience, and the sympathy with which
a sovereign assembly will receive his view of law[6]. That

---

[1] *vv.* 763 foll.   [2] *vv.* 729–731.
[3] *vv.* 696 foll.   [4] *v.* 782.
[5] Whether he is or could be made amenable to the law of Argos, we are not
told, except by himself (*v.* 771), which is inconclusive. But he is beyond the
protection of that law, might well be lynched (*v.* 770), and will certainly be
assassinated.
[6] Refer to *vv.* 564–578, and that speech generally.

they should not hear it, is the one thing now left to wish
for him. But neither to Pylades nor to Orestes does it
occur—how should such a consideration, or any relevant
consideration, occur to two boys, frantic with haste and
despair, of whom neither, we may presume, has taken part
in a political meeting, much less addressed one, in his life?—
it does not strike them, that speech can exasperate as easily
as propitiate, and that to speak or not to speak, as a question
of policy for a given occasion, depends upon *what* you will
say, *how* you will say it, and *who* are to hear!

Or.	Should I go and tell the people—
Pyl.	That thou wroughtest righteously?
Or.	Taking vengeance for my father?
Pyl.	Glad might they lay hold on thee.

The fear of violence, the possible imprudence of quitting
the house, is the only caution which crosses the counsellor's
mind; and decision is taken upon the sentiment, that it is
'finer' to do something! Concerning the balance of public
opinion and the probable course of debate, Orestes has
nothing to tell, nor Pylades to ask. So utterly is all this
ignored, that in relating the visits of his grandfather and uncle,
*Orestes does not even mention the debate, or the part which they
will or may take in it.* The determination of Tyndareus to
prosecute, the single thing of practical importance which has
come out, he does not notice. His one idea is that Menelaus,
who should have saved him from execution, has by Tyndareus
been frightened away[1]. Pylades on his side is equally blind
to the question, whether an Argive, on trial for a murder
committed in Argos, will be recommended to favour by the
companionship of his foreign accomplice; although his own
language[2] must suggest that reflexion to any experienced
or reasonable person. His political wisdom exhausts itself
in the suggestion (such it seems to be) that a democracy, being
notoriously leadable, may be led by himself and his friend[3]!
Nor should we quite pass over, though less pertinent to the

---

[1] *vv.* 736–754.

[2] *v.* 771, with the inimitable πάντα ταῦτ' ἐν ὄμμασιν (*All this depends upon the
eye*) of *v.* 785. [3] *v.* 773.

business, the many revelations of the young men's moral taste:

OP. οὗτος ἦλθ', ὁ τὰς ἀρίστας θυγατέρας σπείρων πατήρ.
ΠΥ. Τυνδάρεων λέγεις· ἴσως σοι θυγατέρος θυμούμενος¹.

All things considered, the persons, their relationship, the situation, and everything, these two sentences would stand well in a competition for the most revolting sentiment ever attributed to a human being. One wonders again, whether Euripides has over-painted; but one may believe not. Among the younger members of the oppressed nobility in the year 408 B.C., among the *hetairoi*² of the *hetaireiai*, there may well have been some moral jewels of the first water.

However, the resolve is taken, and Pylades completes his work by forbidding, as a loss of time, disclosure to Electra. A final incident illuminates grimly the difference between the pair, and the sort of religion, devout but unenlightened, by which the softer and more complicated spirit has been driven into the same path as the more hard. 'Take me,' says Orestes, 'to the grave of my father.'—'What for?'—'To pray his aid.'—'Well, at least he owes it³.' And so, leaning upon the heart 'by habit welded to my own,' upon the comrade 'more precious than a thousand kin,' Orestes goes forth to face the assembled citizens.

A choric ode carries us over the time occupied by the trial. In the next scene Electra, almost at the same moment when she first learns with dismay what her brother has done (*Who was the adviser?* is her significant exclamation⁴), receives tidings of the fatal result. The report of the debate has a species of interest not common in the formal narratives of Greek tragedy. Generally speaking, the narrators have no special character; they are merely competent observers of the facts. But in this case, the reporter is a witness manifestly and extremely incompetent; and his mind is a medium of intense refraction. A rustic thrall, attached to the family as something between retainer and serf⁵, he has by accident come into the city and witnessed the debate. His relation

¹ v. 750. ² v. 804. ³ vv. 796-797. ⁴ v. 849. ⁵ vv. 866 foll.

of the unfamiliar proceedings has therefore, especially for citizens of Athens, all the piquancy of prejudice, ignorance, and misconception. The selection of such a narrator is in my opinion alone sufficient to disprove the supposition (which on other grounds also appears to me not entertainable) that Euripides intended his picture as a satire on the proceedings, reflecting indirectly upon the *ecclesia* of Athens. If he had meant anything of the sort, surely he would have put the description into the mouth of a person, whom an average citizen of Athens, an average member of the *ecclesia*, would recognize as at least competent to understand what he saw, one fitted by experience to estimate fairly the bearings of what was done and the intentions of the actors. A modern dramatist, who desired to stigmatize some proceeding of the House of Commons, would scarcely describe the debate through the mouth of a gillie from Sutherland or a game-keeper from Connemara, who had somehow got into the Strangers' Gallery. The Euripidean narrator is a person who, because of his breeding, regards it as monstrous that the heir of Agamemnon should be tried for his life at all, and who, by his manner of living, has been precluded from learning how an arraignment is conducted, how such an assembly should be managed, and how, if at all, such a criminal may be saved or helped[1]. The only reason or excuse for choosing such a narrator is that a better-informed audience may appreciate his misconceptions, which are in fact as gross and transparent as they possibly could be.

The facts, of course, the things actually done and said, we must suppose him to state correctly ; he is our authority for them. But his comments we shall of course not accept ; on the contrary, we shall presume that they are absurd, and that we are intended to correct them. The facts which he reports are these.

The question 'whether Orestes, a matricide, should or should not suffer death?' having been formally propounded by an officer of the assembly, the lead is taken by the friends

---

[1] See the narrative *passim*.

of Agamemnon. Talthybius, his diplomatic agent[1], speaks
ambiguously, extolling his late leader, but condemning the
offender's conception of filial duty. Talthybius is followed
by 'the lord Diomede,' whose proposal, to inflict instead of
death the 'more scrupulous' penalty of exile[2], is received with
clamours of approbation and also of dissent. Next a professional orator, employed by Tyndareus, argues for the heavier
penalty. The argument is not given, because we have heard
it already; he is not only instructed but prompted by
Tyndareus, and his line therefore is that of the king of
Sparta: private vengeance cannot be tolerated, and severity
is necessary for the vindication of law[3]. But hereupon 'a
different person' starts up:

> No dainty presence, but a manful man[4],
> In town and market-circle seldom found,
> A yeoman—such as are the land's one stay,—
> Yet shrewd in grapple of words, when this he would;
> A stainless man, who lived a blameless life.
> He moved that they should crown Agamemnon's son
> Orestes, since he dared avenge his sire,
> Slaying the wicked and the godless wife
> Who sapped our strength:—none would take shield on arm,
> Or would forsake his home to march to war,
> If men's house-warders be seduced the while
> By stayers at home, and couches be defiled.
> To honest men he seemed to speak right well;
> *And none spake after. Then thy brother rose,*
> *And said—*

what we know that he will say, a repetition, varied for the
audience, of what he said, with such happy effect, to his
grandfather[5]. He (so he says) is the deliverer of Argos; he is

---

[1] κῆρυξ, *v.* 896; we have no description exactly corresponding to this as used
in the fifth century; 'herald' is quite incongruous. A 'military secretary' and an
'aide-de-camp' have partial resemblances. We may note that the same name is
given to the 'clerk' of the *ecclesia* (*v.* 885).

[2] *v.* 900. Note εὐσεβεῖν.   [3] *vv.* 491–525.

[4] *vv.* 917 foll. (Way).

[5] Compare *vv.* 932–942 with *vv.* 564–571, and especially the reference to
'law' in *v.* 941 with that in *v.* 571.

the champion of his fellow-citizens, as men, against the slavery
to which they must sink, 'if murder of the man be permitted
to woman[1]'. And therefore,

> if ye shall indeed slay me,
> *Law is annulled.*

Whereupon he is condemned to death, and this with such
animosity that he can scarcely obtain permission to escape
by suicide, within the day, the horrible Argive punishment
of stoning.

Upon the substance of this story, the course of the
proceedings, and the actual result, the comment of an average,
reasonable man in the Euripidean age, or any other civilized
age, would be, one would suppose, a shrug of the shoulders.
The whole thing is in essence and effect so obvious, so
predictable, that for this very reason (I presume) Euripides
selects an incompetent narrator, in order to animate, by
prejudiced and ignorant comments, what otherwise must have
fallen flat. In any age of law and civilized government,
and before any respectable tribunal that could exist, a defendant, guilty of such a crime that the most he could hope
for was a mitigated punishment, would, *and should*, be held to
prove himself both incorrigible and dangerous, if he insulted
his judges by taking the tone of a public benefactor. The
attitude of Orestes is suicidal and, like all his proceedings,
scarcely compatible with sanity. The main point which the
report brings out, and throws into sharp relief, is that his
condemnation to death, the rejection of the mitigated penalty,
is his own work, the natural outcome of those wise preparations which we have witnessed in the course of the play.

Had he propitiated his grandfather, or even spared to defy
and insult him, had he stayed at home, as Electra or any
person of sense would have advised, his life (it is plain)

---

[1] *v.* 935   εἰ γὰρ ἀρσένων φόνος
ἔσται γυναιξὶν ὅσιος, οὐ φθάνοιτ' ἔτ' ἂν
θνῄσκοντες, ἢ γυναιξὶ δουλεύειν χρεών.

The generality of ἄρσην and γυνή must not be limited to 'husband' and 'wife.'
To defend the position of Orestes, that a son may avenge one of his two parents
upon the other, the claim of superiority in sex is essential.

would have been scarcely in danger. The city was not, as
he wildly imagined[1], bent upon destroying him, nor the friends
of Agamemnon negligent. It is the other side, the friends
of Aegisthus, who are unprepared and conscious of weakness:
they do not attack ; they forego the advantage of the lead ;
they do not even aid in resisting the defenders. Talthybius
and Diomede take the lead, and, acting manifestly in concert,
conduct their cause with skill. For the sake of the defendant,
they must of course not pretend to justify the murder, or
omit to express sympathy with innocent sufferers, such as
the family of Aegisthus. Their claim, their only possible
claim, is to moderate ; and to make this clear is the part
of Talthybius, who, because he balances, because he

was ever glancing still
With flattering eye upon Aegisthus' friends,

is absurdly accused by the ignorant rustic of treachery: 'it is
the way of his class, the diplomatists, always to be on the
prosperous side[2].' Diomede, a person of the highest consideration, follows with the moderating proposal, to inflict only the
minor and usual penalty of exile. Nothing could be better.
And but for Orestes, there might, so far as appears, have
been actually no opposition. He however, as we know, has
secured an opponent, and a formidable one, the spokesman of
his grandfather. This person is described by the narrator
as an impudent wind-bag, confident of applause, no genuine
citizen, a mere tool[3], malicious, always able to mislead,
etc., etc.—all which simply means that he is a professional
orator, raised by his talents, a sort of Lysias who has obtained
citizenship, but detestable to the boorish retainer of the
Pelopidae, both as a new man and as a man of the schools.
The grave argument of Tyndareus, presented with skill, must
of course produce upon the audience a weighty impression.
But again the situation is saved. A respectable, though
uneducated, yeoman, described with partiality but also with

---

[1] vv. 425 foll., 721.   [2] v. 895 ἐπὶ τὸν εὐτυχῆ πηδῶσ' ἀεὶ κήρυκες.
[3] Or 'puppet' ἠναγκασμένος (904), acting by the motion of those who control
him (Wedd).

comprehension, gives vent to his rude but honest feelings, and presents the excuse of Orestes, such as it is, to the utmost advantage. Orestes, he says, has punished a sort of wickedness, which ought, in the public interest, to receive the severest punishment. This is true, and it goes home; for *no one ventures to reply.* The opposition, weak from the first, has collapsed; and the moderating proposal, if now put, is certain of success. But the defendant, being present, must be heard if he will. His interposition is at best mischievous; for the mere sight of the matricide must provoke a reaction. And then, instead of making the humble apology which is expected, he poses as a protector and superior, a restorer of manhood and liberty,—a defender of the law!

And lest these missiles should not stick, he begins by personally insulting the Argives as such. He begins by reminding the arbiters of his fate, that, according to their legendary history, they, as 'Danaidae,' are descended from criminal women, the daughters of Danaus, who (like Clytaemnestra) slew their husbands, and were absolved in the very place where the assembly is now sitting[1]. They are

'Lords of the land of Inachus,
Pelasgians first, but Danaids afterwards.'

Orestes would recall them to the virtue, which they possessed before that vicious blood had corrupted them! The result of this eloquence, though it surprises the rustic narrator[2], could surprise no one acquainted with affairs. The insulted citizens are instantly convinced, as Tyndareus was convinced before, that they have before them a dangerous, irreclaimable miscreant. The extreme sentence follows of course, and includes the sister.

The proceedings are meant to represent what would happen, under the circumstances, in any *ecclesia*, including

---

[1] *v.* 932 ὦ γῆν Ἰνάχου κεκτημένοι,
πάλαι Πελασγοί, Δαναΐδαι δὲ δεύτερον.
The point of the address is explained by the mention (*v.* 872) of the legend that the Argive place of assembly was first chosen for the trial of the Danaids. The legend is introduced for the purpose of the address, and neither must be struck out.

[2] *vv.* 943–945.

that of Athens,—save that the mention of stoning as a legal penalty would at Athens sound harshly[1], and is probably (but not certainly) an anachronism even for Argos. If we must consider, though it scarcely belongs to literary and dramatic criticism, how the Athenian *ecclesia*, as here represented, should be estimated by a historian of law and civilization, we should say, I think, that, for judicial purposes, it had the defects which are inherent in a popular assembly, which would be displayed, for instance, by the House of Commons, if it should unhappily revert to the practice of attainder. It was, for judicial purposes, too much influenced by feeling and incident. The resentment provoked by Orestes, though just, is too violent ; and on the other hand, the sensational explosion of the yeoman obtains for his opinion more effect than judicial minds would allow. As to the justice of the sentence, it is pure matter of opinion. My own judgment, if one must be a judge in the court of Argos as well as in that of drama, is that, in the given circumstances, a truly judicial mind would have awarded death ; but that most tribunals which have actually existed —in consideration of this and that, the youth and nobility of the defendant[2], and so forth—would have awarded exile, as a majority of the Argives would have done, if Orestes had let them. The condemnation to death is, merely as justice, defensible ; and if any spectator regrets it, Orestes and his accomplices soon dissipate that feeling, and make us heartily wish that all three, by stoning or any way whatsoever, had been quickly enough expunged from the world.

One observation however will occur to a modern reader, which more nearly concerns us as critics, because we cannot be sure how Euripides would have received it. To be possible, the story requires that general interdict, by which citizens of Argos are prohibited from intercourse with the criminals[3]. If, during the previous week, those friends of Agamemnon, such as Talthybius or Diomede, who undertake the cause of his children, had been in communication with them, the

---

[1] *v.* 946 ; see Aesch. *Eum.* 189.
[2] See *v.* 784. Pylades is right enough so far.   [3] *v.* 47 etc.

prognostications of Orestes must have been different, and his behaviour might. And in this aspect, the interdict seems to us unreasonable and cruel ; though it is not more so than certain arrangements, such as the refusal of counsel to all criminals or some criminals, which were maintained among ourselves, with general approbation or indifference, down to very recent times; not more perhaps than the rejection of a defendant's oath, which was modified, amid murmurs, only yesterday ; not more than some other things, which it is not our business to denounce. Euripides in this play assumes the interdict, in an aggravated case of murder, as an accepted thing. What he thought of it does not clearly appear ; my own impression, from the course of the story, would be, that he thought it dangerous, if not cruel. It is not known, so far as I am aware, how the practice was related to that of his own age, whether at Athens, at Argos, or elsewhere.—But let us proceed with the play.

The lyric lament of Electra, over the approaching end of her glorious house[1], has little dramatic import, and was probably inserted for the benefit of a musical performer. It does however illustrate the aristocratic sentiment of rebellion against a popular tribunal[2], which is one element in the scenes to follow; and it also condemns in advance, upon the mourner's own principles, the fury which leads her to extinguish, in the person of Hermione, the other branch of the family. About the return of Orestes, and the dramatic arrangement of the scene, some remarks will be found in the Appendix[3]. His new and apparently baseless fancy, that Menelaus has purposely destroyed him and his sister with an eye to the sole succession[4], is a significant supplement to the partial lamentations of Electra.

But in Orestes, the most menacing symptoms are physical. His feebleness, still visible at his approach[5], is reinvigorated by the fatal forces of fever and madness ; exhaustion is replaced by activity, energy, violence, and finally by a strength more than natural, while the organ of thought proportionally fails, and at last is utterly overthrown. Very soon we perceive

---

[1] *vv.* 960 foll.   [2] *v.* 974.   [3] On *v.* 950.   [4] *v.* 1058.   [5] *v.* 1015.

the failure of his memory, when he adjures Pylades, a home-
less outcast, to refrain from suicide, in the name of his father
and of the city from which he has been ignominiously ex-
pelled[1]. Upon the absurd and atrocious proposal to murder
Helen, Orestes hesitates[2]: 'Can it be done with honour?'
And his scruples must be argued away. The still more
atrocious and, if possible, more absurd scheme, of which
Hermione is the victim, he embraces with admiration[3]. This
progression, upward in strength and downward in reason, is
visible throughout, and needs no further comment.

Of Pylades and Electra it is more difficult to say, whether
and how far they realize the true nature of their acts, or
believe the pretexts with which they disguise it. It is always
difficult, and in a moral view unnecessary, to determine
whether such fury as theirs inhibits only, or actually perverts,
the reason. The slaying of Helen, says Pylades[4], is an act
of justice, the glory of which will cover all their previous
offences! The seizure of Hermione, says Electra[5], will enable
them to control Menelaus, and Menelaus must save their
lives! Both notions are too monstrous for criticism, and
(this may perhaps be worth notice) they are also incompatible. The bargain to be driven with the government of
Argos[6], if for a moment we take the conception seriously,
depends wholly upon the co-operation of Menelaus, for which
the price is to be the sparing of Hermione. What then can
be more preposterous than to destroy, before seizing his
daughter, the more precious hostage which the speculators
already hold, in the person of his adored wife? Yet such details
are scarcely perceptible in the wild and appalling enormity
of the speculation itself. The republic of Argos, having
deliberately sentenced certain persons to death for two
murders, will be convinced of their merits, when they have
committed another, or must at all events pardon them, if
they threaten to commit one more! It is as needless as

---

[1] *v.* 1075. In *vv.* 765–767, Pylades, by evasion, confesses that Phocis approves.
[2] *v.* 1106 εἰ γ' ἔσται καλῶς (cf. καλῶς βουλεύομαι in *v.* 1131). Pylades, in
answering with σφάξαντες (*v.* 1107), mistakes, but wilfully, the meaning of Orestes'
πῶς. The turn is borrowed from Aesch. *Eum.* 591–592 (Dindorf).
[3] *v.* 1204.   [4] *vv.* 1131 foll.   [5] *vv.* 1191 foll.   [6] *vv.* 1611 foll.

impossible to calculate, in what exact proportions ferocity
and frenzy, ignorance pure and ignorance wilful, are combined
in such imaginations as these.

Indeed, when they are stated coolly and in prose, they
seem things impossible even to be imagined or suggested.
Perhaps they are such; and it is certainly a criticism to which
the scene is liable. When every allowance has been made
for the characters and circumstances, we may doubt whether
a real Pylades or Electra would have found these pretexts
entertainable; and therefore, since, unscrupulous as they are,
they are not quite capable of murder without a pretext, we
may doubt whether their actions are adequately accounted for.
Almost any story, in which violent passions are made to
produce startling incidents, will be at some point open to
this doubt. The skill of the dramatist in such a case is
shown by holding the doubt in abeyance, by preventing
us from feeling it at the time; and here Euripides is strong.
The qualities of the three persons are so adroitly adapted
for mutual impression, that the natural madness of Orestes,
as Euripides in an earlier scene bids us notice[1], seems to
infect the others; and their acts, though not those of sane
persons, do not at the time seem unnatural. A single
instance may be given. Pylades is an outcast from his family
and his native Phocis, is as completely ruined, he told us,
as Orestes himself[2]. In spite of this, Orestes, as we saw,
when his frenzy begins to work, bids Pylades return to his
'paternal house and comfort of his home[3].' This Orestes
does simply and naturally, because his brain is giving way;
and to a cool observer such an incident would have given
pause. But because Pylades, though not insane, is a wild,
proud fool, full of hot and silly romance, he encounters or
evades the suggestion, not by recalling the facts, but with a
rodomontade about the impossibility of excusing himself to
the Phocians for such a crime as the abandonment of his
friend[4]. In this way, by mutual deceptions, the conspirators
seem gradually to lose, without becoming incredible, all touch

[1] v. 793 Orestes to Pylades: εὐλαβοῦ λύσσης μετασχεῖν τῆς ἐμῆς.
[2] vv. 763–767.   [3] v. 1077.   [4] vv. 1085–1097.

with the world of reality. And the terse, vigorous, impetuous versification helps to sweep us along. Extravagant as the actions are, few, while reading Euripides, will be conscious of any strain upon belief.

Having thus agreed to murder their aunt and to 'capture' their cousin, the malefactors appropriately seal the compact by a conjuration, an invocation of Agamemnon, mimicking with hideous fidelity that ritual of the dead, which Hermione has been performing in pure affection at the grave of Clytaemnestra.

> *El.* Come father, come, if thou in earth's embrace[1]
> Hearest thy children cry, who die for thee.
> *Pyl.* My father's kinsman, to my prayers withal,
> Agamemnon, hearken ; save thy children thou.
> *Or.* I slew my mother—
> *Pyl.*   But I grasped the sword!
> *El.* I cheered them[2] on, snapped trammels of delay!
> *Or.* Sire, for thine help!
> *El.*   Nor I abandoned thee!
> *Pyl.* Wilt thou not hear this challenge—save thine own?
> *Or.* I pour these tears for offerings[3]!
> *El.*   Wailings I!

The structure and style of this passage are closely copied from the invocation of Agamemnon performed by his children in the *Choephori*[4], when they are about to attack his adulterous murderers at the risk of their lives. The effect of it in the present circumstances is different.

This done, the two men go within, to interrupt the progress of Helen's needle-work by cutting her throat. Electra and the obedient Chorus keep watch, to signal the approach of chance-comers, or of Hermione, who, we are told, should by now be returning. From this point to the end of the play the action is precipitately rapid, and the theatrical incidents exciting to the highest degree.

Amid the agitation of the sentinels, we suddenly hear the cry of Helen for help, followed by other noise within. She

---

[1] *vv.* 1231 foll. (Way).   [2] *thee* Mr Way. See also Appendix, *v.* 1236.
[3] *v.* 1239 δακρύοις κατασπένδω σε, *i.e.* the adjuration is intended to have the force, so far as it may, of the ritual χοαί, which in Aeschylus are offered really.
[4] *vv.* 315–509, especially *vv.* 479 foll.

cries again; and almost at the same moment Hermione is seen approaching. Her rite has found acceptance[1], and she returns somewhat consoled. But the noise from the house has alarmed her, and still, though subdued, continues. Electra explains that the young men are appealing to Helen for intercession, and begs the support of her cousin. She, with a touching expression of forgiveness—'I do not will your death'—hastens to the door, where Orestes and Pylades, visible for a moment, seize her, stifle her scream, and drag her within. Electra follows; the gate is shut, and locked (as the sequel shows) from within.

The Chorus break into outcries, but a few moments later relapse into silence[2]; for their anxiety to know, what has been done or is doing within, is raised to intensity by a fresh incident. Some one—Hermione? Helen? we know not who—is frantically pulling at the door. Other vague sounds follow; and then—at the open *metope*[3], high above the ground, half naked, bleeding, and ghastly, appears one of the eunuchs, the Trojan slaves of Helen. He flings himself down[4], remains for a while inanimate, and then crawls painfully to the centre of the scene, where utterly exhausted he lies in a daze. The women gather about him[5].

---

[1] *v.* 1323 λαβοῦσα πρευμένειαν.   [2] *v.* 1365.

[3] See *vv.* 1369 foll.

[4] The abandoned couch of Orestes was probably used to make this practicable.

[5] A *scholium* asserts, that the words of the Chorus which accompany the entrance of the eunuch, *vv.* 1366–1368 ἀλλὰ κτυπεῖ γὰρ κλῇθρα βασιλείων δόμων, | σιγήσατ'· ἔξω γάρ τις ἐκβαίνει Φρυγῶν, | οὗ πευσόμεσθα τὰν δόμοις ὅπως ἔχει, have been interpolated or altered by actors, who substituted for the climbing of the *metope*, as supposed in *vv.* 1369 foll., an entrance by the door. That this latter mode of performance was sometimes adopted, we can perhaps believe; for to the perversions of actors in difficulty there is no limit. But such performance was absurd, as contradicting the text and the situation. It is inconceivable that the conspirators should leave the door in such condition that it could be opened by any one, except themselves; their whole scheme, and indeed their chance of dying a tolerable death, now depends on the possession of it.

Whether, as the *scholium* suggests, the text has been altered in *vv.* 1366 foll., is a question of little moment, but appears to me (as to Paley and others) doubtful. The statement is apparently an inference from the assumption, that κτυπεῖ κλῇθρα, 'there is a noise of the bolts,' refers to actual opening. But it would be satisfied by attempts to open, such as any fugitive must naturally make before thinking

The scenes which follow, those in which the eunuch takes part, are of that perilous kind—the episode of the Porter in *Macbeth*[1] is a famous example—in which a dramatist, having, as he thinks, brought the spectators to an excitement of the graver feelings—pity, horror, and above all suspense—strong enough to stand any strain whatever, deliberately strains it for the purpose of strengthening, by showing them what in ordinary circumstances would arouse inconsistent emotions, such as contempt, ridicule, or disgust. The sense that *we cannot smile*, that we do not, even though we perceive a call, is the supreme test and confirmation of gravity; and to excite this sense by art, as is done in *Macbeth*, is a supreme, though hazardous, resource. The success in a given case will be variously estimated, and notoriously is so estimated in English examples. As a general observation, we may note that mere reading is no test at all. We must see, or imagine, performance, the proposed effect being essentially spectacular. To misconceive the scenic situation will be ruinous; and in the case of an ancient dramatist, such mistake, as we have just seen, is easy. But under any conditions, judgments will differ. I can but give my opinion, which is that Euripides here is not less successful than bold. The scenes, in which the eunuch figures, are the best in their kind which I know.

That the personage is revolting, his garb grotesque, his cowardice, superstition, cunning such as would, in any common

of the climb, and which are essential to the effect of the scene. The phrase βασιλείων δόμων, *royal* house, is exceptional, but not incompatible with the play. By pedigree, though no longer in fact, the family had this pretension (*v.* 1248). The word ἐκβαίνει may perhaps be understood generally (*is coming out*) and not imply *walking*. In any case, what the author meant to be done is certain, and fortunately is indicated by himself. The example suggests both a warning as to the condition of our MSS. in reference to stage-direction, and also a consolation; since the alleged actors, whatever they did, wrote, or said, did not deprive us of the authentic indication in *vv.* 1369 foll. We should note that, to account for this mention of the climb, it must be partly visible. If it occurred only somewhere inside the house (and how should it?), the drama would have no concern with it. And in short, the whole purpose of it, and of the passage generally, is to emphasise the fact, that the house has become a prison as well as a fortress. All who cannot find such an exit, Helen, Hermione, the rest of Helen's train, are doomed.

[1] The question of its authenticity is happily here irrelevant. Its effect has been abundantly proved.

situation, be contemptible and comic,—all this is certain ; and also, that Euripides has exposed all this with unsparing audacity. In the very first words of the creature[1], his relief at having escaped is mingled with astonishment that he should have achieved the climb—no mean feat, we may suppose, even for a man properly trained and dressed—in his Asiatic costume ! When Orestes bursts out upon him sword in hand[2], his grovellings, flatteries, screams, writhing, shudders, and propitiatory jests, differ scarcely at all from those with which the slaves and valets of comedy excite roars of scornful merriment. In the midst of a breathless recital, he must needs mention with an air of importance, that, when the assassins entered, he was engaged in performing upon Helen what he calls the Phrygian custom of the fan[3]. Everything about him is described so that readers will naturally laugh. But did the spectators laugh ? That is the question. If they did, the scene was a gross and offensive failure ; for that Euripides meant to raise a laugh over the fate of Hermione, Helen, or even the murderers, is, to me at least, inconceivable. But did the spectators laugh ? Before we fix our impressions, let us remember that this play was 'famous upon the stage'[4]; and let us be quite sure that we realize the thing, and *see it done*, *as if we were there*. So imagining, and speaking for myself, I cannot conceive the possibility of a smile.

At first the suspense, anxiety, curiosity, the feeling that, as the Chorus say, 'now we shall know what has passed within,' avert and prohibit all emotions irrelevant to the fate of the wretches imprisoned within the horrible wall. The wanderings of the narrator merely irritate our intense desire that he should go on[5]. And then his broken effeminacy, his utter distraction, dislocation, dissolution of mind and body, appearing as part of the horror, take the same colour.

Let us picture the thing. When the door is swung in upon Hermione and her captors, every one feels that the human creatures within—and we know them to be not a few, though all helpless—are lost. In some way, the worse the more

---

[1] *v.* 1369.   [2] *v.* 1506.   [3] *v.* 1426.
[4] *Hypothesis* II.   [5] *vv.* 1394, 1451.

likely, they must all perish, with the demons who are masters of the house. Sooner or later these fiends, if it comes to the worst, as it must, will burn down the house over their heads. Pylades has warned us[1]. *And their victims cannot get out.* This horrid sensation possesses us, and is burnt into our consciousness by the vain attempt made upon the door. Then one, just one, by a way for him miraculous, does get out; one living creature has escaped, or may escape, the impending agony of sword and fire. What, in God's name, does any one care, what sort of dignity the wretched being has, or what manner of dress it is, which hangs in rags upon his palpitating body? *He is out! And what of those within?* What signifies anything, except this? There he lies, mingling, like a sort of Madge Wildfire, bits of his story with scraps of native song[2], unintelligible and irrelevant. 'What are they doing?' say the women, 'Tell us again. We cannot understand[3].' Nor can we; and our baffled excitement becomes a positive pain.

Even when the narrator becomes more lucid, our chief sensation is still, that he cannot get to the point, nor make things clear, when he does. At last this much comes out: some of the slaves have been killed, more maimed, the rest hunted into hiding-places[4]; but Helen has not been killed, or else, which the Phrygian seems to think equally probable, her body has 'disappeared[5].' The assassins, in the very act of despatching her, were called to the door by the arrival of Hermione; and when they got back,—'O earth and air, O day and night!', she was gone, 'vanished by magic clean away!' Wounded then at most (we infer) she, like the other fugitives, must be concealed somewhere in the building. The narrator, favoured, so far as can be made out or as he understands, by the fact that he happened to be in waiting on Helen at the time, and was suffered to remain in the front part of the house when his fellows were thrust out of the way, scrambled up to the *metope*, Heaven knows how, and got out as we know[6].

---

[1] See *vv.* 1149–1150.   [2] *vv.* 1385–1386, 1391–1392.   [3] *v.* 1393.
[4] *vv.* 1445 foll., 1474 foll.   [5] Compare *vv.* 1470 foll. with *vv.* 1490 foll.
[6] The story is not meant to be exactly intelligible, but this seems to be the upshot. The ἐμίμνομεν of *v.* 1475 is a confusion; the narrator, it seems, cannot have been one of these fugitives. And the whole is in the same style.

He has reached this point, when there occurs—the one thing perhaps which now we could not expect[1]. He is pursued. The door is flung back, and Orestes, sword in hand, rushes out, leaving the house open behind him. It needs not his wild gestures and words to tell us, that he is now literally and absolutely mad. His act is enough. And it also proves that his accomplices, who after all are not, properly speaking, insane, can no longer restrain him. Probably, when the door is opened, they are just seen, vainly attempting to prevent his exit[2]. Discovery from the town must be imminent; it may come at any moment, nor, so long as the house is closed, does it matter when. To the prospects, real or imaginary, of the assassins, the only thing material is to keep the door shut; and the escape of one victim is insignificant. Nor indeed is it the purpose of Orestes to stop him : he says so, but he is beyond the capacity of a purpose. In horrid play, like some feline monster, he follows step by step over the scene his crawling captive, the two together presenting humanity in the utmost extreme of moral and physical degradation.

Orestes.	Didst thou not to Menelaus shout the rescue-cry but now ?
Phrygian.	Nay, O nay,—but for thine helping cried I : *worthier art thou.*
Or.	Answer—did the child of Tyndareus by righteous sentence fall ?
Phr.	Righteous—wholly righteous—though she had three throats to die withal.
Or.	Dastard, 'tis thy tongue that truckles : in thy heart thou think'st not so.
Phr.	Should she not, who Hellas laid, and Phrygia's folk in ruin low[3] ?

Such is the dialogue; which, if we fully heard it, might make us laugh, or, more likely, make us sick. But we scarcely should hear it. The action would fascinate our senses. At any moment Orestes may strike. But he has no purpose to strike, he has no purpose at all ; and the slave, perceiving his condition and catching a glimpse of hope, keeps up a run of

---

[1] καινὸν ἐκ καινῶν, *v.* 1503.

[2] There is not, and could not be, any sign of this in the text; but it would express the situation. It is what, I think, a stage-manager should order.

[3] *vv.* 1510 foll. (Way).

slavish quips[1], which the madman answers with cruel zest, and once[2] with a strange commiseration, the echo, as it seems, of some inner self-pity. All this while, the cunning Phrygian is edging and creeping towards the way of escape. Suddenly Orestes changes his tone, bids him go within, and turns contemptuously away. In an instant the wretch springs to the exit, and disappears[3]. The maniac continues for a few moments to rush about[4], uttering boasts, threats, and defiances; and finally, unconscious of what has passed behind his back, darts again into the house. For the last time the door is swung to, and the bolts are heard to go, as it is again locked[5]. At the same instant the women break into cries of consternation, and from within fillets of smoke begin to roll and to ascend. The house is on fire![6]

Nothing else could be expected. In the first propounding of Pylades' plan[7], he talks of burning down the house. That this will be the end, we might guess from that moment; and the end must be now. The open door, which, even in this extremity, Pylades and Electra cannot close upon their accomplice, his madness, now beyond their control and threatening them with nothing less than to be torn in pieces by a raging mob, finish all hesitation. To do their worst, to crown their glory with flames, and then to get rid of their lives, while yet it may be done without torture,—this is all that remains. They fire the house; and by the same token we know, that in a few minutes they will have ceased to live.

---

[1] *vv.* 1517, 1521, 1523.　　　　　　[2] *v.* 1522.

[3] Menelaus, approaching the house, meets him (*v.* 1558); but even without this, we must have presumed that he gets away. It is the only tolerable end of the scene, and the only possible one, unless he were killed on the stage.

[4] *vv.* 1527–1536.

[5] See *v.* 1551, where 'the addition of bars to bolts' implies that we know the door to be locked already. But in any case the fact, and the audible evidence of it, might be assumed.

[6] *vv.* 1537–1544. The Chorus, sobered by the sight, and remembering (not too soon) their responsibility (*vv.* 1539–1540), talk of 'torches,' with which the house 'is to be fired'. But plainly no lighting of torches could produce what they describe (*vv.* 1541–1542), nor account for their sudden terror. They lie to themselves, because the truth appalls them, as well it may. But the thing is visible, and is the natural sequel of what has just taken place.　　[7] *v.* 1150.

But the maniac knows it not. He knows not even that the house is burning. Alone he is left, the only fit actor, to finish the insane programme of the conspiracy. Menelaus, at last returning, has met the escaped eunuch, 'a wreck of terror,' and learnt from him the awful news, that Helen has 'vanished' and Hermione is a prisoner. The 'vanishing' he of course dismisses as an absurdity, an invention (as he supposes) of the crazy matricide[1]. In this he is only so far wrong, that the idea, suggested originally by the imagination of the Oriental[2], has now lodged itself, though with more difficulty, in the burning brain of the Greek[3]. Menelaus however has heard enough to convince him that his wife is beyond rescue, and he hastens to save his daughter. The horror of the real situation he has not time to see completely. Scarcely has he entered, when Orestes appears at the parapet, with Hermione, a light burden to the strength of madness, in his arms. The girl is unconscious, for throughout the scene which follows she neither moves nor cries ; it may be hoped, and is probable, that she is dead. Orestes flings the body upon the parapet, and, standing as in act to decapitate it, calls to Menelaus, who is beating at the door below. Looking up, he perceives the figures, amid gleams of fire and wisps of smoke. 'Torches! And the murderers upon the wall!' He starts back in a daze. Between uncle and nephew, the one scarcely less frantic than the other, there passes a wild parley, Menelaus begging now for the body of Helen and now for the life of Hermione, Orestes answering with furious mockery. The wicked mother should have died, but has been spirited away; the daughter shall die now; Clytaemnestra, Helen, Hermione, a fit succession; for all

[1] *v.* 1559 τοῦ μητροκτόνου τεχνάσματα...καὶ πολὺς γέλως, where τέχνασμα means, not *device*, but *invention, conception*, as of an artist.

[2] *vv.* 1495 foll.

[3] At *vv.* 1533–1536 Orestes still assumes the plain truth, that Helen is either *dead* or else *alive and in his power*. But in the last dialogue (*vv.* 1580, 1586) he, like the Phrygian (*v.* 1496) though more vaguely, seems to assume her miraculous escape. This notion, so far as concerns the real play, is what Menelaus calls it, 'sheer absurdity.' The epilogue (*vv.* 1629 foll.) develops it with ironical gravity.

'wicked women' the punishing sword shall be ready!'[1] The bewildered Menelaus, hoping to get something at least intelligible from an interlocutor not out of his senses, appeals in a louder voice to the invisible accomplice[2]: ' Sharest thou too in this murder, Pylades?' There is a pause; but no Pylades answers, because no Pylades hears. '*His silence saith it!*', explains the maniac,—and the dialogue rushes on, in a hail of crossing invectives, until Menelaus exclaims[3] in desperation ' What am I to do?' The chance word recalls Orestes to the programme, which he abruptly propounds: ' Go, plead with Argos.'—' Plead! And for what?'—' For our lives! Ask the city for that.'—' And that only will save my child!'—' Even so.' Menelaus, though his reason totters, has enough left to perceive by this that all is over. Attempting no reply, he breaks into lamentations: ' Helen! Helen!...Thou!...Won only to be slain!...And all that I did

---

[1] *vv.* 1576-1596. In *v.* 1589 μητέρος, by the context, is ambiguous between ' Clytaemnestra' (mother of Orestes) and ' Helen ' (mother of Hermione). The ambiguity is intentional, and should not be determined either way.

[2] There is no suggestion in the text, either in this scene or in that which follows the appearance of Apollo, that Pylades or Electra is standing with Orestes on the parapet. After the appearance of Apollo, they may join him ; because then anything, however impossible, may occur, the more impossible the better for the effect ; but the evidence is against supposing so. Here, where we are still dealing with realities, they cannot be there, for a reason which we already have divined and which the unconscious madman grimly confirms. The notion that Pylades, though actually standing by Orestes throughout, is made silent (*v.* 1592) because the dramatist had not an actor to spare, implies in Euripides an ineptitude surely inconceivable. If he was in such a difficulty, why expose it, by making Menelaus address to Pylades a question on this hypothesis needless, since the complicity and adhesion of Pylades would be proved by his presence? Nor could the difficulty exist: small ' fourth parts' were allowed; and it would also have been easy, if necessary, to use the tritagonist for Pylades at *v.* 1592, and then to replace him by a mute, so that he might appear at *v.* 1625 as Apollo. It is possible that Pylades appears *for a moment* between *vv.* 1567 and 1574 (where see τούσδε, which, if we press it strictly, though that is not necessary, would imply as much). He may appear for a moment, taking leave of his Orestes with a wild gesture, and plunging again into the house. This would be effective. After this he is certainly seen no more. That Orestes imagines both Pylades and Electra to hear him, both here and at *vv.* 1618-1620, is a natural trait of his insanity. Their actual presence throughout is assumed by expositors only to make natural, what Euripides means to be plainly impossible, the subsequent performances of Apollo.

[3] *v.* 1610.

for her...It is too much!...Helpless in thy hands!'—which
Orestes punctuates with taunts. Then, suddenly impatient,
'Fire the house, Electra!...There!' he screams, as the smoke
goes up thicker; 'Burn down these battlements,...Pylades,
dear Pylades...my surest friend! Here, here!'—'A rescue!',
comes the answering scream of the maddened Menelaus;
'Sons of Danaus, chivalry of Argos, to arms! A rescue,
a rescue! Here is a matricide, foul with his mother's blood,
...who would wrest *his life* from all the power of your state!'

———————————

Curtain quick. So would Euripides direct now. So
would he then have directed, if he could; and such a termi-
nation, in such manner as the conditions of his theatre
permitted, he does actually express. Unfortunately for him,
he had no curtain; and whatever might be the fate of his
personages, his actors, dead or alive, must walk off. Nor was
he free, as a matter of form, even to kill them. The murderers
of his story, the matricide and his sister and his friend, must
indeed certainly die. The story is so shaped, coloured, and
conducted, that no other ending is either conceivable or
desirable. But since, being compelled by convention to
borrow names from ancient history, he has for this occasion
borrowed those of Orestes and Electra, Pylades and Hermione,
history demands that *her* personages, when the dramatist has
done with them, shall be restored intact. According to *her*,
they were married, Orestes to Hermione, Pylades to Electra.
There were probably among the audience persons who claimed
descent from these unions, which had also some political
importance. Helen again, in association with her brothers
Castor and Pollux, was an object of worship. History then,
or legend, must at least in form be satisfied.

These practical demands, in part peculiar to the *Orestes*
among extant plays, but partly familiar to Euripides, he
meets, as elsewhere[1], by the *deus ex machina*, that is to say,
by a final scene, transparently perfunctory and ironical, in
which a supernatural personage, whose very being is incom-

———————————

[1] See for example the *Ion* and *Iphigenia in Taurica.*

patible with the assumptions of the drama, arrests the proceedings, commands the impossible, and dismisses the personages, with suitable directions, to fulfil their legendary destinies. Apollo, with Helen as a goddess beside him, appears, by operation of the crane, in the sky. The smoke ceases to ascend from the roof, Hermione wakes up and rises, Menelaus and Orestes become not only sane, but attentive. Apollo explains the position of Helen, 'daughter of Zeus and therefore destined to immortality,' and sketches for the young men and women a future which follows the legendary lines and includes the legendary marriages. Menelaus, henceforward a king of Sparta[1], is endowed with his wife's heritage there, and reminded, by way of further consolation, that she has given him perpetual trouble[2]. The divine commands are gratefully obeyed; though Orestes, in spite of his restored faith in the oracle (which, he says, he *had* suspected of devilry), will not accept the hand of Hermione, even from a god, without a polite deference to the decision of her father!

> Lo, from the sword Hermione I release,
> And pledge me, *when her sire bestows*, to wed.

Menelaus however is equally tractable, admires the good fortune of his translated wife, and wishes all happiness to his son-in-law. The god gives the word to depart; and to a march-tune, Apollo singing, the company make their several exits.

It is, or should be, needless to expound the nature and spirit of such a *finale*. Of all the like scenes in Euripides it is perhaps the most prodigiously absurd, unreal, meaningless, impossible. So far as the story is concerned, Apollo has nothing to do. All is ended, ended as we expect. He may tell us that Helen is now a goddess of the main, but cannot make the Helen of the play—the heartless beauty, a little

---

[1] In this play, as in the *Agamemnon* of Aeschylus, he belongs to Argos, where according to this play there is no king at all.

[2] v. 1662   φερνὰς ἔχων δάμαρτος, ἥ σε μυρίοις
           πόνοις διδοῦσα δεῦρ' ἀεὶ διήνυσε.

passée, with her humours and her needle-work—into a person conceivable in her new situation. He may marry his Orestes to his Hermione, but cannot make the imagination of such an alliance between the persons so named in the play anything else but revolting. He may marry Pylades to Electra. But although we are told in the play[1], that the two youths in their wisdom, and after the fashion of their kind, had proposed to cement their friendship by this connexion, we, as spectators, do not want their design to be realized ; we know it cannot, and the very thought would be revolting, if it were not so impossible and so ridiculous.

Menelaus, forsooth, is to settle and reign in Sparta! But how would he be received there by the Tyndareus of the play, and how are we to suppose, that an alleged fiat of Apollo would be executed by Tyndareus, upon whom the authority of Delphi, when cited in favour of what he condemns, produced no impression whatever ? Or what of Argos and her citizens, her laws, authorities, organs, and public opinion ? Of all these 'Apollo', the actor suspended upon the crane, can dispose no doubt, if words could do it, in two verses :

> I will to Argos reconcile this man,
> Whom I constrained to shed his mother's blood.

That is to say, he will assure the Argive assembly, as in the *Eumenides* he assures the Areopagus, that he, Apollo, is responsible for the matricide. But how are we to conceive the appearance of such a god before the *ecclesia* depicted in the play ? Or what could he there effect ? He might as well have proposed to attend next day the Athenian *ecclesia* of the year 408, and dictate some decision, morally and politically detestable, about Samos or Alcibiades. The *ecclesia* of the play consists of men like those of the fifth century. *They do not believe in a matricidal god*, and would not receive as Apollo a person professing that character. They would simply order the impostor to be stript of his costume and scourged.

The plain fact is, that, in connexion with this play, an epiphany such as that of Apollo and Helen is absurd, and

[1] *vv.* 1078, 1207.

can serve only to announce, that we have done with serious imagination. We may recur to our former illustration, a supposed play turning on the fate of a man, who commits bigamy in Melbourne upon the strength of his own conviction, or that of his confessor, that marriage with a deceased wife's sister is a nullity. When the hero had received the inevitable condemnation, and had answered it by braining a warder and firing the gaol, what would be the effect of introducing some canonized Doctor of the Law, suspended in the air, to declare from that elevation his agreement with the offender, and to order that he be discharged and promoted to honour?

What sort of epiphany could really be imagined in the days of this play, by what sort of person, and in what circumstances, Euripides is careful to show. Menelaus and his sailors have seen a supernatural person, or so they believe:

> For touching Agamemnon's fate I knew,
> And by what death at his wife's hands he died,
> When my prow touched at Malea : from the waves
> The shipman's seer, the unerring God, the son
> Of Nereus, Glaucus, made it known to me.
> For full in view he rose, and cried it to me[1].

The story recalls, and professes to correct, that of the *Odyssey*, in which the same disclosure is made to Menelaus in Egypt by the sea-god Proteus. Let then the two versions be compared, in reference to the question whether the composers, the epic bard and Euripides respectively, intend, for the purpose of their artistic work, to convey the impression that something supernatural really occurred. In the epic, needless to say, nothing else is for an instant supposable. In Euripides the contrary is as plain. Sailors of Euripides' own day and city might doubtless have been found to say, that on some lonely shore they had seen and spoken with Glaucus. But how many people, and what sort of people, would have believed them? They spoke with some wanderer of the beach, transfigured by superstitious imagination. Like the similar story in the *Iphigenia in Taurica*[2], where two common mortals are falsely identified, by foolish rustics, as Castor and

---

[1] *vv.* 360 foll. (Way).   [2] *vv.* 260 foll.

Pollux, the tale of Menelaus serves to show that, for the purpose of the play, we are to place ourselves at an epoch when, for sober judgments and under circumstances of proof, epiphanies do not occur, and when the epiphany of Apollo in a political assembly is a grotesque supposition, stamped by the mere statement as not serious.

For these reasons and others[1], the *deus ex machina* of the *Orestes* can be no part of the serious drama, but is a pretence, necessary to get off the actors and repair the breach with legend. The scene is not a *dénouement*. And indeed we should remark, that though the use of supernatural personages for the purpose of *dénouement*, that is to say, to effect something *required by the story* but not easy to be worked out, is commonly associated with the name of our author, he did in fact, so far as we know, but rarely so employ them. The *Medea*, the very example cited by Aristotle, is almost the only one now extant, though we should perhaps add the *Hippolytus*. In the *Medea*, a thing *which the author requires for his story*, the escape of the heroine, is achieved by a supernatural device, the dragon-chariot, to which the story does not lead. We have discussed the case in a previous essay[2]. But the Apollo of the *Orestes*, like the Athena of the *Iphigenia in Taurica*, has, for the story, nothing to do. We know that really the house was burnt down, and the persons in it, those who were not dead, perished; we cannot even desire, and we cannot suppose, that anything else should follow; and all the deities of the property-room could not affect our imaginative belief. Apollo is merely for the theatre; and as readers, we have no concern with him at all.

Nor, in all probability, had the first and original spectators of the play. Next to the *Medea*, the *Orestes* is, of all the extant plays, the one which offers the strongest internal evidence that it was not originally conceived as having a Chorus, and therefore was not first planned for the theatre of Dionysus. The presence and co-operation of Electra's fifteen visitors,

---

[1] On the histrionic allusion to the success of the play (*vv.* 1650–1652) see *Euripides the Rationalist*, p. 171.

[2] p. 127.

though not perhaps impossible, like that of Medea's, is utterly
improbable; and it is proportionally improbable that the
story would have been conceived at all, unless the dramatist
had known conditions of performance, for which a Chorus
was not required. And the play, though essentially spectacular, does not in the least require the theatre. The front of
any Greek house, if it did not actually furnish everything
necessary, could be made to do so by slight modification and
a little make-believe.

And it is remarkable that, in the Greek introduction
attributed to the scholar Aristophanes[1], we have what looks
like an actual reference to a 'recasting' or 'alteration' made
'for the sake of the Chorus.' "The arrangement (διασκευή)
of the play is as follows. Against the palace of Agamemnon
is placed Orestes, sick, and prostrated by madness upon a
couch. Electra sits at his feet. The question is asked why
in the world (τί δήποτε) she does not sit at his head; seated
in this closer position, she would have appeared more attentive
to her brother. We may suppose then, that the dramatist
made the arrangement (διασκευάσαι) because of the Chorus.
Orestes would have been awaked, having but lately and with
difficulty got to sleep, if the women of the Chorus had come
up nearer to him. And this is suggested by what Electra says
to them: 'Hush, hush, tread lightly' etc.[2] Probably then
this was the excuse for the position (διάθεσις) chosen." Now
this writer, it will be noted, does not pretend that the problem
and solution given are his own. 'The question is asked'
he says. And surely it is manifest that he misunderstands
the author of the question. He takes it as depending upon
the assumption, which he himself gratuitously makes, that
Electra actually sits 'at the feet' of her patient. There is no
evidence of this detail. Nor does the explanation which
follows agree with such an understanding of the question.
If Electra is at the couch at all, the Chorus, fifteen persons,
when they approach her, are likely to disturb the patient;

---

[1] *Hypothesis* II. The others, I and III, are worthless. The author of III
actually introduces into the story the plot of Sophocles' *Electra*!

[2] *v.* 140.

and whether she sat at the head or the feet could make no appreciable difference. The author of the question, 'why in the world Electra does not sit at Orestes' head,' did not mean to lay stress on the last words ; he meant simply 'why does she not sit by her patient, in the place proper to a nurse.' The traditional arrangement of the opening scene, an arrangement quite consistent with the text, was evidently that Electra from the first should be *standing, and as far as possible from Orestes.* The author of the question, possibly Aristophanes, thought this position not the most natural ; and it is not. But he thought it might have been adopted, and it might, in order not to bring the Chorus to the couch. The blunder of our writer would not be worth notice, but for the doubt which it opens, whether he rightly understands what his author meant by the words ἔοικεν οὖν διὰ τὸν χορὸν ὁ ποιητὴς διασκευάσαι. Our writer, our copyist, probably or certainly took διασκευάσαι in the sense 'arrange,' corresponding to his own ἡ διασκευὴ τοῦ δράματος, 'the arrangement of the play' ; and I have translated it accordingly. But the question and solution have more meaning, purpose, and point, if we take διασκευάσαι in the literary sense, 'recast, retouch, alter.' The author perceived what is the fact, that *with a Chorus* the opening of the play cannot be quite naturally arranged. And *knowing, or believing himself entitled to assume, that the play was originally designed without one,* he suggests that the arrangement actually adopted was *a modification,* introduced for the sake of the Chorus. Euripides, he means, has framed an opening, which seems unsuitable to theatrical conditions ; it may be his 'excuse', that originally he did not contemplate those conditions.

This is the more probable, since we are also told (and on very high authority) that our *Medea* was a 'revised' or 'recast' version, the original being attributed to a certain Neophron[1]. I think it not improbable that the transformation of our *Medea* from a domestic to a theatrical play[2] had something to do with the origin of this puzzling tradition.

---

[1] τὸ δρᾶμα δοκεῖ ὑποβαλέσθαι τὰ Νεόφρονος διασκευάσαις, ὡς Δικαίαρχος κ.τ.λ. *Hypothesis of the Medea.*   [2] See above, pp. 125 foll.

However this may be, internal evidence in both cases warrants, in my opinion, the assumption that neither the *Medea* nor the *Orestes* was originally planned for a Chorus. One or two friends, deeply attached and intimate friends of Electra, would certainly be needed in the opening; *and there is a trace of them in the text.* When Electra says[1] ' Did you see (εἴδετε), how Helen cut only just the tip of her hair?', whom does she address? The Chorus are not yet come; and according to the text as it stands, we should naturally suppose Electra to be now alone, except for her sleeping brother[2]. The audience are not to be thought of; it would be comic. We can perhaps suppose what now seems necessary, that some attendants of Helen remain for a moment when Helen goes in, and receive Electra's remark. But the supposition is strained; and my belief is that this ' Did you see?' is simply an oversight. It was originally addressed to confidants of Electra, who, if they were not 'on' from the first, came on before this was said. The arrangement was altered, when room had to be made somehow for the introduction of the importunate fifteen; but the ' Did you see?' was inadvertently left.

Confidants, intimates, one or two, we can even conceive without extravagance as present throughout, and as parties to the horrors of the later scenes. Unless the recasting was in this part very extensive, some such figures were always required. The smaller the number, the more natural or acceptable would be the assumption[3], that their devotion to Electra is proof against the strain which is put on it. But this we cannot determine. Happily we need not at all events suppose that Euripides, of his own will, assumed the acquiescence and co-operation of fifteen.

From a domestic version of the play, Apollo, as well as the Chorus, would of course disappear. The confidants, if they had not gone before, would at all events fly, as naturally they should and must, when they become aware that the house is, or soon will be, on fire (*vv.* 1537–1539); and we

---

[1] *v.* 128.   [2] See the stage-directions of Mr Way.
[3] *vv.* 1103–1104.

should be relieved of the preposterous assumption, necessarily attributed to the actual Chorus (*v.* 1540), that they can do nothing 'safer' for themselves than to remain where they are. At *v.* 1624 Menelaus would rush off; Orestes, seizing the body of Hermione, would leap back from the parapet into the house; and the piece would end formally where, for every purpose of serious art, it now virtually does.

APPENDIX.

I. NOTES ON THE ANDROMACHE.

vv. 24 foll.

κἀγὼ δόμοις τοῖσδ᾽ ἄρσεν᾽ ἕνα τίκτω κόρον,
πλαθεῖσ᾽ Ἀχιλλέως παιδί, δεσπότῃ γ᾽ ἐμῷ.
καὶ πρὶν μὲν ἐν κακοῖσι κειμένην ὅμως
ἐλπίς μ᾽ ἀεὶ προσῆγε σωθέντος τέκνου
ἀλκήν τιν᾽ εὑρεῖν κἀπικούρησιν δόμων.
ἐπεὶ δὲ τὴν Λάκαιναν Ἑρμιόνην γαμεῖ
τοὐμὸν παρώσας δεσπότης δοῦλον λέχος,
κακοῖς πρὸς αὐτῆς σχετλίοις ἐλαύνομαι κ.τ.λ.

24. ἄρσενα τίκτω L, ἄρσεν᾽ ἐντίκτω reliqui codd., ἄρσεν᾽ ἕνα
Barnes; ἰδίως ἕνα φησὶ παῖδα γενέσθαι schol.—28. δόμων BO (γρ.
κακῶν B), κακῶν rell.—See Prof. Murray's apparatus, to which I
refer throughout.

ἕνα and δόμων are probably right. The omission of ἕνα, the
conjecture κακῶν, and Elmsley's κἀπικούφισιν for κἀπικούρησιν, assume
that the ἐλπίς of *v.* 27 is Andromache's hope that Molossus might
live; but if this were so, we should next hear of his present danger,
which is not mentioned until *v.* 47. Translate, 'There was a time
when, low though I had fallen, I was used as a wife, in the hope
that, by the preservation of a child, he might gain some support
and strengthening to his family. But since he married...' etc. With
προσῆγε (= ἐπέλαζε) supply αὐτῷ, τῷ δεσπότῃ, and cf. πλαθεῖσα. For
σωθέντος τέκνου cf. Aesch. *Eum.* 660 (Dindorf) τίκτει δ᾽ ὁ θρώσκων,
ἡ δ᾽ ἅπερ ξένῳ ξένη | ἔσωσεν ἔρνος, οἷσι μὴ βλάψῃ θεός. Until
Neoptolemus married, the family was anxious that he, the only
child of an only child and having but *one* child himself, should have
more quasi-legitimate children, ἀλκήν τινα, *support of a kind*, by a
woman who, if a slave, at least had been a princess. But after the
birth of Molossus (about 8 years old at the time of the action) there
were only disappointments. After his marriage (*v.* 29) her importance
and the connexion ceased.

The phrase ἄρσενα κόρον (*a male boy?*) requires explanation. It suggests that τίκτειν κόρον does not here mean primarily and properly *parere filium*, but *parere fastum, parere iniuriam maris* (from the ancient and familiar equivocation of κόρος, = υἱός or ὕβρις), *i.e.* to become a mother in the circumstances of Andromache. Virgil apparently understood it so, and represents the sense, though not the equivocation, in *Aen.* III. 320 foll. Andromache speaks:

> O felix una ante alias Priameia virgo,
> hostilem ad tumulum Troiae sub moenibus altis
> iussa mori, quae sortitus non pertulit ullos
> nec victoris eri tetigit captiva cubile.
> nos patria incensa diversa per aequora vectae
> stirpis Achilleae *fastus iuvenemque superbum*
> *servitio enixae tulimus*; qui deinde secutus
> Ledaeam Hermionen Lacedaemoniosque hymenaeos
> me famulo famulamque Heleno transmisit habendam.

Here the very peculiar phrase *enixae tulimus fastus iuvenemque*, which has raised difficulty, is dictated by τίκτω κόρον in the double sense. In other points also the passage is influenced by that of Euripides, and has been composed with the *Andromache* in mind.

v. **147.** No lacuna here. *Vv.* 147—154 *answer* (154) the last words of the Chorus, which Hermione, surprising them, hears. They speak of her as a 'tyrant' (142); they are not slaves, nor is she properly their mistress. She *replies* that the princess of Sparta may say and do in Phthia whatever she pleases.

v. **169.** Read οὐ Πρίαμος, οὐδὲ Χρυσᾶς ἀλλ' Ἑλλὰς πόλις. χρυσὸς MSS. for which Prof. Murray refers (*sed quaere*) to *Tro.* 995. —Χρυσᾶς, *of Chrysa*, the Homeric town, is an adjective formed to balance Ἑλλάς. Chrysa was the seat of the Trojan Apollo, and Ἑλλὰς πόλις, as opposed to Χρυσᾶς, signifies the people whose centre and leader was *Delphi*—a fact, but not fortunate for Hermione.

vv. **215—231.** Though suspicious of transpositions, I think the seven lines 215—221 must follow the next seven, 222—228. Thus 'if your husband had lived in Thrace, the drenched-*with-snow*'— χιόνι τὴν κατάρρυτον, where χιόνι is emphatic by position—is explained by the words preceding, 'you would fain keep your husband from *a drop of rain*.' As the snow to the rain-drop, so is the liberty of Thracian husbands to that of others. Thus also the reminiscence of Hector comes in naturally after 'even if she have a bad husband' (213). And the admission that women are more licentious than men (220) has the purpose of dragging in the mention of Helen (229). In 221, ἀλλὰ προύστημεν καλῶς is still obscure, corrupted probably in consequence of the transposition. Perhaps προστῶμεν, *let us stand up for them*, is preferable to προσταῖμεν (Hermann).

v. 344. The suggestion that Menelaus will have difficulty in obtaining a second son-in-law is perhaps the acme of the irony in this speech. Menelaus is not unprovided.

vv. 397—398. Genuine, though defective. All that follows refers to τὰ ἐν ποσὶν κακά, the question whether Andromache shall sacrifice her child or herself: ἥτις (399) has its antecedent in ἐμοί (404). Punctuate 403—404 thus : νυμφεύομαι— | τί κ.τ.λ. In 397 the error is rather in λογίζομαι than in ἐξικμάζω (= *wring out*, from ἰκμάς). Andromache uses bitterly some very humble metaphors from slave-work.

v. 462. εἰ δ᾽ ἐγὼ...πράξειας ἄν is addressed not to Menelaus but to Hermione within (cf. παῖδα σήν 460), indicated by the gesture of turning to the house. There would be no dramatic point in the prophecy of retribution on Menelaus, which does not come. The punishment of Hermione is already begun ; cf. 492.

v. 480. Read κακὰ for κατὰ, construing as κακά ἐστι: 'Two minds to decide the steering are mischievous.' The plural κακά marks the point.

v. 483. For ἑνὸς ἃ δύνασις read ἓν ὅσα δύνασις, *i.e.* ἕν ἐστι ὅσα δύνασίς ἐστι, 'In private or in public (if success is desired) wherever there is power, there is unity.' For the metre see 491.

v. 557. ὕπαρνος is a pun ; hence τις, *in a manner*. Primarily it means 'as a sheep with your lamb,' but also, as from ὑπ-αρνεῖσθαι, 'one who protests' or 'may protest'; for the form cf. κάταρνος. The ὑπό- signifies objection. The second sense explains and is explained by 558 : in the absence of the family and her master Neoptolemus, Andromache can *protest* to the jurisdiction, as she has protested (358—360). The pun has a dramatic purpose: Peleus' first impression is, that the proceedings of Menelaus must be some incomprehensible jest.

vv. 650—659. A hideous irony, considering the relations of the speaker to Neoptolemus and Orestes, his murdered and murdering sons-in-law. In this scene, almost every passage exhibits something of this kind.

vv. **668—677.** Genuine, not interpolated. The consummate impudence of ὡς δ' αὔτως ἀνὴρ | γυναῖκα μωραίνουσαν ἐν δόμοις ἔχων, from the husband of Helen (!), must be Euripidean. The argument is as inapplicable to the facts as all the rest, but not more; and it serves equally well the speaker's only real purpose, to provoke the anger and contempt of Peleus.

vv. **701—702.** Much like the saying that 'any man could be a Shakespeare *if he had the mind.*' The dislike of Euripides for military power did not prevent him from perceiving the futility of vulgar sarcasms on military talent. Common men could be commanders, if they had the daring and the will.

v. **709.** 'Get away, with your *barren* daughter!' Certainly; that is why Menelaus has arranged to take her away.

v. **733.** πόλις τις. No allusion to contemporary politics (Argos?) should be sought. The pretext is too flimsy to have meaning.

v. **745.** σκιὰ ἀντίστοιχος, 'the shadow which walks (στείχει) the reverse way' (to that of the sun), and 'can do nothing but speak' (tell the time)—does not this allude to the principle of the sun-dial?

vv. **752—756.** Dramatically significant. If Menelaus really sought the life of Andromache, of course she would not be out of danger. His easy surrender has alarmed her, as it would alarm any reasoning person. But Peleus is past reasoning.

vv. **766 foll.** This ode, like the preceding and following scenes, is full of irony, of points on which the circumstances furnish a commentary not designed by the uninformed speakers. The advantage of being well-born (*vv.* 766—771) is supposed to be exemplified by the case of Andromache; the feeling of the Chorus is that not so much concern would have been felt about themselves. But this matter is seen in a different light by us, who know now for certain, what sort of advantage and protection is accruing, by virtue of her nobility, to Hermione. Only a princess of the first importance would, or perhaps could, be used and treated as she is by her father and her cousin.

v. **891.** At the approach of Orestes, the attendants and Chorus arrange themselves so as to conceal from him, if possible, the dishevelled Hermione; see *vv.* 877—880, where ὁρωμένη indicates that the speaker has observed a stranger. Hence he can pretend not to be aware of her presence, until she rushes forward.

v. **900.** This pious appeal to the god of Delphi is an admirable touch.

v. **929.** The optative εἴποι, without ἄν, is a survival, in a fixed colloquial formula, of the archaic optative for imperative, meaning strictly, not *as some one would say*, but *as let some one (be supposed to) say*. See Aesch. *Ag.* 945 (Dindorf), and the Indices to my editions of the *Agamemnon* and the *Choephori, s.v.* Optative.

v. **937.** Surely genuine; it is not intended, nor proper, that Hermione should sustain the pitch of dignity. This whole speech, with its general suggestion that somebody else (the Chorus, for instance, as the nearest persons) is really responsible for Hermione's errors, is merely an extravagance of fright. *Vv.* 943 foll. are sentiments which the dramatist would depreciate and ridicule. The women receive her insinuations with a sort of pitying contempt (954).

vv. **964—992.** Note that he actually drops here his pretence about 'Dodona' (885). Being now quite sure of his prey, his sole object from this point, and only reason for delay, is to preclude her from future rebellion by laying as much foundation as possible for the story—which of course will be his version—that she eloped with him, and was in fact his accomplice. Hence the recital, worse than useless so far as she is concerned, of his old claim on her hand; it is for the benefit of the Chorus. She, whose one thought is to get away 'before my husband arrives,' evades the suggestion very well, *as she thinks*, by the reference to her father, but speaks ambiguously, lest, as she fears, her cousin may still refuse his aid. The untoward incident naturally increases her anxiety to end the scene; and at *v.* 989 she actually begins to go, Orestes following.

vv. **995—1008.** To suppose this intended for the hearing of Hermione, or heard by her, is impossible. At the first hint of it, she would have shrunk from Orestes in horror. Nor in fact would she hear it. The movement is this. The *exit* begins at *v.* 989 (see

preceding note); at *v.* 992 Hermione and her waiting-woman, hastily
preceding, pass out, *vv.* 993—994 being spoken 'after' her.   *In
the remaining fourteen verses she is not addressed*, which alone would
show that the situation is changed.   At *v.* 994 Orestes, slowly
following her, stops; and while she continues, as we presume, to
hurry forward, delivers the rest for the benefit of the other women
(the Chorus) and with the same purpose which prompts the
reminiscences of *vv.* 964 foll., that is, to provide for the future
development of a suspicion that she shared his plot.   That is what,
when all comes out, many in Phthia and elsewhere would certainly
believe.   He runs no risk by the menace.   Having delivered it, he
instantly goes; and before it could even be comprehended, he is off,
in the carriage (see *v.* 992) which of course is ready.   The duenna
(τροφός, see 803—878), a slave devoted to the personal service of
Hermione, naturally goes with her, a point not unimportant to the
effect of the scene.   By permitting this, Orestes, in the real
circumstances, loses nothing whatever; and he gains at the moment
the appearance of good faith.   In the sequel there is necessarily
a flaw, but small and purely theatrical.   The women, who hear the
menace, ought, as they admit (*v.* 1053), to report it in the house at
once, though it would make no practical difference if they did.   But
in the theatre they cannot, *because they are the Chorus and must here
sing an interlude*.   Flaws of this kind however are so common and
inevitable in choric drama, that Greek audiences must have become
indifferent to them.

vv. **1031** foll.   Note the unusual and, I believe, elsewhere
unknown version of the murder of Clytaemnestra.   Ἀργόθεν πορευθείς
is a detail not explained by other accounts, and ἀδύτων ἐπιβὰς
κτεάνων, though apparently corrupt, points to some other divergence.
The story alluded to here must have been told somewhere, and was
probably told in the preceding play.   The peculiarities were no
doubt designed to suit in some way the particular characterisation
of Orestes.

v. **1053.**   See on *vv.* 995 foll.

v. **1113.**   τυγχάνει δ' ἐν ἐμπύροις means, I think, 'he succeeded in
the sacrifice,' *i.e.* 'obtained favourable omens' for his consultation
from the victim or from the ashes of the altar,—an effective touch.
Not 'he was engaged in sacrifice,' as if with ellipse of ὤν.

v. 1120.

χωρεῖ δὲ πρύμναν· οὐ γὰρ εἰς καιρὸν τυπεὶς
ἐτύγχαν᾽ †ἐξέλκει δὲ† καὶ παραστάδος
κρεμαστὰ τεύχη πασσάλων καθαρπάσας κ.τ.λ.

The interpretation 'drew (his sword)' is not justifiable. ἐξήρκει 'he bore up' (Kirchhoff, cited by Murray) is possible, but remote. Is it possible that ἐξέλκει is, or covers, an adverb of the type of πανδημεί, αὐτοβοεί, and meaning *externally, with an external wound* (ἕλκος)? We should then punctuate thus: οὐ γὰρ εἰς καιρὸν τυπεὶς | ἐτύγχαν᾽, ἐξελκεὶ δέ· καὶ παραστάδος κ.τ.λ.

v. 1151. I see no reason to doubt that ὅσπερ αὐτὸν ὤλεσε means 'the same who killed Achilles himself,' referring to Ἀχιλλέως...παῖς (note emphasis on παῖς) above. The purpose is to mark the responsibility of *Phoebus* for both deaths; cf. *v.* 1212 διπλῶν τέκνων μ᾽ ἐστέρησ᾽ ὁ Φοῖβος. But who then is the Δελφὸς ἀνήρ? It points to a variant version of the death of Achilles, according to which the actual slayer was not Apollo but *a Delphian*, named or unnamed, presumed to be the agent of Apollo. Such a version would be natural to Euripides; indeed some such version would be necessary for the admission of the incident into his realistic story. But where was it so related? Probably by Neoptolemus in the preceding play, in the scene suggested by *v.* 977 ὁ δ᾽ ἦν ὑβριστής.... See *vv.* 51, 1002, 1194.

v. 1192. Ἑρμιόνας Ἀΐδαν. This strange expression for 'the deadly Hermione' alludes, I think, to the associations of her *name*; see σῶν λεχέων τὸ δυσώνυμον, *v.* 1189. Hermione or Hermion in Argolis was one of the places supposed in legend to contain an opening into the underworld (Hades). Hence its connexion with the bringing up of Cerberus by Heracles; see Eur. *Heracles* 615. This simplifies *vv.* 1189—1193, though there is still some obscurity and probably error.

v. 1195. †ποτε Φοῖβον βροτὸς† κ.τ.λ. Read perhaps ποτὶ, 'and that you had never laid upon Phoebus, a mortal upon a god, the slaying of your Zeus-born father.'

v. 1223. Note the ambiguity of the phrase ὦ κατ᾽ ἄντρα νύχια Νηρέως κόρη, which *may* signify that Thetis was immortal and now

v. 18

inhabits a sea-cave, but may also refer only to the underground chamber of the tomb-chapel represented on the scene, the κατασκαφὴς οἴκησις of Soph. *Ant.* 891 etc.   According to the epilogue, Thetis was a goddess, but for the realistic story she must be supposed merely a woman ; see p. 37, note 6.   The ambiguity is precisely of the same kind as those respecting the rescue of Theseus in the *Heracles* ; see pp. 176 foll.

II. NOTES ON THE HELEN.

v. 5, in connexion with *v.* 8, must suggest *prima facie* that 'this house,' the house of the drama, is in Pharos. For a precise parallel see *Andromache* 21, 25. Taken by itself, *v.* 5 would merely imply that Proteus *had* lived in Pharos, though Theoclymenus lives on the mainland; and if such a distinction between the two houses were anywhere indicated, we might suppose that the apparent bearing of *v.* 5 on *v.* 8 was an oversight. But when we find that, throughout both prologue and play, the house is always that of Proteus, and that no separate house of Theoclymenus is anywhere mentioned or suggested, we may be sure there is no oversight, and that the audience are really meant to suppose, in some sense and for some purposes, that the dramatic house is on the island. The *king of Egypt*, who received there Paris and Helen, was also named in legend Proteus (Herodotus 2. 112 foll.); but, with this conception of the personage, there is no place in the story for the island of Pharos. The incongruous and unnatural suggestion, that *this* Proteus, *the king*, lived, like the sea-wizard of the *Odyssey*, in Pharos, was, I believe, invented by Euripides simply to make a sort of basis for his domestic allusions.

v. 9. With the rough metre of this verse compare that of *v.* 291 ἐς ξύμβολ᾿ ἐλθόντες ἃ φανερὰ μόνοις ἂν ἦν, and of *v.* 700 Μενέλαε, κἀμοὶ πρόσδοτέ τι τῆς ἡδονῆς. The similarity indicates that all three are genuine, not corrupt. See also *v.* 86 ἀτὰρ τίς εἶ; πόθεν; τίνος ἐξαυδᾶν σε χρή, which is in the metre of comedy, and *v.* 88 Τελαμών, Σαλαμὶς δὲ πατρὶς ἡ θρέψασά με, which goes beyond the ordinary license of tragedy. In such a work as this, we may well suppose either a certain negligence, or the deliberate and critical imitation of faults. This should be considered throughout in dealing with the text.

v. **21.** Note that the emphatic suggestion of a doubt about the legend of Leda is, for this play, irrelevant and absurd. The play assumes the truth of it (*vv.* 214, 257, 616—619, 1144—1150, especially the last verse). This strengthens somewhat the supposition, that the εἰ σαφὴς οὗτος λόγος is to be taken as applying, partly at least, to the word δίωγμα, the metrical stress on which, to a native ear, would, I think, be obvious and significant.

v. **179.** The epithet κυανοειδές, referring to the dark sediment carried and deposited by the Nile, is the nearest approach I can find in the play to a mention of the subject which Aristophanes (*Thesm.* 856—857) nevertheless selects for his leading point of attack. Manifestly it affords no explanation whatever of his gibe, even if readers of *Helen* happened to remember the epithet.

vv. **237—243.** Here as elsewhere (p. 114) we should remember that the opposed goddesses, Aphrodite and Hera, are apparently represented by images on the scene.

v. **437.** The old Portress, a purely comic figure, and utterly inappropriate to her supposed situation in the palace of the king of Egypt, may fairly be supposed to belong to the actual household of Eido. Probably the real slave played the part. Any one could play it; and the worse it were done, the better for the effect.

v. **513.** The quotation of the σοφῶν ἔπος is a compliment to some poet, like Shakespeare's quotation of Marlowe (*As You Like It*, III. 5. 80); perhaps to Agathon.

vv. **616** foll. Leda's chicken, he thinks, has suddenly found her wings.

v. **756.** This sentiment has no relevance to the dramatic situation, but is very pertinent to 'Theonoe,' the intelligent and enlightened heiress of wealth acquired by trade.

v. **771.** Note the amusing ambiguity of δὶς λυπηθεῖμεν ἄν. To Menelaus, having before him the very same woman (to all appearance) who was actually with him in his voyages, the 'repetition' must seem singularly awkward. Helen sees the innuendo and retracts her question.

vv. **919—923.** Note that this 'mantic' passage points not only to the significance of the pseudonym *Theonoe*, but more directly to

HELEN 277

the real name *Eido* and its possible connexion with εἰδέναι. In both aspects it is a mere jest. Euripides, and presumably his friend, had a poor opinion of the art. See *vv.* 744 foll., and note on *v.* 756.

v. 936. κεἰ μὲν θανὼν ὅδ᾽ ἐν πυρᾷ κατεσφάγη κ.τ.λ. If we must translate this by 'had been slain as victim to a grave,' it seems, as commentators remark, so irrelevant as to be unintelligible. Why should it be assumed that Menelaus, had he died, would have perished in this way? May it not conceivably be a bold and loose passive, signifying 'had received σφάγια offered to his pyre,' that is to say simply, 'had been buried'?

vv. 944—946. If these three verses are assigned to the Chorus-leader, what point has the distinction and antithesis between οἱ λόγοι and Helen (σύ)? I suspect that only *v.* 944 should be given to the Chorus-leader, who commences the usual distich, but is impatiently interrupted by Theonoe, 'eager to hear Menelaus.' We must then take οἰκτρά, *pitiable*, in a contemptuous sense. This use is not apparently classical in literature, but may have existed in conversation, or might be invented for the immediate purpose. The implied sarcasm on the conventional distichs with which the Chorus mark critical pauses—perhaps the least happy feature in Attic tragedy (*Orestes* 542, 605, *Hel.* 996)—is in keeping with the play and the situation. If Theonoe here speaks, it is natural that Menelaus should reply to her invitation without any vocative (ὦ παρθένε or the like); otherwise I think we should expect one.

v. 1085. Note that Menelaus, after all his brags, though here left *on* the altar-tomb, is eventually found *under* it (*v.* 1203), having taken this refuge on the approach of Theoclymenus,—a suitable incident in the comedy of the deception, and probably imitated from some unlucky scene.

v. 1168. He makes a point on his name 'heard by the god,' *i.e.* by his sainted father; cf. *Alcestis* 995—1005. The name was originally given (*v.* 9), because the pious father had been 'heard,' as he hoped, in his prayers for a satisfactory son. It is again played upon in *v.* 1643, where his impious threats bring upon the scene the intervening deities.

vv. 1348 foll. The attempts to show that Euripides professes to connect the subject of this ode with that of the play, depend on the supposition that ὦ παῖ (*v.* 1356) is addressed to Helen. This seems on the face of it improbable. A return to the theme of the play would surely be marked by some expression not liable to be misapplied. For reasons explained in the essay, we should not seek any internal pretext for the ode, though, if one could be found, it would make no difference to the general effect of it as an arbitrary digression.

In the uncertainty of the text, the point of *vv.* 1353—1357 must remain doubtful. But I think it almost certain (1) that ἐπύρωσας should be retained, (2) that συσσεβίζουσα (Seidler for οὐ σεβίζουσα) is right, (3) that ὦ παῖ is addressed, with playful familiarity, to Aphrodite. The general sense, as many have supposed, is that Aphrodite, though she had committed a grave offence in practising upon Pluto (ὄν), nevertheless 'stayed the wrath' of the injured Mother by the prominent part which she took in the powerful propitiation (*v.* 1358) of the rites.

As I have said in the Essay, I do not find in Euripides any true parallel to this ode, in its relation to the play. In considering this question, we must distinguish, as not parallel, such examples as the meditation on children in the *Medea* (1081 foll.), or the Pythian ode in the *Iphigenia in Taurica* (1234 foll.). In these, though the interludes are no part of the dramatic story, the themes are suggested by the play, and harmonize with it. No one could feel it to be surprising, that the topic of children should be thought of in connexion with the story of Medea, or the topic of Delphi in connexion with that of Iphigenia and Orestes. The link of thought is visible and obvious. And generally in Euripides, the freedom of the interlude seems to be limited by this natural and reasonable condition. But in the *Helen*, as it seems to me and to others, there is not the least reason why the legend of Demeter and Koré should occur to the mind at all. The topic is totally foreign. The narrative form also, and the contrast between this and the preceding odes, increase the abruptness of the effect. It must therefore (I think) surprise and perplex the audience, unless they had an extraneous cue.

vv. 1366—1368.

<blockquote>
εὖ δέ νιν ἄμασιν
ὑπέρβαλε σελάνα
† μορφᾷ μόνον ηὔχεις.
</blockquote>

Here ὑπέρβαλε seems wrong (see *v.* 1351), but probably gives the sense, ἔβαλλε or something similar. 'The moon shed upon them fair daylight,' that is, upon the gods, the performers of the rites (v. 1357), the passage on the efficacy of the rites (vv. 1358—1365) being parenthetic. The final verse is with reason regarded as gibberish. Even if the clause had sense in the context, it could not be appended thus abruptly. What we want is apparently a description of the moon; perhaps μορφὰ μονονηχής, 'floating' or 'swimming in lonely beauty,' like a swan, the stars being extinguished by her brilliance. For the form see ἀλινηχής.

v. 1374. Read perhaps

κάλλιστα δῆτ' ἀνήρπασ' ἐν τύχῃ 'πόσις'·
κάλλιστα δ' αὐτὸς ἥρπασεν τύχῃ πόσις,

or something like this. For the bearing of the first line, 'she (Theonoe) was indeed very happy in catching up the point of πόσις,' see p. 117. The punning turn of the transition would fit the general colour. But Dindorf's suggestion—'versus ab interpolatore fictus lacunae explendae causa'—is very probable.

v. 1627. May not the speaker (a man, see p. 54) be the sailor himself? That he should interfere in the circumstances would be the most effective of protests. The Chorus being, I think, excluded, there is no one else, unless we suppose a fourth actor, since one is required for the epilogue (v. 1642).

III. NOTES ON THE HERACLES.

v. 4. The references, here and *vv.* 252, 794, to the miraculous Theban legend of the armed men who sprang from the dragon's teeth, though not connected with Heracles, are very much to the purpose of the play. Such traditions are a natural precedent for fresh inventions in the same style. So also the 'offspring of Zeus' in *v.* 30. In *v.* 164 a rank of hoplites is described by the abrupt and obscure metaphor δορὸς ταχεῖαν ἄλοκα, comparing the sudden rise of the spears to the growth of blades from a furrow. I suspect that it alludes to a rationalistic interpretation of the γηγενὴς σπαρτῶν στάχυς (*v.* 5), where note the last word.

vv. 240. *Helicon…Parnassus*: apparently meant for bombast. Parnassus is more than 30 miles away; and neither hill can have been supposed by Euripides to be as near Thebes as is here implied.

v. 257. Take κάκιστος τῶν νέων together: 'worst of the new generation, because a foreigner.' οἱ νέοι are the faction now triumphant, those who have brought in Lycus (*v.* 37 etc.). The expression is characteristic of the aged speakers, and should not be changed. The object of ἄρχει, so far as it has any, is τῶν Καδμείων.

v. 452 may perhaps be retained. 'Where is he that shall slaughter these poor things, murdering, alas, the very life of me?' Literally 'the slaughterer of them, *or in other words* slayer of me.' See a similar expression in *v.* 537 τἄμ' ἔθνησκε τέκν', ἀπωλλύμην δ' ἐγώ, 'when my children were to die, it was *I* that was to perish.' Both mark the special relation of the mother.

v. 471. δαιδάλου (*i.e.* Δαιδάλου) ψευδῆ δόσιν (MSS.) is probably right. The mace, we are to understand, was said to be a miraculous weapon, a gift to Heracles, direct or indirect, from the magical craftsman, Daedalus. Megara of course does not believe this.

v. 687. These 'nymphs of Delos,' who 'at Apollo's gate go circling round and sing in his honour,' are, I think, simply the swans of the famous 'round pond,' κυκλοτερὴς λίμνη, before the temple at Delos, the λίμνη Δηλιάς of *Ion* 167, which see also for the swans. Hence the reference (*v.* 692) to the 'swan-song' of the old men themselves. For the singing of swans to Apollo, cf. Aristoph. *Birds* 769. Mr Blakeney suggests this.

v. 729. Read perhaps

ἐς καλὸν
στείχει—βρόχοισι δ' ἄρκυον γενήσεται—
ξιφηφόροισι τοὺς πέλας δοκῶν κτενεῖν,
ὁ παγκάκιστος.

"He is going right, where his 'trap' will find a 'snare,'—a man who thought to slay his neighbour with aid of sworders, the wretch!" The βρόχοισι is a bitter allusion to Lycus' gibe (*v.* 153). The instrumental ξιφηφόροισι refers to the armed guards, the hated symbol of tyranny. This involves no change but that of ἀρκύων to ἄρκυον, and remedies, among other things, the expression βρόχοι ξιφηφόροι, not justified by *Med.* 1278 ἀρκύων ξίφους, even if that is certainly genuine and right. Note further that the *sword* is not Heracles' weapon in this play.

v. 732. Euripides gives this for the sentiment of a savage. The sequel makes it hideous. It would not have been put into the mouth of Theseus, or of the sane Heracles.

v. 825. ἑνὸς δ' ἐπ' ἀνδρὸς σώματα στρατεύομεν (MSS.), 'Our war is against the *persons* of one man only.' I believe this, strange though it sounds to us, to be right. The σώματα of Heracles are the 'persons' belonging to him, his wife and children. It might include his slaves, but these are not considered.

v. 826. φασιν. That a goddess should treat this matter as uncertain is surely, from every point of view, absurd. But it is proper to the dream. Mr Blakeney calls attention to the irony.

v. 835. παιδοκτόνους, and *v.* 839 καλλίπαιδα, include Megara. See p. 196, note 3.

v. **845.**   Read perhaps τὰς for τάσδ', and φιλοῖς for φίλοις, thus :

> τιμάς τ' ἔχω, τὰς οὐκ ἀγασθῆναι φιλοῖς.

'And my office is such as one would not be apt to admire.' The archaisms τὰς for ἃς, φιλοῖς for φιλοίης, and optative without ἄν, all characterize the expression as a fixed locution or proverb. For the optative see on *Andromache* 929. The whole phrase perhaps comes bodily from some old author.

v. **1170** (and **1415**) νέρθεν. As these ambiguities are of cardinal importance, I will repeat here the substance of what is said about them in the text. The expression νέρθεν (or γῆς νέρθεν) regularly means *the underworld*, Hades, and in tragedy almost always does. It is so used, with intention of course, in this very play (*vv.* 497, 621). The context in these cases happens to show the meaning; but even without any special indication, a reference to Hades would be presumed, unless excluded. And it is intended by the dramatist, that a reference to Hades shall be presumed (by the uninstructed and unwary) in the allusions of Theseus and Heracles to the rescue. But the term νέρθεν is nevertheless ambiguous. The word in itself means only *below* or *from below*. And the fact, that the four allusions are all ambiguous, is sufficient, when we contrast the language of the play elsewhere, to prove that the ambiguity is intentional.

These passages therefore, so far from impugning those conclusions, as to the purpose of the poet, which are required by the whole play, are not only consistent with them, but positively support them.

v. **1386.**   *Cerberus.* I have purposely abstained from discussing in detail, what may have been the rationalistic version of this legend, to which Euripides here alludes; partly because, so far as I can discover, we have not materials to determine it, but chiefly because the details are for Euripides irrelevant and immaterial, as he shows by not giving any. The various forms of the legend, in their inconsistency and extravagance, invited the rationalists, and we have evidence that it engaged them early. Pausanias, who himself mentions as many as four places which claimed the honour (Troezen 2. 31. 2, Hermione 2. 35. 7, Taenarum 3. 25. 5, and the sanctuary of Zeus Laphystius in Boeotia 9. 34. 4), frankly abandons the monster, and favours the version of Hecataeus. According to this, 'the

Hound of Hades' was not a dog at all; 'hound' was merely poetical and signified 'attendant,' as when the Hydra is called κύνα Λέρνας by Euripides himself (*Heracles* 420 and 1274); the creature was really a deadly snake, which inhabited the cave of Taenarum, and was brought to Eurystheus by Heracles. This early attempt, however, cannot be much commended, if only because it takes no account of the variations in place; we can hardly suppose that the king of Argos collected remarkable reptiles. We may fairly assume, and Euripides indicates, that between Hecataeus and the date of his play there had been improvements, particularly by Herodorus, who treated the legend of Heracles. For one thing, the rationalists had fairly faced the 'dog'; in the Taenarian case, Euripides plainly supposes a dog, properly so called. Also, we may assume, they had perceived the advantage thus obtained in embracing rival localities; if Eurystheus commanded the services of a great hunter, nothing could be more reasonable than that he should collect a pack. More dimly and uncertainly we may perhaps divine how they dealt with the 'three heads.' Three places *in the Peloponnese* seem to have contended for the animal, Taenarum, Hermione, and Troezen. Two are upon 'headlands' and the third near to a headland. What more easy, it might be said, than a confusion between τρικάρανοι κύνες and τρικάρανος κύων? A similar twist, *mutatis mutandis*, is indicated (*Heracles* 419) for the legend of the Hydra, the 'heads' of which doubtless belonged to different snakes. Whether it was supposed that the various dogs lived in, or were connected with, caves, one cannot say; but that would not be necessary. If Heracles brought back a dog from an expedition to Taenarum, somebody, Herodorus would say, was sure to pick up the notion that it was 'the dog of Hades,' and was got from the lower world. In reality, it was just a hound 'of the Spartan kind' desired by Eurystheus as a breeder.

But it is needless and useless to pursue with guesses speculations which, as Euripides saw, had a fundamental vice. Whatever the facts supposed, they would not fairly account for the rise of a legend *without the exercise of imagination*; and to make the process really probable, the imagination, through which the facts were passed, should be a wild, confused, and in short *an insane imagination*. Given this, the transformation is possible and psychologically interesting. Also, which is the main point, it becomes a possible foundation for tragedy. And on the other hand, given this, to fix the facts in detail is superfluous. When we have been told that the journey of Heracles to Taenarum had *some* connexion with the bringing of a dog to Argos, and that the dog was left for a time at Hermione, we have, with an insane Heracles, all that we want. We have a sufficient origin for the miraculous account; the development we may suppose as we please.

IV. NOTES ON THE ORESTES.

v. **349.** πολλῇ ἁβροσύνῃ should (I think) be retained, with the
scansion − − | ∪ ∪ −. The crasis, though peculiar, is not more so
than that, for example, of *v.* 599 εἰ μὴ ὁ κελεύσας ῥύσεταί με μὴ
θανεῖν, where the article is nevertheless indispensable. Absolute
regularity in such matters is not to be expected.

vv. **409—410.** ' I know whom you mean ; but I prefer not to
name them.'—' Because they are *Semnai* ! But polite remarks may
be spared.' The reply of Orestes signifies his natural and irre-
pressible impatience of the vulgar scruple. A man, who for a week
past had been liable to fancy that he *saw* Erinyes, would be beyond
the fear of naming them, as Orestes in fact is ; see *v.* 582.

vv. **421—422.** μητρὸς οἴχονται πνοαί is difficult. The context,
especially *vv.* 400—405, indicates that *v.* 421 should mean ' How
long is it since *the funeral*?', since the commencement of the visions,
not ' since the death.' And indeed μητρὸς οἴχονται πνοαί seems
hardly a possible phrase for ' your mother died.' Probably therefore the πνοαί are the smoke of the pyre, which ' passed away '; see
Aesch. *Ag.* 820 (Dindorf), where burning Troy προπέμπει πίονας
πλούτου πνοάς. The statement ἔτι πυρὰ θερμὴ τάφου must in any
case be rhetorical and exaggerated.

v. **470.** At the approach of Tyndareus, Orestes (*v.* 467) crouches
behind Menelaus. Tyndareus, entering so as to approach Menelaus
on the left, desires to put himself *on his right* (πρὸς δεξιὰν στῆναι
v. 474) for the purpose of a well-omened salutation. He therefore
crosses, and in this movement discovers Orestes, who is still kneeling.
Menelaus, who holds his hand, now bends down and whispers to him,
encouraging him, we may presume, to seize the chance of propitiating
his grandfather. This is the action which evokes the προσφθέγγει
νιν ; (*v.* 481) of Tyndareus. Menelaus has not ' spoken ' to Orestes
aloud. Orestes probably does not rise until *v.* 542.

v. **658.** This reference to the sacrifice of Iphigenia is, so far as I have noticed, the only anachronism in the play, the only incident of the story which could not (one would say) be supposed in the society described. Negligence on such a point is so unlike Euripides, that we should suspect some explanation, probably not now ascertainable. The legend of Aulis had received various fantastic developments (such as the miraculous transformation or translation of Iphigenia), which had no doubt produced in their turn the usual crop of rationalistic equivalents. What Euripides here assumes, I cannot say ; but he does not mean, in all probability, that the niece of his Menelaus was actually and deliberately killed as a victim.

v. **694.** Punctuate thus :

σμικροῖσι γὰρ τὰ μεγάλα πῶς ἕλοι τις ἄν ;
πόνοισιν ; ἀμαθὲς καὶ τὸ βούλεσθαι τάδε.

'How can great (objects) be attained with small (means)? *By effort?* A foolish hope!' When the power is inadequate, it is useless to *struggle* ; you must use *cunning* and watch your opportunity. See the whole context. If πόνοισιν is joined to the previous sentence, the word is superfluous, and the metrical emphasis upon it not justifiable.

v. **950.** Some of these 'friends' probably appear with Orestes (otherwise they would hardly be mentioned) and silently take their leave, with embraces and the like, upon the stage. Hence the fact, apparent in the text, that until *v.* 1020 he does not face Electra. There he *turns to her*, and the despair '*in his eyes*' evokes her 'second' cry (οἳ 'γὼ μάλ' αὖθις). A guard or guards also probably appear, and then retire. In the preceding scene, just before the trial, it is for the first time indicated (*v.* 760) that the watchers of the house are *visible*. The dispositions proper to such an occasion were of course familiar to the audience, and would be represented as far as the conditions allowed.

v. **1182.** Read perhaps τίν' ἡδονήν ; not τιν' ἡδονήν—'To defer (telling) good news is no pleasure,' a formula of impatience. The other reading is interpreted thus : 'Speak, since the fact that thou art about to speak consoling words has in itself a sort of pleasure.' This seems rather odd and obscure.

v. **1236.** Read perhaps

ἐγὼ δ', ἐπεὶ 'βούλευσα κἀπέλυσ' ὄκνου.

'And I too (set hand to the sword), inasmuch as I counselled and incited.'—ἐγὼ δ' ἐπεβούλευσα MSS.

v. 1267. A curious question, but of no great importance, arises here. κόρας διάδοτε διαὶ βοστρύχων πάντῃ (κόραισι δίδοτε MSS.) is supposed to mean that the Chorus are to look 'through their hair' or 'their eyelashes.' Mr Wedd (*ad loc.*) is evidently dissatisfied with this, and it seems absurd. Why should the hair of the women be over their eyes? Or how should βόστρυχοι mean 'eyelashes'? If βόστρυχοι is the right word, we should suppose some secondary sense. Possibly iron-work, crowning a wall, decorative spikes or a *grille*, may have been so called; and the forecourts of great houses may have been partly enclosed in this way. Nothing of the kind need, or should, have been actually exhibited, the boundaries of the *aulé* being supposed outside the scene. The Chorus at this point go to the *parodoi*, and some of them probably are at times heard only, and not visible.

v. 1554. Aristotle (*Poetics* 25. 19) cites the character of Menelaus in this play as an instance of what he calls 'depravity of character without (inner) necessity,' that is, a degree of wickedness not required for the working out of the plot. He classes this fault with 'irrationality' (ἀλογία), by which is here meant the assumption of an unlikely behaviour, where the practical result might have been reached in a probable way and naturally accounted for.

As to 'irrationality,' it is a blemish, and should be avoided; though in truth few stories, and hardly any stories suitable for dramatic treatment, are wholly free from it; and an artist who was very punctilious on this score would assuredly not earn, and possibly not deserve, the gratitude of his audience. On many matters, we would far sooner accept an unlikelihood than be troubled with an explanation. In the very case cited by Aristotle, the 'Aegeus in Euripides' (meaning probably the Aegeus of the *Medea*, whose odd proceedings at Corinth are singularly opportune) we may doubt whether one spectator in a thousand would care to be prepared for the incident; we have other things to think of. The principle however is undoubtedly sound; incidents should be accounted for, so far as they conveniently may.

But as to the 'unnecessary depravity,' even the principle is dubious. As Professor Butcher observes (*Aristotle's Theory of Poetry and Fine Art* p. 224, and elsewhere), the rules about character laid down in the *Poetics* are 'too rigorous on their ethical side,' and cannot be accepted without qualifications, which Aristotle himself does not sufficiently indicate.   It can by no means be admitted, that vice in character should be limited to what is necessary for the mechanism of the plot; such a canon would condemn some of the best stories in the world, the best in every possible sense.

This being so, we have the less interest in considering, whether the principle, if conceded, would be applicable to the case cited, the Menelaus of our play; nor is it easy to do so, without a more full explanation from the critic.   The bad acts of Menelaus are necessary to the plot; so far we may go with Aristotle.   Before the trial, he leaves Orestes alone, and thus without an adviser; after the trial, he does not reconduct him to the house; he keeps, for a time, out of the way.   Both actions are necessary to the plot.   The first leaves an opening for the counsel of Pylades, the second for the atrocities of Pylades and Electra.   Further, though the first action is, in the circumstances and the hurry of the moment, excusable, the second is inexcusable, grossly indelicate and unkind.   And as a fact, both actions proceed from the same vice of character.   Menelaus would not have done either if he had not been extremely defective in sentiment, callous in feeling, a low, vulgar, 'practical' man.

There Euripides leaves the matter.   He does not provide any reason, except the character of Menelaus and his actual relations with the public of Argos, why Menelaus did not walk through the streets, from the assembly to the house, by his nephew's side.   The criticism of Aristotle should mean (1) that a better Menelaus might (for some reason) have been kept away, and therefore (but this is questionable) a better Menelaus would have been more proper to art; and (2) that, at all events, his going away and his staying away should have been otherwise accounted for than they are. To consider this view, we should like to hear from Aristotle, what other way precisely he would have preferred.   Pending this explanation, it is not, I hope, impertinent to express a doubt, whether one could improve upon Euripides.

It is of course true that, in some species of drama, there would not be room for such a character as our Menelaus, nor for any of the characters in the play, nor for the facts and the story generally. And the principles of the *Poetics*, if taken rigorously, may point to the conclusion that the species of drama, which does admit such characters, facts, and story, is inferior, if not illegitimate.   We will not pursue further the various possible inferences.

INDEX

The figures in black type refer to pages

For EU product safety concerns, contact us at Calle de José Abascal, 56–1°,
28003 Madrid, Spain or eugpsr@cambridge.org.

www.ingramcontent.com/pod-product-compliance
Ingram Content Group UK Ltd.
Pitfield, Milton Keynes, MK11 3LW, UK
UKHW010348140625
459647UK00010B/916